French Tanks
of the Great War

This book is dedicated to Jennie Long, for her endless patience
and everything else as well . . .

French Tanks
of the Great War

*Development, Tactics and
Operations*

Tim Gale

Pen & Sword
MILITARY

First published in Great Britain in 2016 by
PEN AND SWORD MILITARY
an imprint of
Pen and Sword Books Ltd
47 Church Street
Barnsley
South Yorkshire S70 2AS

ISBN 978 1 47382 350 1

A CIP record for this book is available from the British Library.

Printed and bound in England by
CPI Group (UK) Ltd, Croydon, CR0 4YY

Typeset in Times by CHIC GRAPHICS

Pen & Sword Books Ltd incorporates the imprints of
Archaeology, Atlas, Aviation, Battleground, Discovery,
Family History, History, Maritime, Military, Naval, Politics,
Railways, Select, Social History, Transport, True Crime,
Claymore Press, Frontline Books, Leo Cooper, Praetorian Press,
Remember When, Seaforth Publishing and Wharncliffe.

For a complete list of Pen and Sword titles please contact
Pen and Sword Books Limited
47 Church Street, Barnsley, South Yorkshire, S70 2AS, England
E-mail: enquiries@pen-and-sword.co.uk
Website: www.pen-and-sword.co.uk

Contents

List of Plates

A Renault gun-armed light tank in US Army service, demonstrating its manoeuvrability.

Schneiders detraining.

A late-model Schneider on manoeuvres with French infantry.

An early-model St Chamond.

A St Chamond moving through a destroyed French village.

A late-model St Chamond being used to raise war bonds in the interior of France.

Interior of a Schneider tank.

Interior of a St Chamond.

A machine-gun Renault undertaking testing.

Two US tank crewmen in their Renault tank.

Renaults moving to the front line.

A group of Renault gun tanks.

Renault tanks in US Army service.

A Renault Company moving to the front in Northern France.

A Renault in Spanish service during the Rif War in the 1920s.

A surviving Renault tank at Les Invalides in Paris.

Acknowledgements

The genesis for my interest in the French army in the Great War was a course taught by Professor William Philpott at the Department for War Studies, King's College London (2001), and little did I know that this topic would come to dominate my academic work from there on in. Throughout my doctoral studies Professor Philpott was a constant source of support, on many levels, and I really cannot thank him enough for his wisdom and assistance. My friends in the KCL First World War Operations Research Group have also been a constant source of support and constructive criticism, in particular those working on the French army, Drs Jonathan Krause and Simon House. My research assistant, James Hartstein, has been invaluable and I must also thank Michel Souquet (*Tanker*) for his erudite corrections on my original account of Lieutenant Boudon's experiences and James H. Reeve for his assistance in relation to some of the more obscure aspects of the *Artillerie Spéciale*. I must also thank Rupert Harding of Pen & Sword for commissioning this book, as well as Stephen Chumbley for editing it and Barbara Taylor for providing the maps.

Above all though, I must thank my partner, Jennie Long, for supporting me to the fullest degree possible during long periods of research and writing, which is why this volume is dedicated to her.

Tim Gale
May 2015

List of Abbreviations

AFGG	*Les Armées françaises dans la grande guerre* – French official history of the First World War.
AL	*Artillerie Lourde* – Heavy artillery.
ALC	*Artillerie Lourde Courte* – Heavy howitzers.
ALGP	*Artillerie Lourde Grande Puissance* – High-power (i.e. long-range) heavy artillery.
ALL	*Artillerie Lourde Longue* – Heavy artillery guns.
ALVF	*Artillerie Lourde sur voie ferrée* – Railway heavy artillery.
AS	*Artillerie Spéciale* – The French tank service.
AT	*Artillerie de Tranchée* – Trench artillery.
BCA	*Bataillon de chasseurs alpin* – Mountain chasseurs battalion.
BCL	*Bataillon de chars légers* – Light tank battalion.
BCP	*Bataillon de chasseurs à pied* – Light infantry battalion.
CA	*Corps d'armée* – French army corps.
CAC	*Corps d'armée colonial* – French Colonial Army Corps.
CC	*Corps de cavalerie* – French cavalry corps.
Cdt.	*Commandant* (usually refers to a Major).
CM	Machine-gun company.
CP	Command Post
DI	*Division d'infanterie* – French infantry division.
DM	*Division marocaine* – Moroccan (infantry) Division.
DSA	*Direction du Service Automobile* – Army Motor Service.
EM	*État-Major* – Staff (EMA – Army Staff).
Esc	*Escadron* – Squadron.
GAC	*Groupe d'armées du centre* – Central Army Group.
GAE	*Groupe d'armées de l'Est* – Eastern Army Group.
GAF	*Groupe d'armées du Flandres* – Flanders Army Group.
GAN	*Groupe d'armées du Nord* – Northern Army Group.
GAR	*Groupe d'armées de reserve* – Reserve Army Group.
GB	*Groupe de bombardement* – Air bomber unit.
GBCA	*Groupe de Bataillons de Chasseurs Alpins* – a mountain chasseurs unit.

GPA	*Grand Parc d'artillerie* – Central artillery park.
GQG	*Grand Quartier Général* – French equivalent to GHQ.
GQGA	*Grand Quartier Général des Armées Alliées* – Allied GHQ.
ID	Infantry Division (German).
IR	Infantry Regiment (German).
JMO	*Journal des Marches et Opérations* – French army unit war diary.
PA	*Parc d'artillerie* – Artillery park.
PAD	*Parc d'artillerie divisionnaire* – Divisional artillery park.
PC	*Poste de commandement* – Command post.
PAOC	*Parc annexe d'organisation de Champlieu* – Part of the AS base at Champlieu.
PO	*Poste d'observation* – Observation Post.
PV	*Pigeon voyager* – Carrier pigeons.
RAC	*Régiment d'artillerie de campagne* – French field artillery regiment.
RAL	*Régiment d'artillerie lourde* – French heavy artillery regiment.
RAP	*Régiment d'artillerie à pied* – French foot artillery regiment.
RAS	*Régiment d'artillerie d'assaut* – French tank regiment.
RI	*Régiment d'infanterie* – French infantry regiment.
RIC	*Régiment d'infanterie coloniale* – French colonial infantry regiment.
RIT	*Régiment d'infanterie territoriale* – French territorial infantry regiment.
RMZT	*Régiment mixte de Zouaves et Tirailleurs* – North African infantry regiment.
SHD	*Service Historique de Défense* – French military archives at Vincennes.
SRR	*Section de Réparations et de Ravitaillement* – Tank re-supply and breakdown section.
TM	*Transport de matériel* – Material transportation unit.
TP	*Transport de personnel* – Personnel transportation unit.
TSF	*Télégraphie sans fil* – Wireless telegraphy.
VF	*Voie ferrée* – Railway.

Preface

This volume follows on from my previous book on the French tank service (the *Artillerie Spéciale* – AS), *The French Tank Force and the Development of Armoured Warfare in the Great War* (Ashgate, 2013). Although inevitably many of the same areas are covered in both books, I have tried to make them as complementary as possible by treating topics with a different emphasis in each book. Thus the convoluted interactions between the French civilian and military bureaucracies and their conflicts over the various tank programmes will be discussed here but not in as much detail as in *The French Tank Force*. By contrast, this book has more detail about the combat operations of the AS and incorporates research I have done subsequent to the publication of my previous book. I have also been able to address some very important engagements of the AS that I was unable to cover in *The French Tank Force*, such as the tanks' participation in the Battle of the Matz in June 1918. In addition, the operations of the AS with the US Army and its participation in the battles of Flanders and the Serre in late 1918 are covered here for the first time.

Because of the format of this book, I have not used footnotes but listed my references in Further Reading. However, unless otherwise indicated, all information herein is taken from the papers in the French military archive at Vincennes and the archive references are given. Documents from the archives have not been specifically named in all circumstances because of limitations of space but important documents will be named in full. Should you wish for specific references, please contact me via the publisher. Readers may also find useful the extensive guide to researching the French Army in the Great War and using the French military archives that I have written for the British Commission for Military History, which can be accessed by the public via the BCMH website.

General Key for all maps.

BR British

FR French

US United States

XXXXX Army group

XXXX Army

XXX Corps

XX Division

II Battalion

I Company

German

Infantry

Cavalry

Armoured

Railways

Canals

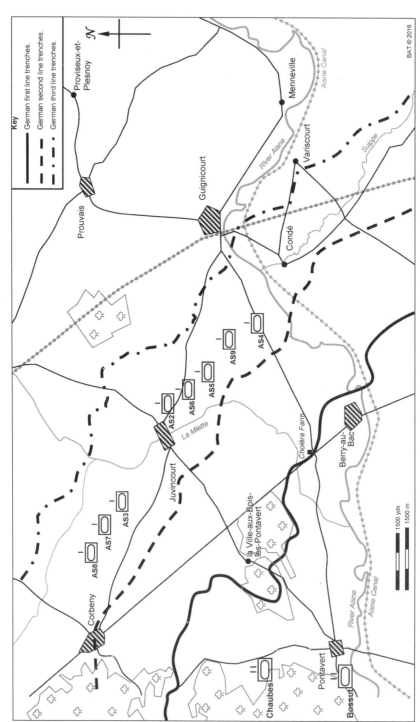

1. The Nivelle Offensive 1917 – proposed tank advance.

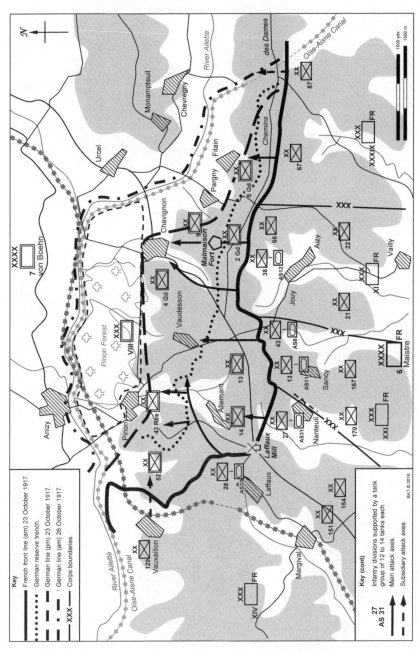

Key

—— French front line (am) 23 October 1917.

········· German reserve trench.

— ― — German line (pm) 23 October 1917.

–·–·– German line (am) 26 October 1917.

XXX —— Corps boundaries.

Key (cont)

27
AS 31   Infantry divisions supported by a tank group of 12 to 14 tanks each.

⟶   Main attack axes.

⇢   Subsidiary attack axes.

2. *The Battle of Malmaison, 23–27 October 1917.*

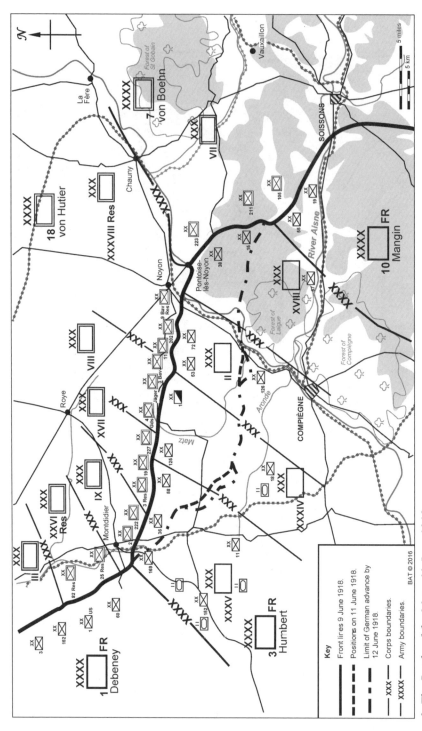

3. *The Battle of the Matz, 11 June 1918.*

Key

Front lines 9 June 1918.
Positions on 11 June 1918.
Limit of German advance by 12 June 1918.
xxx — Corps boundaries.
xxxx — Army boundaries.

BAT © 2016

5 miles

5 km

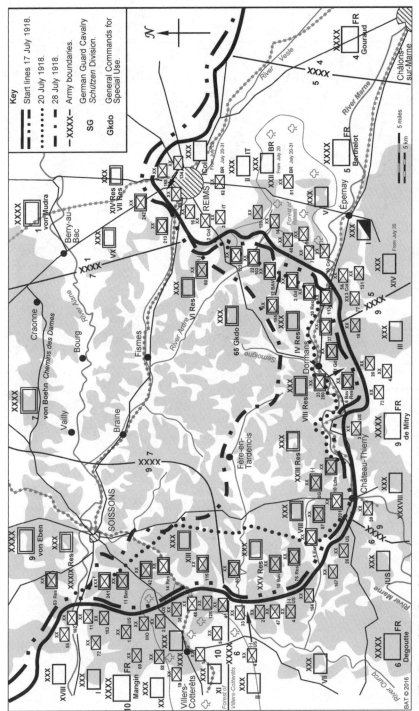

4. The Second Battle of the Marne, 17–28 July 1918.

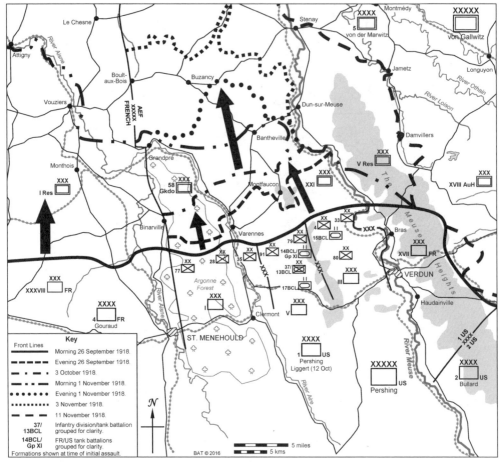

5. The American Offensive in the Meuse-Argonne, 26 September–11 November 1918.

Chapter 1

The French Tank Force in the Great War – The *Artillerie Spéciale*

By the summer of 1915, the French army was desperately seeking solutions to the problems thrown up by wide-scale trench warfare on the Western Front. In particular, 1915 was a very hard year in a very hard war for the French and there was frantic intellectual activity within the French army to find solutions to the tactical problems being grappled with. It was in the autumn of that year that an obscure French artillery colonel, Jean Baptise Eugene Estienne (who preferred to be known as Eugene Estienne), wrote to the French commander-in-chief, General Joseph Joffre, with plans for the construction and use of a fleet of armoured vehicles. This would be the beginning of the French tank programme which, despite many trials and tribulations, would end up as the world's most advanced armoured force, with both a sophisticated doctrine and a very efficient organisation. In this volume I will be examining primarily the combat operations of the French tank force, the *Artillerie Spéciale* (Special Artillery – AS), although I will also discuss some aspects of the issues around procurement and manufacturing. The AS is little known in the UK, a reflection of the general lack of knowledge of the French army in this period, despite being an important component in the French army's successes on the Western Front and an important part of the general history of the development of armour.

Estienne's Idea
Estienne wrote to Joffre twice during the autumn of 1915 explaining his ideas for an armoured vehicle (called at that point a *cuirassé terrestre*, a land battleship) but these letters were not passed on to Joffre by his staff. Undeterred, Estienne wrote another letter on 1 December 1915,

this time addressing it to Joffre personally, the letter including some preliminary drawings and plans. Joffre, unlike his staff, immediately recognised this was an idea worth pursuing and Estienne, accompanied by his assistant Captain Hubert Lefebvre, was invited to meet with General Maurice Janin, Joffre's deputy chief of staff in charge of material, eleven days later. This meeting was the birth of a new arm for the French army; its tank force which would play a major role in the last two years of the war.

Estienne's Career
Before considering this meeting, Estienne's military career prior to the war is worth describing in detail, as his personality and abilities had a major influence on the development and success of the AS. His pre-war career had given him wide experience of technological military issues, as well as giving scope to his considerable inventiveness. These experiences were to prove crucial to Estienne's mastery of the issues surrounding the development of the French tanks.

Estienne had entered the army in 1884 as an artillery lieutenant, after receiving an extensive scientific education, followed by a year at the Fontainebleau artillery school. By 1891, he was a captain and supervising the military factory *Atelier de Fabrication de Bourges*, which gave him experience of military manufacturing and its associated production processes. He was a keen inventor, his inventions included a rifle-harness to enable infantry to fire whilst advancing which, although ingenious, was not adopted for service. Throughout his army service, he was a prolific contributor to French military journals and wrote a variety of scientific papers, many of which were on the application of telemetry and geometry to artillery fire. By 1907, he held the important post of commander of the *Centre d'Instruction d'Artillerie* at Grenoble. As a known innovator and well regarded for his organisational abilities, he was appointed to organise the French army's aviation service in 1910. Although Estienne successfully oversaw the building of an aircraft construction centre and a pilot school at Vincennes, the government's interest in military aviation waned and he was shunted off to command the air squadron at Lyon in 1912. The government changed its mind on military aviation at the close of 1913 and Estienne was recalled to Paris to become *Directeur de l'établissement d'aviation militaire de Vincennes*. Thus Estienne had benefited from direct experience of military manufacturing as well as the difficulties of establishing a new arm within the army; his experience organising the army's military aviation, in particular, alerted him to the problems involved in initiating innovation in the French army.

Estienne was ahead of most of his peers in the French artillery service in one very important respect; he was a keen exponent of indirect artillery fire in an army whose artillery tactics were predicated on direct fire. He had also been a student of recent wars. A close friend from the military aviation service, Lieutenant Bellenger, served as a French observer in the Balkans, reporting to Estienne on the effectiveness of field fortifications and machine-gun fire. Estienne's examination of reports from both the Russo-Japanese War and the Balkan Wars led him to believe that fieldcraft and long-range infantry weapons were making direct artillery fire significantly less effective. His solution was indirect artillery fire based on air observation, famously saying before the war 'the aeroplane is the eye of the artillery'. He published a report on how a section of observation aircraft could be organised within each artillery regiment and the advantages that this would bring to the artillery, although this was completely ignored within the army. Another aspect of the Balkan Wars that had intrigued Estienne was the power of field fortifications and how to breach them, without entering into full-scale siege warfare. Having seen the power of contemporary field fortifications, Estienne told his officers in August 1914 that he thought an agricultural tractor could be modified to carry a 120mm gun across broken terrain, this initial idea being more of a self-propelled gun rather than a tank. Shortly after this discussion, his regiment was mobilised and any development of his ideas about armoured vehicles would have to wait.

Estienne's War
Estienne arrived to command the *22 Régiment d'Artillerie* (a field artillery regiment, armed with 75mm guns) on 3 August 1914, accompanied by two *Blériot* aircraft (which could be dismantled and then transported by lorries) and three pilots. Two aspects of the August fighting demonstrate Estienne's capabilities in relation to both morale and organisation. Estienne, having written on the power of morale before the war, was 'an inspiration' to his regiment, according to the regimental history, during the difficult retreat of 1914. There was a good example of Estienne's command style on 23 August 1914, when Estienne, attached to an adjacent division, intervened to advise the 5 DI's regimental commanders to organise themselves, rather than wait for the division's commanders who had 'run off'. Estienne also managed to

keep his regiment in good order during the very trying retreat of 1914, something not managed by a significant number of his peers.

On 6 September 1914, Estienne was promoted to command 6 DI's artillery and he subsequently successfully concentrated the divisional artillery on a German fortified artillery position, identified by air reconnaissance, on the edge of Montceau-les-Provins. His bombardment largely destroyed the German position, allowing the French infantry to occupy the area without any significant loss.

Estienne's experience on the Western Front during 1915 could only accentuate the need for a means to move infantry quickly through fortified areas. He had told several officers of his artillery regiment in August that 'victory will go in this war to that of the two belligerents that is the first to place a 75 cannon on a vehicle that can move on all terrain' and further thoughts on this had led him to write to Joffre.

At his meeting with Janin, Estienne proposed using armoured vehicles *en masse* in a surprise attack without a preparatory artillery barrage: the *cuirassé terrestre* would advance in front of the infantry, clearing trenches as it moved. These vehicles, weighing around twelve tonnes, would move at up to nine kilometres per hour, carrying a 37mm gun and two machine guns. They would need to be able to traverse various obstacles on the battlefield and be able to cross trenches. Thus from the beginning, the tanks were conceived primarily to assist the infantry. Estienne cannily added to his pitch a claim that was bound to attract attention in the cost-conscious French army; would not 30,000 tonnes of tanks be more useful than 30,000 tonnes of shells, he asked.

General Maurice Gamelin, head of GAE's 3 Bureau (Operations), was tasked with examining Estienne's proposals and he reported to Joffre on 24 January 1916 that he was satisfied that this was a viable project. Within three days, his staff had produced detailed specifications for the vehicles and a projected time frame that would have the first tanks available for combat in spring 1917, qualified by uncertainties over the time needed for initial experimentation. These specifications required that the tanks would have good cross-country mobility, including the ability to climb 40-degree inclines, and on level ground the tanks were expected to have a speed of seven kilometres per hour. The tanks needed to be able to crush barbed wire and cross trenches that were one and a half metres wide. They needed sufficient mobility to be able to change objectives quickly and to move extensively across the battlefield. Essentially, the tanks were envisaged in this report in the conventional terms of the traditional cavalry role, particularly as the report emphasised the need for the tanks to have good battlefield mobility. The potential problem that large shell-craters might present was recognised at this early stage but this was to remain an un-resolvable problem throughout the war for all tanks. The tanks' armour was expected to defeat small-arms fire, including machine guns, and shell and grenade fragments, but there was no method of making the tanks proof against direct artillery fire.

Initial opposition to Estienne's project came from various parts of the military, most importantly from General Léon Mourret, the commander of technical services in the *Direction de Service Automobile* (DSA). (The DSA oversaw all motor transport in the French army and jealously guarded its power.) There was certainly a high degree of inter-agency rivalry in both the DSA and Mourret's attitude to Estienne and the AS. However, Mourret's reluctance should also be seen in the context of all sections of the army having to fight over the finite resources that were available to them. It was not self-evident that the tanks would either work or, if they did, whether their effectiveness would justify the resources given to them. Mourret, for example, was hard pressed to provide the level of service from the DSA that the army was demanding. Just in relation to engines, the tank project had to compete with the demands of motor transport as well as the increasing demand for aero engines. Joffre estimated in October 1915 that he was going to need 1,400 lorries delivered within six months, by which time the DSA's total requirement would be over 2,000 lorries, with a need for 600 replacements each month. On top of these requirements for the artillery, the air service would need at least 500 tractors and 300 lorries to function effectively. The colossal number of horses killed in the first years of the war added further pressure to the French industrial system, as, for example, the increasing number of heavy artillery units that were being raised could no longer rely on horse power and required sections of lorries to mitigate the shortage of horses. Thus, Mourret and the DSA were now competing with the artillery, the air service and the engineers. The continuing debate about where the priority for engines should lie had a considerable impact on the manufacture of tanks, as their engines were often diverted to other uses.

There was also a debate to be had about whether the French army could afford the human resources needed for the tank project, as the initial tanks considered would need a crew of at least six. In practice, most of the tanks were crewed by NCOs, thus removing valuable junior leaders from other branches of the French army. By 1916, the army was in particular need of such men for the infantry and losing them to an untried branch was clearly a risk for GQG. It is also worth noting that the project would not be insignificant in terms of costs; the estimate in early 1916 was that 400 Schneider tanks, with their associated armament, would cost in excess of 24 million francs.

While discussions were undertaken within the military and the government, Estienne started to canvass various industrialists to take on his project. The problem he encountered was that French industry had no real experience with tracked vehicles; although the army had experimented with a wire-cutting tractor, as well as converting a Filtz tractor to carry machine guns, neither prototype was a success and there was no civilian manufacturer of tracked vehicles in France before the war. Even the great French industrialist and inventor Louis Renault was not persuaded by Estienne to shift his attention to armoured vehicles, at their initial meeting in December 1915. Renault simply had too many military projects already underway and his factories were working to their full capacity. Thus it can be seen that some of the reservations about the tank project in France should be judged as perfectly reasonable at the time.

The Schneider Tank
The same afternoon he was rejected by Renault, Estienne visited Eugene Brillié, an engineer at the Schneider-Creusot works (*Société Schneider*), who told him that the Schneider factory had been experimenting with Holt agricultural tractors bought from America and he was thus interested in developing Estienne's ideas. After their meeting, Brillié persuaded the factory to begin the project and Joffre then informed Albert Thomas, in charge of the *Sous-secrétariat d'artillerie* (part of the *Ministère de la Guerre*), that 400 tanks should be ordered immediately, subject to satisfactory trials, to be delivered by the spring of 1917. After some satisfactory experiments with a Holt tractor on 21 February 1916 at Vincennes, Thomas told Joffre that an order would be placed with the Schneider factory for 400 tanks, to be delivered by 25 November 1916. After a slow start-up period, the factory would deliver 100 tanks per month and production commenced in great secrecy at the *Société d'Outillages Méchaniques et Usinages d'Artillerie* (SOMUA) factory in Paris. It therefore took less than three months from Estienne's initial approach to Joffre for this ambitious project to be taken up by the French army. However, without Estienne's continual pressure, including being willing to bypass parts of the military hierarchy, it seems likely that the tank project could well have lost its impetus.

The tank designed by Schneider, weighing 13.5 tonnes, was essentially an armoured box on tracks, with a sloped prow at the front to help avoid ditching and for cutting barbed wire. The tanks were armed with a short-barrelled 75mm gun, mounted on the front right side, giving a rather restricted field of fire, with one machine gun on each side. The tank had a crew of six; a gunner and loader, two machine gunners and a mechanic, with the commander driving the tank. As the tanks could not be made immune to direct artillery fire and armour-piercing shells, their armour was designed to withstand only fire from infantry weapons and to have limited protection against blast and shrapnel. The Schneider's main fault was that its forward-mounted fuel tank (containing over 50 gallons) was fitted above the engine, a necessity due to the use of a gravity feed, a good example of the technical constraints of the time.

Being at the front of the tank, the main petrol reservoir was liable to be ruptured when hit by shell fragments, spraying the interior of the vehicle with petrol. As the engine was uncovered inside the crew compartment, this could lead to serious fires with few effective means to put them out. As the crew were in constant close proximity to the engines and there was little in the way of ventilation, heat within the tanks was to remain a problem. This problem was compounded by the lack of an exhaust pipe in the first Schneiders manufactured, the exhaust gases venting through a small hole in the tank's roof. This resulted in a smoky and very hot interior; Estienne reported that many of the Schneiders' interiors had heated to near boiling-point during the engagements in May 1917. Another problem was the power-to-weight ratio available from contemporary petrol engines but, even by contemporary standards, the Schneider's engine was underpowered. Its in-line four cylinders only produced 60 HP at 1,000 rpm, which was near its maximum engine speed. Although it could reach eight kilometres per hour in third gear on the flat, even the slightest inclines brought the speed down to half of that.

The St Chamond Tank
In April 1916, after production had commenced on the Schneider, Joffre received an astonishing letter from Albert Thomas. Thomas informed Joffre that his department had placed an order with the St Chamond factory (the informal name for the *Société des Forges et Aciéres de la Marine et d'Homécourt*) for 400 tanks, which were designed by the well-known artillery designer Lieutenant Colonel Émile Rimailho. Neither Joffre nor Estienne had been consulted in any way about this tank and

it is indicative of the reaction to the St Chamond tank from its users that many in the AS suggested that the primary concerns of this new design were for it to be bigger (over twenty tons), more sophisticated (with an electric transmission) and better armed (with a 120mm gun, four machine guns and a crew of nine) than the Schneider design. This is not an unreasonable criticism, as much is made in Thomas's note to Joffre of the large size of the St Chamond and the beneficial effects on morale this would have. As Léon Dutil points out, given the limited French industrial production available, it would have been better for the two design teams to collaborate but this never occurred. It is equally difficult to see why the pursuit of two medium tank designs simultaneously was sensible in the first place.

In September 1916, Joffre examined two prototype St Chamonds, one with a Creusot 75mm gun, and the other with a 120mm *modèle 90*. Joffre wisely rejected the ministry's proposal for the St Chamond to be armed with a 120mm gun, which he could see was totally unsuitable, and insisted a 75mm gun was used, so that it would have common ammunition with the Schneiders. Recent British combat experience with their tanks had also suggested that a very large gun was unnecessary. Estienne was as unimpressed as Joffre when he finally got to examine the St Chamond prototype and immediately saw the problems with the tank's engines and tracks during demonstrations, pointing out that the tracks' ground pressure was twice the recommended maximum. At least this inspection gave him the chance to firmly quash the DSA's desire to put a flamethrower in the tank.

Although Rimailho's design was largely good in relation to firepower and armour, the automotive components of the St Chamond proved to be very problematic, largely due to the effort to make the tank as large and well-armed as possible. This illustrates the difficulties that can be encountered if you give a very competent weapons designer a project that should have been seen primarily as a vehicle project. The deficiencies of the St Chamond are immediately obvious; the tracks were too short and narrow for the body, it was soon nicknamed the 'elephant on the legs of a gazelle'. The tracks were only 35 centimetres longer than those of the Schneider, although its body was two metres longer, leaving a dangerous overhang on the front of the tank. This large body and extensive armament made it weigh just over 23 tonnes, a weight its engines were too underpowered to move reliably. A four-cylinder Panhard petrol engine, producing nearly 90 HP, was used to drive two electric motors, one for each track, via an ambitious electric transmission. Although this eliminated the crashing gear-change problems that plagued all early tanks, it was beyond the capabilities of the French engineers to make it reliable until mid-1918 and it added considerable weight to the tank. (However, once the transmission was adequately refined by mid-1918, it was retrofitted to the remaining Schneiders and proved a great success.) In particular, the driver interface was very complex, drivers needing to juggle a confusing number of levers and pedals. The St Chamond was appreciably faster than the Schneider over completely flat ground but in practice it was not able to travel faster on the battlefield. One intelligent feature was the provision of an observation position at the rear of the tank and another advantage it had over the Schneider was its greater manoeuvrability due to its independently-driven tracks.

The general technical problems were never entirely resolved and although the St Chamond continued in use throughout 1918, it would be difficult to argue that it was a success. (It is notable that the French were not able to export any of the remaining St Chamonds at the end of the war.) However, if the three primary attributes of any tank are considered, firepower, mobility and protection, then the St Chamond would have been formidable had its mobility had been addressed prior to its armour and armament. It is worth noting that both French tank designs were armed with a much more useful main armament than those produced by the British, who were using 57mm guns or even just machine guns in the case of the Mark I and IV 'Female' tanks. Indeed, the 75mm gun used in the St Chamond remained the most powerful gun fitted to any tank until the middle of the Second World War. Rimailho was in this respect ahead of contemporary thinking about tank armament, as was his argument for the development of guns specifically designed for tank use. However, in the event, tank guns rarely engaged targets at long range during the war, as will be discussed.

Building the Tanks
The actual construction of the medium tanks was to prove very difficult. Albert Thomas had originally promised to deliver the entire order of 400 Schneiders before the end of 1916. In the event, most of the Schneiders were delivered during 1917, with the final deliveries only taking place in 1918. In relation to the St Chamonds, there were even greater delays; in fact the delivery of the initial order for 400 tanks was never completed, with only 294 being delivered to the army during the war, the last three of these arriving as late as September 1918. The ministry

was never able to deliver the 100 Schneiders per month it had offered and during the main part of the delivery schedule it averaged only just over half this number. From January to June 1917, 306 Schneiders were delivered, averaging fifty-one per month. The largest monthly delivery was in March (eighty-six tanks), with the least being in June (twenty-two tanks). By contrast, there were more St Chamond deliveries between January and March 1918 (143 tanks) than there had been from April to December 1917 (117 tanks). However, this was all considerably later than had been planned, Thomas having undertaken to deliver all 400 St Chamonds by December 1917, extravagantly promising to manufacture three tanks per day from September onwards. The ministry also began to count tank deliveries in terms of tanks that had left the factories, rather than tanks actually delivered to the front in a usable condition. This made the delivery schedule look better but was obviously of no use to the army. For example, by June 1917, there had been 185 St Chamonds manufactured but only eighty-three of these had been delivered to the army, the others remaining unusable at the Cercottes depot due a variety of manufacturing defects. The situation was even worse in December 1917, when there were only seventy-nine St Chamonds in operation with GAN, despite the fact that the entire order of 400 had been manufactured. (The problems connected with manufacturing are further discussed in Chapter 3.)

The *Artillerie Spéciale* is Formed
Estienne was returned to his artillery duties while the initial technical developments were being undertaken and, in March 1916, he took command of 3 CA's artillery, subsequently serving at Verdun, his corps being under the command of a future commander-in-chief, Robert Nivelle. Estienne rushed to England in June 1916 to inspect the British tank project and came back asking for three months to organise the 'tracked vehicles', this being approved by Joffre. However, it took until August 1916 for the first set of AS personnel to arrive at Fort Trou d'Enfer at Marly-le-Roi. Michel Goya's research has shown that the majority of AS officers initially recruited were from the cavalry; although each infantry division was asked to provide one lieutenant or second lieutenant, each cavalry division was expected to provide five officers, including a captain. This is hardly surprising as the cavalry was better able to spare officers than the infantry but it was soon clear that there was a need for officers with mechanical and other technical knowledge. The army was asked to provide half this requirement from

the heavy artillery and the DSA, the balance being taken from the depots of the Interior. Some officers were even drafted in from the navy, although most continued to be taken from the infantry and the cavalry, the other ranks being recruited from the artillery depots. The ability to drive motor vehicles was not common at this time and 200 drivers had to be brought in from the DSA and the artillery.

By October 1916, Estienne had a small but highly proficient staff; Colonel Jean Monhoven, an acknowledged tactical expert from one of France's elite colonial regiments (2 RIC), was to supervise and advise on tactics, while *Commandant* Joseph-Aimé Doumenc, one of the most competent officers in the entire DSA and primary organiser of the successful French supply effort at Verdun, gave advice on technical matters. The staff had in addition three captains, as well as thirty-eight NCOs and other ranks, with seven automobiles and a motorcycle. A major AS camp was subsequently set up at Champlieu, near Compiègne, and this remained the primary AS HQ until it was forced to move by the German advance during the Spring 1918 offensives. As well as Champlieu and Marly, there was an AS camp in Cercottes, north of Orléans, which took delivery of the tanks from the factories and prepared them for their units. As the AS was slowly forming, a new disruptive element became apparent as Estienne encountered the full force of the obstructive French civilian bureaucracy.

The Consultative Committee
Interestingly, Estienne had warned Joffre in his original letter that using a *Commission d'examen* to consider armoured vehicles would be incompatible with producing the first vehicles both quickly and in total secrecy. However, a supervisory committee was duly formed; the *Comité consultatif de l'artillerie d'assaut* (hereafter referred to as the *Comité*), comprising of representatives from the various departments involved in the French tank programme. Its *Président* (Chairman) was Jules-Louis Breton, leader of the *Sous-Secrétariat d'Etat des Inventions*. The other *Comité* members were Estienne and a technical adviser from the AS, General Mourret and Lieutenant Colonel Picoche for the DSA, Lieutenant Colonel Deslandres and *Commandant* Ferrus from the artillery, *Commandant* Boissin, from the technical section of the engineers, Mario Roques and Captain Leisse from the *Ministère de l'Armement*, with Lieutenant Hubert as secretary to the committee and three other officers in support. There were also three representatives from the St Chamond factory, including Lieutenant Colonel Rimailho,

and one each from the Schneider and Renault factories. This resulted in a very unwieldy body, as there were often over twenty representatives, with very different agendas, attending meetings. It has already been noted that Mourret was not enthusiastic about the tank project and this attitude was shared by a number of other members of the *Comité*. In particular, Lieutenant Hubert had a low opinion of Estienne and closely allied himself with Roques and the *Ministère de l'Armement* but this was somewhat balanced by the fact that *Commandant* Ferrus was a friend and long-term associate of both Estienne and Louis Renault. However, initially the *Comité* was not entirely unhelpful and a number of design faults were rectified as they became apparent during testing. Concerns immediately arose over the Schneider's armour, particularly in relation to it being proof against the German SmK armour-piercing rifle round. It was agreed that additional armour (an extra 5mm) would be fitted, although this modification was to take place after the tanks were delivered. The initial St Chamond engines needed immediate revision by the factory because they were simply not powerful enough for the tank. Estienne's relationship with the *Comité* was to become considerably more difficult over the following year but for the moment his main effort was directed to preparing the AS for its first combat operations. These are the subject of the next chapter.

A Note on Terminology
In official French army documents, Renault tanks are usually referred to as light tanks (*chars légers*), while the Schneider and St Chamond tanks are confusingly called both medium and heavy tanks, although the British Mark I–IVs were also referred to as heavy tanks. From around mid-1918, with the expected introduction of genuine heavy tanks into the French army, the Schneiders and St Chamonds were generally called medium tanks. In what follows, the Schneiders and St Chamonds will be referred to throughout as medium tanks. Although the majority of light tanks were manufactured at the Renault factory, a number of other manufacturers were later brought in to boost production, as will be discussed. However, all French light tanks in this volume will be referred to as Renaults, as the design remained the same, regardless of the manufacturer. The medium tanks were initially organised as the French artillery was, thus a tank *groupement* is equivalent to a battalion, a *groupe* to a company. *Groupes* of medium tanks are referred to in official documents as both 'AS' followed by a number and '*groupe*' followed by a number. All have been changed here to read such that '*groupe 40*'

will be AS40. The Renault units were organised along infantry lines in battalions and companies; all AS units with three numerals are Renault companies, i.e. the first company of the first Renault battalion was AS301 of 1 BCL (*1 Bataillon de chars légers*).

Following the convention of wartime French military documents, French armies will be referred to with Roman numerals, while all lower formations (corps, divisions, regiments etc.) will have Arabic numerals. The exception is in relation to the medium tank *groupements*, which were given Roman numerals. All other armies' formations will be referred to in Arabic numerals.

In relation to personnel, the category of officers in French during the war does not usually include *sous-lieutenants*, as these were counted separately. However, I have included this grade in 'officer casualties' rather than keep it separate. The tank crews were largely NCOs, being French *brigadiers* and corporals, although in French casualty lists they are referred to as 'other ranks'. They will be thus referred to in relation to casualties as 'men'.

Most French terms have been translated into English. Thus, for example, *position d'attente* is translated as waiting position and *position de départ* is translated as departure or jump-off position. *Chef de bataillon* (infantry) and *Chef d'escadron* (cavalry) are equivalent to the British rank of major but have usually not been translated as they give a useful indication of the officer's original arm of service.

Chapter 2

'Very Bad Conditions' – The Nivelle Offensive, 1917

Early French tank tactics

While the testing and manufacturing of the first tanks was underway, Estienne and the AS were developing their tactical ideas. Estienne initially wanted to use the tanks in a surprise attack across a broad front, without a preparatory artillery barrage. The tanks would take up prepared positions prior to the attack, preferably at night, and advance into combat *before* the infantry, without the customary barrage. The infantry would advance to the first enemy trench-line only after the tanks had taken it and then half the tanks would continue the advance to the next enemy position. The remaining tanks would destroy or suppress any enemy infantry left in the captured trench-line, as the infantry moved to consolidate the position, and then advance to support the tanks attacking the second trench-line. These tactics, in theory, would enable a very swift advance to the German field-gun line, within an hour, thus preventing an effective enemy response. Estienne also wanted some tanks to be fitted with sledges that would carry infantry that could dismount quickly to defend ground taken by the tanks.

The first instructions on tank tactics from GQG in August 1916 were essentially a refined version of Estienne's ideas. The tanks were to enable a general offensive to take possession of the enemy's main gun line within several hours, across a broad front. All that would be left to the infantry was to occupy the positions taken by the tanks, with the cavalry expected to exploit the success. The offensive would have to be over ground suitable for tank movement; in particular areas too damaged by heavy artillery fire were to be avoided. The tanks should be used across as wide a front as possible, while the depth of the attack would be determined by the number of tanks available. It was considered sufficient to have one tank per 200 metres covering an enemy trench; as the German first trench-line would usually consist of three trenches, with the second having only one, this required four tanks per 200 metres of front (twenty tanks per kilometre), along with a general reserve of ten tanks, giving thirty tanks per kilometre of front.

As this was to be a surprise attack, all of the tanks would advance simultaneously on their respective objectives. Those tanks attacking the trenches after the first would have to advance through the preceding positions without fighting, thus ensuring both speed and conservation of ammunition. A major problem-in-waiting was acknowledged; once the tanks left the French lines it was going to be nearly impossible to exercise any command and control. It was also recognised that getting the tanks to the front line without being noticed by the Germans was going to be challenging.

Having spent time developing these ideas, the French were furious when they learnt that the British were intending to use their tanks well before the French tanks would be ready. Estienne had emphasised to the British, when he visited the Lincoln tank factory in June 1916, that the tanks should be kept back until both countries could deploy large numbers of them as part of a major offensive. Learning that Haig was intending to use British tanks on the Somme, the French made representations to E. S. Montague, the British Minister of Munitions, asking him to intervene with Haig. Haig was not prepared to delay using his tanks until the following year, which was when the French tanks would be ready, and a small number saw action in the closing stages of the Battle of the Somme in September 1916. Arguments have raged ever since as to whether Haig should have exposed this new weapon to the Germans in such a small-scale manner. Recent research suggests that the Germans would probably have discovered the Allied tank programmes before the spring of 1917 (when the French tanks would have been ready to go into action), so unveiling them earlier was probably of no great advantage to the Germans. For the Allies, it should have been an opportunity to understand the shape that tank warfare might take but it was almost impossible to judge what parts of the British experience were generally applicable and which were particular to that engagement. General Pierre des Vallières, commander of the French military mission to British GHQ, made an initial report on the British tanks which suggested that direct artillery fire was not a problem for the tanks, which was highly misleading, as the French tank crews would find out. Another plus for the AS was that the British tanks had been successful enough to convince even the most sceptical in France that their tank programme was worthwhile.

Whether the British were justified in using tanks in the Battle of the Somme or not, Estienne and his staff were forced to develop a new tactical approach, in which the tanks would become direct artillery support for the infantry. Estienne wrote to Joffre in October 1916 setting out his revised ideas on tank tactics. The role of the *Artillerie Spéciale* was to precede the infantry and be 'their guide and light'. The tactical and administrative unit was established as the *groupe*, which consisted of four batteries, each with four tanks plus the *groupe* commander's tank. Each *groupe* had a frontage of 800 metres in combat, with 200 metres per battery. The battery was to be the unit of manoeuvre, i.e. the batteries would be given individual objectives within their *groupe*'s area of operations. *Groupes* were organised administratively in *régiments de marche* (extemporised regiments), each with a *section de parc*, which was responsible for repairs and ammunition and petrol supplies.

Operations using tanks were to be carefully planned using aerial reconnaissance photos, with detailed orders for each battery. Tanks would usually be moved at night to their starting positions, possibly with artillery fire to mask the noise of the tanks' motors. Despite being armed with cannons and machine guns, the tanks' main combat power was their ability to keep advancing under enemy fire. The primary role for the tank cannon was to fire, while moving, on enemy machine guns. Despite the fact that their guns were capable of much greater theoretical ranges, the Schneiders were not expected to engage targets beyond 200 metres, with the St Chamonds not normally firing at targets beyond 600 metres. Even though the latter had a 75mm field gun, there was no expectation that it would be able to engage enemy machine guns in the second trench line, long-range fire being reserved for firing on retreating enemy infantry to disperse them. The tank commander was expected to direct the cannon fire while driving the tank, although the machine gunners were to acquire their own targets. As both medium tank designs had a very limited main arc of fire (the Schneider's main gun had a forward arc of 20 degrees, with the St Chamond's gun having a forward arc of only 5 degrees), the machine guns were primarily for protecting the tanks' flanks. As the tanks were only to use their guns at short range, an attack in fog or during the early morning was advisable. Estienne summed up the purpose of a tank's gun as 'only fire when you can't march', a pre-war infantry slogan.

The tank attack was to be made in three distinct phases. The first phase would see the tanks assisting the infantry to take the trenches of the enemy first position. The enemy batteries behind the first position would then be attacked by the tanks with short-range flanking fire, in conjunction with the infantry. The last phase comprised of the tanks advancing and taking the second enemy position. The entire attack should be completed in two or three hours, with the tanks advancing up to six kilometres. The British experience had also shown the primary importance of close infantry and tank co-operation. An infantry company was therefore to be attached to each tank battery, principally tasked with the removal of obstacles and the consolidation of captured positions. There was one particularly disastrous consequence of the first British tank attack for the French and it was that the Germans had responded by appreciably widening all of their trenches. This immediately removed the ability of the French medium tanks to cross the German trenches, as their tracks were not long enough. As it was too late to change the existing tank designs, the tanks were now going to require infantry to help them cross trenches, which became a vital task for the supporting infantry.

Now that the AS had a workable idea of how to approach battle, the difficult decision was to be made as to where and when the French tanks would make their debut. A tank operation was planned for February 1917 against German positions near Beuvraignes, on III Armée's front, with three *groupes* under *Chef d'escadron* Louis Chaubès. The general German retreat in March 1917 made this attack redundant and the operation was cancelled. Although it was very frustrating for the geared-up tank crews not to get into action, the tank crews and their commanders gained valuable experience of moving tank units in and out of deployment areas, as well as in relation to supply. General Franchet d'Esperey, the commander of Northern Army Group (GAN), wanted to use some tanks in an attack on the retreating Germans but, for no particularly good reason, Nivelle refused to agree to this operation.

The Nivelle Offensive

The French tanks would debut in the Nivelle Offensive of April 1917, as part of an operation that was intended to break through the German lines across a wide front and to all intents and purposes end the war in the Allies' favour. Nivelle's experience at Verdun had convinced him that he had worked out how to break the deadlock on the Western Front. With his new artillery methods refined at Verdun, 'We now have the formula,' he notoriously boasted, a claim that would come back to haunt him.

Nivelle's plan was for a large Franco-British offensive, which would fix the German Army in place along the Noyon salient while another strong attack broke through on another part of the front. Many senior French officers believed that the general German retreat in March required a complete reconsideration of the offensive, but Nivelle refused to recast his plans in anything but the most minor detail. A newly-formed army group, *Groupe d'armées de reserve* (Reserve Army Group, GAR), commanded by the experienced but undistinguished General Joseph-Alfred Micheler, was to provide the main thrust of the offensive. GAR consisted of three armies; V and VI Armée were to 'completely rupture' the enemy front, with X Armée acting a reserve that would advance through them and exploit their success. The French infantry would take the first and second German positions within three hours and then be ready to attack the third. Although this appears very optimistic with the benefit of hindsight, the offensive was actually more effective than is generally allowed; for example, the Germans were unable to repair those areas of their defences that had been hit hardest by the French artillery

Cyril Falls wrote that Nivelle's offensive might have been successful, 'given favourable conditions and good fortune' but, unfortunately, Nivelle had neither. Poor French security had already alerted the Germans of a forthcoming major operation but on 4 April the Germans obtained details of the offensive, from a captured NCO from *3 Zouaves*. As a major element of the Nivelle offensive was surprise, this proved to be a catastrophe and within a matter of days the number of German observation balloons on view across the front doubled. The captured intelligence combined with the fourteen-day French preparatory bombardment to give the Germans every opportunity to carefully arrange their defences and to bring forward reserves and artillery.

Nivelle intended to replicate the success he had enjoyed with his artillery at Verdun in 1916 but now across a large part of the French front. At Verdun, Nivelle had used concentrated artillery fire to completely smash a corridor for the French infantry through the German defences. While the French artillery had been undeniably effective at Verdun under Nivelle, a large part of this success was the ability of the French to concentrate large quantities of artillery on the front. As Nivelle's attack at Verdun had been on a three-division frontage, he was able to muster a formidable amount of heavy and super-heavy artillery, including five *groupements* of heavy guns, each containing from eleven to fifteen batteries, and an ALGP *groupement* that was specially formed to fight at Verdun. However, this concentration of heavy and very heavy artillery fire at Verdun was impossible to replicate across a front as large as that of the Nivelle Offensive. By comparison, for the Nivelle Offensive, V Armée had 1,100 heavy artillery pieces, along with a number of super-heavy artillery batteries, for its sixteen-division attack on 16 April. There was another vital factor at Verdun that could not be replicated for the Nivelle Offensive; the good observation that the French had across nearly the entire Verdun area. The latter was an area both well-known to the French army, with accurate maps and good vantage points for their artillery observers, factors that did not apply on the Aisne front. On the Chemin des Dames, the German positions were on a reverse slope and thus not directly observable from the French positions, other than by air, making aerial observation vital to the success of the French artillery and the whole offensive. Thus there was a serious problem created when the French aeroplanes were only able to fly for two to three hours a day because of the poor weather in the last stages of the preparatory bombardment. Conversely, the Germans had excellent observation of the French positions, particularly from the plateau of la Californie, near Craonne. In addition, the bad weather seriously degraded the roads, so that the operation had to be further postponed, until 16 April.

Most of the tanks available were attached to V Armée and were to fight in the Juvincourt and Berry-au-Bac area. V Armée had the mission to break through the German lines in one bound, on the Hurtebsie to Reims front, and then roll through the German defences. To do this, V Armée had sixteen infantry divisions, spread across five corps, with support from additional heavy artillery and two tank *groupements*. This raises the question as to whether the French should have committed the majority of its tank force in one go in its first combat operation. In other words, should the French have first used their tanks in an attack of limited size as the British had done in September 1916? It was clearly impossible to anticipate in advance all aspects of deploying the tanks, a completely new weapon, into an existing tactical situation. Thus the French were presented with a dilemma; a small-scale action would have given useful information while limiting the risks but would have given the Germans considerable information about the new weapon, without obtaining a decisive result. This was the result of the British tank attack at Flers and it was very fortunate indeed that the Germans chose to learn so little from that experience. For the French, surprise had been lost to them by the British and therefore it seemed reasonable to aim for the shock of large-scale tank employment. The Nivelle Offensive was expected to be the most decisive battle since the Marne in 1914 and there was no point in holding back a potentially effective weapon in this crucial operation.

French V Armée was opposed by four Bavarian divisions (10, 5 and 9 Reserve, Ersatz), each occupying a front of up to four and a half kilometres. The German defences were approximately seven kilometres in depth, consisting of three successive positions separated by two to three kilometres, with the fourth position being nine kilometres back. The first position was of three lines, each having several trenches. The second position had three parallel trench lines, while the third had only one line of trenches, although these were well developed. There were numerous machine-gun nests between the three positions. Each German division had four battalions in the first position, two in the second, with three battalions in reserve, ready to occupy the third rapidly if necessary. Most of the artillery was employed between the second and third positions, with a number of advance batteries between the first and second. Anti-tank defence was to be handled by indirect-fire batteries and several isolated field guns (for direct fire), placed at the rear of the second position. The ground over which the tanks and infantry would advance rose gradually up to the German positions, one reason why the tanks had been put in this area, but the battlefield was overlooked by high ground both to the north-east and south-east which was under German control. Thus the German defences were considerably stronger than had been envisaged in the initial tactical thought of Estienne and the AS.

Planning for the Tank Battle
The official tactics for the tanks in the offensive were as set out in AS *Ordre général No.1* of 1 January 1917 (with an appendix issued on 20 February 1917). In combat, each tank would have a frontage of 50 metres, with the battery having a front of 200 metres (with the battery commander second in line from the right) and the *groupe* having a front of around 1,000 metres. (Although one of AS5's tank commanders, Charles-Maurice Chenu, said that his *groupe* got into their combat formation on 16 April with 100 metres between tanks.) There was one section of the infantry attached to each battery, with three or four men with each tank and the rest of section closely following behind it. The post-war tank general Jean Perré pointed out that in a real battle the consequences of such tight frontages were 'fatal' for both the tanks and the supporting infantry and we will see that this was the case.

General Olivier Mazel, commander of V Armée, set out the plan of attack for the tanks in March. There were to be eight *groupes* for the attack, organised in two *groupements*; Groupement Bossut and

Groupement Chaubès. The tanks were to be employed to support the infantry in the attack on the third and fourth German positions, those expected to be largely undamaged by the artillery preparation. Groupement Bossut, commanded by *Chef d'escadron* Bossut, was to be attached to 32 CA, Groupement Chaubès, commanded by *Chef d'escadron* Chaubès, to 5 CA, all of the tanks concentrating at the village of Cuiry-les-Chaudardes the day before the attack.

Groupement Bossut (with 32 CA) was to march in one road-column from Chaudardes to Pontavert, cross a narrow bridge over the Miette River and then move to the second German position at Mauchamp Farm, where they would deploy into combat formation. Two of the *groupes* would move towards the south-west of Prouvais Woods, with two *groupes* moving towards the south-east corner of Claquedents Woods, the last *groupe* moving towards the north-west corner of the woods. The accompanying infantry was to be four companies supplied by 165 RI, under the direct orders of Bossut. Groupement Chaubès, with 5 CA, was to move from Chaudardes, through Beaumarais Wood, over the first and through the second German position and then attack the third, to the north of Juvincourt. There were three accompanying infantry companies under the direct command of Chaubès. Four infantrymen would advance with each tank, with the remaining infantry following with the first wave of attacking infantry. The tanks were expected to give strong support to the attacking infantry in taking the last enemy positions, thus prolonging the latter's attack. However, it was emphasised to the infantry that the tanks were there to support the attack, rather than as a substitute for the infantry and the latter were given strict orders not to wait for the tanks or get distracted by them.

However, Jean Perré argues that these official tactics could not hold back the aggressive spirit of the tank officers, largely derived from the influence of the cavalrymen within the AS. Groupement Bossut's commander, Louis Bossut, was a famous equestrian prior to the war and became a decorated cavalryman in 1915, being made a *chevalier de la légion d'honneur* by Joffre. Bossut was one of the earliest volunteers for the AS and had been commander of AS2 since December 1916. His conception of tank combat was that of the surprise charge, an idea that was already prevalent when he arrived at Champlieu. On the eve of his death, he wrote to his brother that he viewed the tanks as 'steel horses'. Michel Goya argues convincingly that Bossut conceived of himself, along with many AS officers, in the tradition of the Napoleonic cavalry, charging at the head of his men. The cavalry element within the AS was certainly dominant when Lieutenant Fourier arrived for initial training at Châlons, in November 1916, all of his classmates were from the cavalry. The casualty lists for 16 April 1917 show that of thirty-four AS officer casualties, thirteen came from the cavalry, eleven from the infantry, nine from the artillery and one from the DSA. However, the dominance of cavalry ideas was not entirely a matter of numbers; it reflected both a continuance of the pre-war high status of the cavalry and the unknown shape that tank fighting would take. There was a heated, albeit friendly, rivalry within the AS mess between the various branches of the army but Fourier leaves no doubt that the cavalry officers set the tone for tactical thinking in the early AS. As they came from another technical arm, artillerymen often found themselves in important positions; Louis Chaubès, commander of Groupement Chaubès on 16 April 1917, was from the artillery.

There were five *groupes* in Groupement Bossut; AS2, 4, 5, 6 and 9 (eighty-two Schneider tanks), with Groupement Chaubès having three *groupes*; AS3, 7, 8 (fifty Schneider tanks). Within Groupement Bossut in 32 CA, AS4 was attached to 42 DI, with the other four *groupes* being attached to 69 DI. The left of 69 DI had AS2 and 6 in 151 RI's zone, which was to attack the Nassau trench (in the third German trench line) in front of Claque-Dents wood. AS2 was on the division's left flank, with the *groupe*'s left flank on the Juvincourt to Amifontaine road. AS5 was attached to 162 RI and was to attack the left part of the Wurtzbourg trench, along with AS9 (in 267 RI's zone) attacking the centre of this trench line. The south end of the Wurtzbourg trench was to be attacked by AS4 in 94 RI's zone, part of 42 DI's attack. All of Groupement Chaubès' *groupes* in 5 CA were attached to 10 DI, initially tasked with taking the Thuringe and Spire trenches, then passing over these positions and continuing the advance. Since the tanks were supporting the second phase of the division's attack, they were only to advance past the attacking infantry three and one-half hours after the main attack started.

The tanks would be supported by *Sections de Réparations et de Ravitaillement* (SRR – resupply and repair units); SRR1 with Bossut and SRR3 with Chaubès. The SRRs would follow the *groupes* to re-supply of fuel and munitions, as well as supplying assistance for any breakdowns that the *groupe* mechanics were unable to repair. SRR1 had two unarmed St Chamonds, one Schneider, two Baby-Holt tractors and a breakdown crew on foot. SRR3 had two Schneiders and two St Chamonds, under the direction of a technical officer from the *groupement*, and was to follow the route taken by AS3. It may seem strange to use the rather unreliable St Chamond as a breakdown vehicle but the Schneiders and the Holt tractors were not powerful enough to tow a St Chamond. Even in a non-combat role the St Chamond proved unreliable; one of SRR3's St Chamonds threw a track just east of Maizy and was thus out of action on 16 April. On 16 April, the St Chamonds of the SRRs were unable to make progress on the broken-up battlefield and contributed little of use. The infantry companies attached to the tanks were expected to help them over first the French lines and then the next two German lines. Once these tasks were completed, they were to continue advancing with the tanks, while also keeping the passages on the trench lines open for the SRRs to advance.

The assembly position for both *groupements* was to be the village of Cuiry-lès-Chaudardes, just north of the Aisne. Both *groupements* left Champlieu on 11 April and disembarked at Courlandon station the following morning. Groupement Bossut arrived at Cuiry-lès-Chaudardes that evening, after a difficult nine-kilometre march in driving rain on a very dark evening, with Groupement Chaubès arriving the following night. As the offensive was again delayed by the weather, the tank crews took the opportunity to make further checks and preparations.

Major Bossut had no illusions about the task facing the *groupements* and he told his brother on the evening before the operation that 'despite all that I've been able to do, our attack will be in very bad conditions'. It was known within the AS that a German prisoner had admitted that the Germans were both aware of the French tanks and the intention to use them on V Armée's front. This removed the vital element of surprise which, coupled with the very bad weather, gave Bossut much to worry about.

Estienne and Bossut had had a fierce argument about how the latter would command his *groupement*. Estienne wanted Bossut to command his *groupement* from a rear command post but Bossut believed that it was essential for him to lead the first tank attack. He also pointed out that the *groupement* would be impossible to command once it started its advance and this proved to be the case. Estienne was eventually persuaded to allow Bossut to lead the attack in a specially-modified command tank. Bossut put his second-in-command, Captain de Gouyon, in charge of the *groupement* once it was in action and the latter was placed with the infantry staff, which was following the second infantry wave. The infantry staff had the usual compliment of telephones, runners, signallers and pigeons to communicate with the rear area but de Gouyon was only given a small group of runners and a flag to communicate with the tank units forward of him.

Groupement Bossut

The *groupements* set off in the early morning of 16 April to their assembly position, west of Pontavert, arriving there at 05.30. At 06.30, half-an-hour after the infantry attack had started, Groupement Bossut left its assembly position and moved in a two-kilometre column along the Pontavert to Guignicourt road. The march was slow and difficult because of the large number of infantry and artillery elements going forward, as well as the vehicles from the supply convoys. The column first attracted heavy artillery fire at 08.00 when it reached the Miette bridge, having been spotted by German aircraft, which although severe only hit one tank. Immediately upon crossing the bridge, Captain Noscereaux (commander, AS5) was seriously wounded when his tank was hit and he had to be evacuated. There were numerous breakdowns on the way; one tank from AS4 ditched as it was leaving the assembly position and one from AS9 had engine problems just after crossing the Miette bridge. The passage over the French lines was surprisingly easy but it then took forty-five minutes for the head of the tank column to get over the first German trench. Major Bossut was dismounted at this stage, directing his *groupement*'s tanks, only returning to his tank once the heavily-shelled area was passed. By 10.15, the *groupement* was already separated from most of the accompanying infantry, largely the result of the heavy German artillery fire, the tanks thus losing their essential infantry support before they had even deployed into their battle line.

At approximately 11.00, the first tanks of the leading *groupe* (AS2, commander Captain Pardon) were beginning to deploy when Bossut's tank was hit by an artillery shell and caught fire. Bossut and two of his crew managed to get out of their tank but all had suffered fatal injuries. There was little Pardon could do but to carry on with the attack and his *groupe* was shortly at the second German position. Only seven tanks of the fourteen in the *groupe* managed to get over this position, the other tanks breaking down, four permanently. The other three tanks took up to two hours to get moving again. In the interim, part of the German trench line was occupied by a small contingent of French infantry from 151 RI.

Just before noon, the five remaining tanks of AS2 reached their objective (Hill 78) where they spent half an hour signalling the French infantry to move forward in support. However, the infantry were unable to advance because of heavy machine-gun and artillery fire, although it is likely that many failed to see the tank signals due to the bad visibility on the battlefield and the primitive measures taken for signalling. The

Schneiders had had their rear doors painted white on the inside, so that they could be opened and closed as a signal, but this, like the flag given for signalling, was only going to be useful for short-range signals along the infantry's line of sight. At 13.00, the tanks gave up trying to persuade the infantry to follow them and they advanced towards their action zone west of Claquedents Wood. Here they ran into a German 77mm field gun, which engaged them at 500–700 metres. The tanks fired at this gun without halting, hitting and destroying it, although the gun hit two tanks and immobilised them. The crews from the immobilised tanks dismounted and then captured a German first aid post, where they took around sixty prisoners, including an officer. The tank crews then converted the post into a defensive position. The remainder of the *groupe* now found itself under accurate German artillery fire from both Juvincourt (to the north-west) and Claquedents Wood (to the north-east), with the additional problem of receiving some French artillery fire that fell short. The engine of Pardon's tank failed around 13.15 and the tank was then hit whilst the crew evacuated it, killing or wounding the entire crew, including Pardon who was fatally wounded. Over the next fifteen minutes, two more tanks were hit and caught fire, while another ditched in a shell-hole. By 14.00, the three remaining operational tanks from the *groupe* had reached their next objective, where they attempted, once again in vain, to signal the infantry to advance. Three of the previously immobilised tanks from the *groupe* were repaired in time to fight off a German counter-attack and then advance on Mauchamp Farm from the third German trench line at approximately 14.30.

AS6 (Captain Chanoine) was following AS2. On arriving at the second German position with sixteen tanks, Chanoine's *groupe* encountered the same problems that AS2 had and AS6 lost two tanks to breakdowns. In the hour between 11.30 and 12.30, the *groupe* was engaged at 1,800–2,000 metres by two German batteries, with five tanks being hit and catching fire. To lessen the *groupes'* exposure to artillery fire, Chanoine moved his unit east, which decreased the intensity of artillery fire, although he was also helped by the advance of AS5, which threatened the enemy batteries and thus eased their fire on his *groupe*. After a German counter-attack of 14.30 was broken up by his *groupe* and the remaining tanks of AS2, Chanoine took the opportunity of a brief respite in the action to form one unit out of the remnants of the two *groupes*. Around 15.00, he saw to his rear some French infantry advancing on the second German position, between Mauchamp Farm and the Miette River. Withdrawing to support them, he discovered 151

RI's command post, commanded by Colonel Moisson, which was operating to the left of 69 DI. The infantry regiment had been tasked with taking the first German line at Cholèra and then the second and third positions. Remarkably, by 16.00, its lead battalion had taken its objectives, capturing numerous prisoners, machine guns, trench mortars and three field guns. However, the regiment had been unable to push any further than Béliers Wood. Moisson and Chanoine extemporised a limited attack with the tanks and the French infantry. Although the attack was successful, a tank was hit by close-range artillery fire, which persuaded Chanoine and Moisson that the tanks should retire back to the French lines, the former ordering the rest of the *groupement* to retire as well (Chanoine had taken command of the *groupement* as Forsanz was missing but how he managed to get this order to the rest of the *groupement* is unclear). This was clearly a wise decision as both the tanks and the French infantry were no longer in any condition to make any further progress; 151 RI had lost 700 men and a great many officers by early evening. On the way back four tanks ditched in shell-holes, although these were recovered by the SRR crews the following day.

When AS5 (Captain Dubois) arrived with fifteen tanks at Béliers Wood it divided into two columns, having lost several tanks to ditching in large shell holes and one destroyed by enemy artillery. AS5 received further heavy artillery fire from the German third position and six tanks broke down as they crossed the German trenches, three of them permanently. The nine remaining tanks continued their advance and the *groupe* attempted to make contact with 162 RI without success. However, the Germans were distracted enough by the appearance of the tanks to enable the French infantry to occupy the Wurtzbourg trench line. Dubois sent three tanks out to reconnoitre but they all fell victim to shellfire, with two being damaged and one destroyed. In the interim, Dubois had managed to make contact with Colonel Bertrand of 162 RI, who informed Dubois that the infantry regiment had already lost over 800 men and thus would be unable to support the tanks. By 17.00, the *groupe* had moved into a position behind a small wood to give themselves some protection from the increasingly intense artillery fire that they were being subjected to. An enemy counter-attack came from the direction of the railway but this was beaten-off by the tanks' gunfire. Dubois and Bertrand were organising their position for defence when orders for the tanks to retire came through from Chanoine. Dubois stripped the machine guns from his immobilised tanks, gave them to the infantry and then moved back to the assembly position. As the tanks retired, they came under heavy artillery fire, leaving seven tanks immobilised in front of the French front line.

AS9 (Captain Goubernard) lost two tanks to breakdowns leaving the assembly position and was then halted at Cholèra Farm for nearly an hour, as the German artillery fire on the preceding *groupes* had seriously damaged the passages over the trench lines. While waiting for a new passage to be made by the infantry, the tanks were attacked several times by German aircraft, although to no effect. The *groupe* arrived at Mauchamp Farm with eleven tanks, a further three having broken down on the way. Just before 13.00, the *groupe* deployed for battle and, although the broken up terrain was difficult going for the tanks, the artillery fire was lighter than elsewhere. As the *groupe* got its remaining eleven tanks to the Wurtzbourg trench, they were obliged by the state of the ground to form into a column in order to cross this trench line, where they were subjected to fire from heavy artillery and large-calibre trench mortars. Almost immediately, four tanks were immobilised and six were set on fire. The crews dismounted their machine guns, set them up in the nearest French-occupied trenches and then slowly retreated to the French lines, all the while under constant and accurate German artillery and machine-gun fire. Only one tank was still in action when Goubernard returned from liaising with the infantry and he ordered it back to the French lines, at which point it broke down. Heinz Guderian was not exaggerating when he wrote in *Achtung-Panzer!* that AS9 was 'wiped out'.

AS4 (Captain Forsanz) arrived without incident at Cholèra Farm. Upon seeing the planned passage alongside Mauchamp Farm had not been prepared, Forsanz split his unit into two *demi-groupes* in order to get into the combat zone. One *demi-groupe* with two batteries, having lost one tank to artillery fire, moved to the left towards the German second position. The other *demi-groupe* on the right lost two tanks to breakdowns but picked up two tanks that had got separated from their *groupes*. By mid-afternoon, only five tanks from the *groupe* had reached the German second position (with elements of 94 RI), although they were quickly followed by three more tanks, the other two of the second echelon having been hit by artillery fire and set on fire. A further two tanks were hit and caught fire after the *groupe* had crossed the German second position. By this stage, 94 RI had gained several hundred metres of ground with support from the tanks but the French infantry was unable to hold this ground due to very heavy machine-gun and artillery fire. These infantry had the disturbing experience of seeing a number of tank crews becoming 'living torches' as they exited their blazing tanks. An added difficulty for the French troops was that the banks of the Aisne-Marne canal were still in enemy hands, thus allowing constant and effective enfilading fire from the Germans. Forsanz could see that further tank action would be fruitless and he decided to retire back to Cholèra. Groupement Bossut's part in the battle was now over.

Groupement Chaubès

Groupement Chaubès left Cuiry-lès-Chaudardes on the early evening of 15 April to move to its assembly area in Beaumarais Wood, which it left at 06.20 the following day. AS3 (sixteen tanks) was in the lead, with AS7 (sixteen tanks) following and AS8 (eight tanks) bringing up the rear. German observation planes spotted the tanks of AS3 as soon as they came out of the cover of Beaumarais Woods and the tanks were then subjected to accurate artillery fire. In consequence Captain Beltz (commander of AS3) ordered his *groupe* to spread out, which prevented any tanks being hit but the accompanying infantry battalion took significant casualties. Two tanks were hit and immobilised by artillery while they waited to cross the last French trench but, within twenty-five minutes, the leading tank of the *groupe* was at the first German trench. Upon their arrival, the tanks discovered that the trench was substantially wider than had been anticipated and the tanks now had to wait for the infantry to come up and prepare the crossing for them. Although the German artillery fire had by this point lessened, heavy machine-gun fire prevented the supporting infantry from making a crossing point for the tanks. Beltz sought another passage over the German trenches but while doing so his tank was hit by a shell fragment and immobilised. The rest of the *groupe* continued to seek a new passage but the heavy shellfire resumed and they moved back and then turned off their engines. Astonishingly, although the tanks remained stationary for nearly thirty minutes, none were hit as the German artillery fire had become very sporadic. Unfortunately, then AS7 came rumbling by and provoked the artillery fire to resume at full strength, which caused four tanks of AS3 to catch fire. Beltz ordered the crews to dismount and become machine-gun detachments for 89 RI in a nearby occupied German trench, where they helped repel a German counter-attack. By 17.00, both enemy and friendly artillery fire began to slacken and it was clear to Beltz that the French attack was now over. He ordered the weapons to be stripped from the immobilised tanks and carried back in his five remaining tanks. They were badly hampered by German artillery fire while undertaking this dangerous task and, after a particularly violent barrage, four tanks were set on fire, leaving the remaining tank badly damaged but still mobile. The latter, despite a badly-damaged petrol tank, made its way back to the French lines where it ditched in a shell hole. By nightfall, most of the *groupe*'s surviving crews had managed to return to the French lines on foot.

The next *groupe*, AS7 (Captain de Boisgelin), was hit by intense artillery fire while it was passing Temple Farm. The passage over the French lines proved easy but as the *groupe* advanced it became clear to Boisgelin that AS3 was in serious trouble at the first German trench line. He spread out the tanks of AS7 to alleviate some of the effects of the artillery fire and then moved to the left but they came under increasing artillery fire as they approached AS3. The two *groupes* presented a comparatively compact target and the fire was severe, with one tank catching fire and many others being immobilised. Under such withering fire, there was little Boisgelin could do but retire back past Temple Farm, while some of his crews took their machine guns and joined the other dismounted crews from AS3 in the German trenches. One tank remained to collect and transport dismounted weapons back to the French lines, while the others moved off. This tank returned during the night to the assembly position to discover that only four other tanks from the *groupe* had made it back, leaving four tanks immobilised on the battlefield and seven destroyed by fire.

Only eight tanks of the last *groupe*, AS8 (Captain Blic), were able to start the attack as the other eight broke down or ditched in marshy ground on the way to the jump-off point. Almost as soon as the *groupe* began to move, it came under heavy artillery fire, the Germans having got their range when engaging the preceding *groupes*. Just after 07.00, one tank was penetrated by a 105mm shell, which exploded inside, killing or wounding the entire crew. Forty-five minutes later, the leading tank of AS8 was still 500 metres south of the German trench line and being subjected to intense artillery fire. To avoid getting caught up with the other two *groupes*, Blic ordered his unit to move to the left and spread out. However, it soon became clear that the passage over the German trenches would take hours and Blic made the reasonable decision to retire, ordering the *groupe* back to Beaumarais Wood but leaving several dismounted AS machine-gun detachments in place. While returning to the French lines four tanks were hit by artillery fire, three of these being recovered later after 'great effort', leaving only four tanks to get back to the safety of their own lines under their own steam.

After a heroic and difficult recovery effort by SRR3 during the evening of 16 April, the *groupe*'s losses amounted to five tanks, which had all been destroyed by German artillery. Groupement Chaubès left thirty-three tanks in total on the battlefield.

The French captured a German artillery commander's report after the Nivelle Offensive, which detailed its action on 16 April against Groupement Chaubès. German 111 Field Artillery Regiment, commanded by Colonel Moeller, was stationed in the Craonne sector, approximately ten kilometres to the north-west of Berry-au-Bac. Moeller had at his disposal a variety of medium and heavy-calibre guns in seven batteries. The German artillery observers had excellent visibility from their positions on the la Californie plateau, north-east of the German trench line that the tanks were attacking. Interestingly, Moeller reports that that the 150mm howitzer was by far the most effective gun against the tanks, each 150mm battery scoring on average four direct hits for the expenditure of just over fifty shells. Even one direct hit by an artillery shell of this calibre was disastrous for a tank. When Major Bossut's brother, Pierre, went searching for his brother's tank, what he found was so badly damaged that he only recognised the wreckage because of his brother's flag. The German 77mm batteries and the 210mm mortar battery were not as effective, although the large-calibre mortar had never been intended to engage moving targets. Moeller's single artillery regiment knocked-out seventeen of Chaubès' tanks in total, destroying the *groupement*, out of the total of twenty-six destroyed, for the expenditure of 277 shells.

Results of the Nivelle Offensive
It appeared that the first action of the French tanks had been both costly and not particularly promising. While Groupement Bossut had got some of its tanks much further than the French infantry, not a single one of Chaubès' tanks had got beyond the first German trench line. British tank pioneer Colonel Stern met with Estienne and a number of his senior officers, the week following the 16 April attacks. Stern reported that the French officers were very disappointed and that 'they generally seemed highly dissatisfied with the French tank'. This was hardly unreasonable as the first French tank action had been at a considerable human and material cost. The AS had lost thirty-four killed, thirty-seven missing, and 109 wounded, the casualties including a significant number of officers. The loss of equipment was just as alarming; thirty-one tanks from Groupement Bossut and twenty-six tanks from Groupement

Chaubès had been destroyed by German artillery. Only Nivelle, desperately seeking some evidence for the success of his offensive, was unequivocal in his praise, describing the AS as having a 'place of honour' amongst the combatants. Although all the written reports conceded that the tanks and their crews had made a 'heroic and stoic effort' in the 'horrible conditions' of that day, the tanks had failed to impress most of the French infantry commanders and their men. For example, V Armée's report was much less enthusiastic than Nivelle's and it noted that the tanks had appeared too late to help the infantry, as well as saying (erroneously) that it appeared that the tanks could not successfully advance under artillery fire. As the tanks appeared to be difficult to command *en masse*, the report suggested that the tanks should only be used for local attacks in small numbers. (This suggestion is worth noting as events would show that this was the very worst way of employing the tanks and it eventually became clear that that using them *en masse* was the most effective tactic. This is a prime example of how difficult it was to make firm conclusions from the limited combat experience that was then available.) The GAN report concluded that the tanks had made a useful contribution to the operation, particularly by stopping numerous German counter-attacks, but that the French infantry simply had been unable to advance through the heavy German artillery and machine-gun fire, thus negating most of the tanks' gains. 5 CA's report echoed the GAN report and agreed that the tanks had been a great help to its infantry but exploitation had been impossible due to the weight of German artillery and long-range machine-gun fire. In consequence, it made some useful observations. The report recommended that aircraft should be attached to the tank units to ward off enemy aircraft and direct counter-battery fire on anti-tank gun positions. The approach march needed to be carefully reconnoitred and made ready for moving across. It was important that terrain should have areas of cover to disguise the tanks' movement, which should be, if possible, from cover to cover. It also underlined the importance of preventing the tanks from outpacing their infantry support.

Estienne and the AS were now in a very difficult position within the French army, as the tank project was a significant consumer of valuable resources that now appeared might be better used elsewhere. How Estienne and the AS turned around this very unpromising situation is the subject of the following chapter.

Chapter 3

The Turnaround at Laffaux
and the Aftermath of the
Nivelle Offensive

If all the available French tank units had been used on 16 April 1917, as intended, then the subsequent story of the AS might have been very different but Estienne had a stroke of luck when his final available *groupement*'s attack on 17 April was called off. Groupement Lefebvre, commanded by *Chef d'escadron* Hubert Lefebvre, had been prepared for an attack near Moronvilliers, in IV Armée's zone, but this was called off on the day due to the general failure of the offensive in that area. How Estienne and the AS completely changed the apparently hopeless situation they were in is the subject of this chapter.

Groupement Lefebvre
Groupement Lefebvre consisted of three *groupes*: AS1 and 10 with Schneider tanks, and a composite *groupe* of AS31 and 33 (referred to hereafter as AS31), with St Chamonds. (The unit was a composite one because of the impossibility of getting enough St Chamonds ready for combat, an early sign of the design's difficulties.) One significant advantage the *groupement* had over those of Chaubès and Bossut was that it had been training (under the personal direction of Estienne) with the *17 Bataillon de chasseurs à pied* (17 BCP – an elite unit of light infantry) since 3 January 1917, an advantage that would become very apparent in this engagement.

The *groupement* was placed under VI Armée's command on 25 April and was moved to Crouy six days later, for a planned attack east of Laffaux. (AS10 remained at Crouy in reserve.) AS1 (Captain Robinet) was attached to a dismounted cavalry division (Division Brécard), attacking south of the Guerbette valley and Fruty. AS31 (Captain Calmels) was attached to 158 DI attacking east of Fruty. Although there were difficult approach routes and an extensive area filled with large shell-holes to go through, the going for the tanks was generally good and, crucially, the assembly areas were hidden from German observation. The *groupement* used the first three days of May to liaise with the infantry in whose areas they were operating and to check equipment, as well as establishing an ammunition depot and make a detailed reconnaissance of the area.

This second tank operation had to be a success if Estienne and the AS were to continue and it was by necessity executed in a very different manner from the first. Estienne and his staff took the opportunity to analyse the 16 April attacks in detail and make sure that mistakes were not repeated. This is the first demonstration of the remarkable ability within the AS to learn from experience and rapidly introduce effective innovations. The lengthy approach march on 16 April had been identified as one of the most egregious mistakes and it was not to be repeated. For this engagement, three batteries from each *groupe* were placed close to the French lines before the battle in order that they could advance with the infantry, not after them. Each of these batteries was given specific tasks and objectives (unlike on 16 April where objectives had been only given to the *groupes*), with one battery held in reserve with the *groupe* commander. To better integrate the tanks with the infantry and at a lower level, the command post of each *groupe* was placed with the relevant infantry division's CP. The *groupe* commanders were given some tactical flexibility by virtue of having a reserve component, an approach that was also applied to the *groupements*. As it was generally agreed that the line formation of the *groupements* on 16 April was impossible to control, the *groupement* on 5 May was echeloned in depth, thus (in theory) enabling the *groupement* commander to reinforce success and concentrate effort, as well as being easier to exercise control.

On 16 April the tanks had been mainly in danger from German artillery fire and considerable thought was put into alleviating this. An aircraft was tasked with keeping the *groupement* commander informed about his units' movements, as well as to direct counter-battery fire on enemy anti-tank batteries. A further six fighters were attached to protect this plane, in addition to chasing off any enemy artillery-observation aircraft. Each tank was given a flare pistol to call down smoke shells from the artillery to mask their movement. Another innovation was to leave part of the accompanying infantry under the direct control of the *groupe* technical officer, thus ensuring better support for the tanks.

The Battle on 5–6 May

On the early morning of 5 May, AS1 was at its assembly position, the officers and men using the next couple of hours to have final liaison meetings with the infantry and making final checks on their itinerary. At 04.45, the *groupe* moved into action and the first battery arrived at the German lines within half an hour, losing no tanks despite being under continuous artillery fire. Here it encountered the first wave of French infantry that had been stopped by heavy German machine-gun fire. The tanks quickly destroyed numerous machine guns and enabled the infantry to continue their advance. One tank captured a large group of Germans sheltering in a trench and then forced the prisoners to help un-ditch a tank and take its wounded crew back to the French lines.

The third battery supported the infantry in capturing Laffaux Mill and then repelled an immediate German counter-attack, causing the attackers to retire in some disorder. Two tanks got as far as a ravine three kilometres from their jump-off point, before the lack of infantry support caused them to retire.

The fourth battery was not as fortunate; when it arrived at the Rossignol trench-line three tanks broke down there. One crew dismounted with its machine guns and defended an occupied trench whilst one of the others destroyed two German machine-gun posts with its cannon. The remaining tank carried on alone, giving the infantry fire support as well as destroying any undamaged wire in its way, before successfully attacking the Château de la Motte. The tank only retired when it was relieved by the French infantry, who occupied the château, the latter losing this position shortly afterwards to a counter-attack.

The second battery, which had been in reserve, was then ordered to recapture the Château de la Motte but the operation was cancelled at the last minute. This attack was rescheduled for the following evening as conditions in the morning were too poor for a tank attack due to heavy overnight rain. However, as the French infantry were still disorganised from the previous day's fighting, as well as being scattered across the battlefield, it became clear to the tank and infantry commanders that it was impossible to co-ordinate their units and the attack was again cancelled, the tanks remaining only to ward off any counter-attacks.

The first combat action of the St Chamonds of AS31 (Captain Calmels) was very trying, as the tanks had considerable difficulty in just getting to the assembly area, the *groupe* losing four tanks to breakdowns in the process. In fact, so many St Chamonds broke down that Calmels was forced to commandeer a Schneider battery to act as his reserve. Calmels thus had only twelve St Chamonds operational by the start of the engagement, along with four Schneiders from AS10. The St Chamonds successfully helped the French infantry to overcome the wire barriers and suppressed enemy fire but the tanks broke down one after another. One battery entered combat with only two tanks, as the other two were out of action before even reaching the jump-off position. One of the former then broke down and the remaining tank was forced to return since the supporting infantry were halted by machine-gun fire. However, the St Chamonds were not totally ineffective; two tanks attacked a blockhouse that had halted the French infantry, killing fifty Germans and causing another thirty to surrender. In another action, one tank opened fire at 200 metres on a German counter-attack and drove it off. At mid-morning, the Schneider battery tried to support an infantry attack on the Rade trench line but when the tanks arrived, the Germans were still in possession of the trench line and, with no infantry support, the tanks were forced to retire, one of them breaking down temporarily in the process. This position was attacked again the following day by two St Chamonds but these had no better luck and they both broke down returning to the French lines.

By the end of the day on 5 May, the *groupement* had taken casualties of thirteen officers and forty-two men, although only three were killed, with 17 BCP losing thirty-two men. AS1 had sent fifteen tanks into combat, of which twelve returned; one broke down in the French lines, the other two outside. AS10 sent four tanks (one battery) into combat and all had returned. AS31 sent twelve tanks into combat and nine returned, one tank being destroyed by German artillery.

Results of Groupement Lefebvre's action
The results were thus significantly better than those of 16 April and the casualties even more so, with only one tank being destroyed by enemy artillery fire. General Marie-Eugène Debeney, a major figure in the French Army, reported that the results obtained by the tanks had been 'encouraging'. This was the result of the careful planning by Estienne, as well as some other helpful factors.

The well thought-out and prepared routes had allowed the tanks to move swiftly and the French air force had complete mastery of the skies. Unlike on 16 April, French counter-battery fire had effectively suppressed the German artillery and its observation positions, notably reducing this risk to the tanks. With the tanks positioned so close to the

German lines, had arrived at them too quickly for the German artillery to respond. The operation demonstrated that good liaison between the infantry, artillery and the tanks was essential, although infantry-tank liaison *during* the battle had proved just as difficult as on 16 April, despite extensive preparation by the infantry commanders and AS officers. Even so, one of the French aircraft had made contact with the *groupement* commander and greatly assisted his control over his tanks, as well as directing covering artillery fire. The attached *chasseurs* from 17 BCL managed to establish telephone communication between the front line and commanders at the rear, in addition to using visual signals effectively. This is a significant example of better training giving noticeable dividends in battle. In conclusion, this was not a particularly successful operation overall but the tanks' success was enough to give the AS some breathing space to reorganise and it removed the very real threat of disbandment of the organisation.

The Consequences of the Nivelle Offensive
The consequences of the Nivelle Offensive for the French Army were to be far reaching and within a matter of weeks there was widespread disorder within the army. Although the offensive had produced proportionally higher casualties for the Germans than previous ones and had severely damaged the morale of much of their army, Nivelle had made extravagant promises of success and these were what the offensive was judged against in France. Political pressure on the government, largely the result of alarmist and incorrect reports about French casualties, forced the Ribot cabinet to intervene, first appointing General Henri-Phillipe Pétain as Chief of the General Staff at the end of April, in an attempt to restore confidence in the army across the country. This weak compromise only lasted two weeks and, on 15 May, the French government tried to save itself by relieving Nivelle of command and appointing Pétain as commander-in-chief.

For the AS, the Nivelle Offensive operations had exposed two major issues; the tactical approach and the deficiencies of the tank designs. In regards to the problems of tactics, many of the changes enacted for the attack on 5–6 May appeared to have successfully addressed these but it was now apparent that the tanks were in far greater danger from artillery than had been foreseen. The French were considerably surprised by the fact that the German heavy artillery had comprised a greater threat to the tanks than their field artillery had. The tanks were expected to be vulnerable to direct artillery fire but it was alarming news that the majority of losses were from indirect fire. The loss of two tanks to an isolated 77mm gun using close-range direct fire was an ominous portent for the future, largely unnoticed at the time.

The tanks were not designed to withstand direct artillery fire, which would have required unmovable amounts of armour, but the tanks' armour was completely proof against ordinary bullets and although the German SmK round could theoretically penetrate it, this never proved more than a minor hazard. The Schneider's weaker rear armour was penetrated on a number of occasions on 16 April, raising cause for concern. There had also been instances where German aircraft fire penetrated the Schneiders' roofs but this does not detract from the success of the tanks' armour. 16 April had shown tanks surviving a considerable weight of artillery fire; Bossut's tanks were under fire for two hours at the second German trench line without losing any personnel. The single casualty to artillery on 5 May seemed to confirm the effectiveness of their armour. The tanks' tracks were revealed to be very vulnerable to any nearby explosions, which almost invariably immobilised the tank. Once stationary, tanks were in serious danger; Groupement II reported that the damaged tanks it had left on the battlefield were subjected to systematic fire from the German artillery until destroyed. It is for these very reasons that Estienne advised using the tanks in the low visibility of dusk, rather than in broad daylight as they were on 16 April, a point made in his report of the operation. In addition, he made the sensible recommendation that the tanks should never be left under German artillery fire for more than an hour.

Most of the other tactical faults were largely the result of the lack of combat experience with tanks. For example, the time it would take to move the tanks into their deployment positions was considerably underestimated, resulting in the *groupements* arriving late. There were issues with the infantry-tank liaison because the infantry support was improvised over too short a period, with only 17 BCP sufficiently trained to be of use to the tanks and even this unit encountered severe difficulties in its support role. The main problem for effective liaison between the tanks and the infantry was the sheer weight of German artillery and machine-gun fire on the battlefield, as would be the case for the rest of the war. Although it must have been very frustrating for the tanks crews to find it so difficult to liaise with the infantry, it needs to be remembered that the infantry had an unenviable task. 17 BCP's regimental history notes the unwelcome fact for the infantry that tanks attracted enemy fire, particularly that of machine guns, which the tanks were immune to, unlike the infantry. In nearly every case, the supporting infantry on 16 April and 5 May was incapable of helping their tanks because they were being pinned down by heavy fire. This could not be addressed by the AS and would require the French army to change its tactical approach.

Although we have noted previously that the cavalry arm maintained a certain prestige within the early AS, this should not be taken to mean that Bossut and the prevailing cavalry ethos were to blame for what happened on 16 April. Certainly, some aspects of Bossut's plans were clearly influenced by his cavalry background, such as his insistence on leading his men from the front, but most of the difficulties encountered were not the result of poor planning. Léon Dutil convincingly argues that the operation was as carefully planned as it could be; the AS had been working on this attack since February and there had been numerous liaison meetings between the AS and the senior infantry commanders before the battle. Bossut and de Gouyon had spent an entire four days at V Armée HQ, planning their attack in consultation with Generals Micheler and Gamelin. The tactic of moving the *groupements* in large columns across the battlefield proved disastrous on 16 April but the AS was expecting that the first two German positions would have been destroyed and their artillery silenced as the tanks advanced. In the event, neither of these events occurred, leaving the tanks far more exposed than could have been reasonably foreseen by Bossut or Estienne. It does seem likely that if the *groupes* had attacked simultaneously, rather than separately, the German artillery would not have been able to concentrate its fire on each *groupe* in turn and thus the spacing of the attacks was a mistake in the plan, particularly in relation to Groupement Chaubès. Estienne realised after the battle that the tanks should not have been moved into combat on a fixed time-scale but only after the German observation posts had been taken. This is an example of a lesson that only experience could reveal.

What should have been planned for was the heavy traffic on the roads during the offensive, which would have caused delays even if the weather had been better. However, this was immediately recognised and on 5 May the tanks were moved in batteries to the starting positions. Guderian argued that the tanks should have set off earlier in order to keep pace with the infantry but it is difficult to see how this would this have made any significant difference on the day; the tanks got two kilometres further than the infantry and they would have been even more isolated if they had advanced earlier.

It was not the absence of liaison with the other arms that proved the crucial problem on 16 April, so much as the absence of surprise, which is fault of Nivelle's planning rather than a fault of the AS. Bossut had correctly recognised that there would be no command and control of the *groupements* once they got past the French lines. The last 32 CA HQ heard from Bossut was a message sent via a pigeon that arrived around 10.00, saying that he was sorry but that the tanks were running behind schedule. De Gouyon, nominally in command of Groupement Bossut, was unable to communicate with the *groupe* commanders and thus exercised no discernible influence on the battle. The *groupe* commanders had difficulties even communicating with each other; the loss of Bossut and his two subordinates left Captain Forsanz theoretically in charge but he was unable to communicate with the *groupement* because it was so spread out, leaving Forsanz commanding the *groupement* in name only. *Commandant* Chaubès remained at the infantry command post throughout the battle, as ordered, but he exercised no control over his *groupement*. Captain Chanoine (AS6) reported to V Armée HQ, in the late afternoon of 16 April, that he knew that Captain Forsanz had taken field command of the *groupement* but Chanoine had received no communication from him. He knew nothing about the state of the other *groupes*, other than AS2, whose remaining tanks he had taken command of.

Despite the terrible and dispiriting losses, there were many reasons to see the French tanks' debut as actually rather more promising than it first appeared. The tanks had in some places advanced over two kilometres further than the infantry and then passed over the second German positions. The Nivelle Offensive was a failure because of inadequate artillery preparation but this should not obscure the relatively good initial tactical performance of the AS, particularly considering how difficult the conditions were. There was also a quite unexpected bonus to the French from the mixed results of their first tank offensive; the Germans were seriously misled by their success against the tanks. There seemed to be no compelling reason for OHL to develop tanks of their own and the direct-fire anti-tank batteries were disbanded, anti-tank measures being largely left to the SmK-armed infantry and the heavier artillery, thanks to its success against the tanks on 16 April. The changes to tactics made by the AS over the two weeks between 16 April and 5–6 May are impressive both in their scale and their success. Pétain's remodelling of the French Army over the months following his appointment allowed the AS time to further improve its tactics and modify, to the extent this was possible, the tanks. Pétain quickly recognised the value of the AS and it was to receive his full support for the rest of the war. While the tactical issues appeared to have effective solutions, the various technical and training deficiencies that the first AS operation had unveiled clearly required immediate attention and we will now discuss the reaction to the Nivelle Offensive within the AS.

The Aftermath
With the winding-down of the Nivelle Offensive and the subsequent temporary lull in offensive operations, the situation for the AS did not look good: it was even rumoured within the organisation that it was to be disbanded and the men returned to their regiments. Although we have seen that there was a marked improvement in the performance of the AS between the action on 16 April and those of 5–6 May, there was clearly much work to do. Two main concerns were now paramount; the tank designs themselves and the training of the crews.

Training became a priority as the relative success of AS1 on 16 April had made clear how vital this was. It is important to note that even this *groupe* did not start training as a unit until mid-November 1916, when only eight Schneiders and four St Chamonds were available. The time spent in training for the rest of the *groupes* had been only enough to familiarise the crews with their machines at a very basic level. The other initial *groupes* (AS2 to 5, all Schneiders) had been formed between December 1916 and January 1917. The Schneider *groupes* AS6 to 9 were formed in February 1917, along with the first St Chamond *groupe*, AS31. AS32 and 33 (St Chamonds) were formed the following month. Thus most of the AS troops in action during the Nivelle Offensive had only been training together for a maximum of eight weeks. In particular, Estienne was very concerned about the poor performance of the AS drivers, writing that they had simply not had enough training in the tanks or experience of driving them. This had resulted in numerous drivers getting their tanks stuck in shell holes or one of the many other obstacles that could be found on the battlefield. However, there were also a number of cases of negligent driving; several tanks reversed into ditches or shell holes because the drivers failed to post someone at the rear for observation. Estienne recognised that visibility from the tanks was very poor, which had forced many drivers to operate their tanks with their hatches open, thus incurring numerous head injuries.

Estienne was very concerned with the performance of the tanks' guns but this was to prove very difficult to address. The accuracy that could be obtained from stationary artillery pieces was impossible from a tank's gun; the short-barrelled gun (in the case of the Schneider), poor observation from inside the tank and the moving platform all militated against accuracy. In Estienne's report on the action at Laffaux on 5–6 May, he stated that the tank gunners had all been 'satisfactory', although their training had been 'simple'. The St Chamonds had generally expended more machine-gun rounds and shells than had the Schneiders. Two of the former had fired over 100 shells whereas no Schneider fired more than forty-eight shells. By comparison, on 16 April, none of the Schneiders had fired more than eighty shells. However, ammunition expenditure amongst the tanks on 5–6 May varied enormously and it is therefore difficult to draw any firm conclusion. Estienne told a British delegation that the short-barrelled 75mm gun was 'inaccurate' due to its low velocity and that without a telescope or a sight 'there was little chance of them hitting a target even at 150 yards'. Much thought went into what size and type of gun should be fitted to the tanks; the French considered that a 47mm gun with a 2kg projectile was 'infinitely superior' to the 75mm piece, a recommendation shared by Mourret and the DSA. There is an interesting report in the Stern archives that details the French army's testing of various artillery pieces for the tanks which suggests why the 47mm was not ultimately adopted and, more importantly, illustrates how inaccurate the tank guns available were. Firing from only 100 metres at a large target (17.5 square metres), the standard 75S gun managed only two hits out of twenty shells fired. However, the modified 75S (as being fitted to the Schneiders) scored 100 per cent with seventeen shells fired whereas the 47mm only managed sixteen hits out of nineteen. The 47mm gun did have slightly better grouping than both versions of the 75S but, crucially, it had a much slower rate of fire. As rapidity of fire was considered to be of great importance for a tank gun, this swung the argument against the 47mm gun and the modified 75S continued in service. The primary difficulty in directing accurate tank fire, from both the main gun and the machine guns, was a result of the poor visibility from the inside of the tanks, one report stating that 'the tank is almost blind'. The limited number of view-ports that the tanks had were impossible to use if a tank was under artillery fire and some form of optical device was clearly necessary for both the gunner and the driver. Mourret recommended fitting a sight to improve the aiming of the cannon, an elementary version of which was produced by the workshop at Champlieu, and the *Service des inventions* commissioned an effective optical sight, although this was still not ready by the end of June. The fuel pump remained unreliable and was never made entirely satisfactory.

However, the greatest problem for the AS in both actions had been the mechanical reliability of the two tank designs. In relation to the St Chamonds, Estienne reported that it was mainly their inadequate tracks that had caused the numerous breakdowns, a problem he had identified with this design from the beginning. Other faults included the fragility of the petrol tanks, which frequently detached themselves from their mountings due to vibration within the tanks. The St Chamond factory's *Directeur général*, Thomas Leurent, had to write to Breton and the *Comité* disputing the numbers of St Chamonds that had broken down on 5 May because there was so much criticism within the AS of the tank's reliability.

The Schneiders were not quite as fragile as the St Chamonds but there were a number of inherent problems with the design. So high was the interior temperature that there was a suggestion by some crews that their petrol tanks had caught fire spontaneously, having heated to critical temperature over the long advance on 16 April. There is no evidence that this happened on any other occasion and it is just as likely that these tanks were hit by incendiary shells, which set fire to the petrol tanks. Just as worrying, the Schneider clutches were prone to burning out when moving across difficult terrain for any length of time. Estienne noted that the tanks would have to be limited to short actions in the future, due to the interior heat exhausting the crews within four or five hours. (Many of the crews on 16 April had been in action with their tanks since 02.00, some not leaving the battlefield until mid-evening. Of course, the crews had taken the opportunity to get out of their tanks whenever possible but many had been operating their tanks for over twenty hours. This is a considerable feat of endurance by any standards.)

Another unwelcome surprise to the AS was how easily their tanks caught fire; the experience of battle suggested that once a shell had breached a tank's armour, the tank was very likely to catch fire if it was hit again. As neither the Schneider nor the St Chamond had armour on the underside of their hulls, any HE shells that exploded underneath them could set the tanks on fire. Lieutenant Fourier was badly burnt when a shell exploded just under his St Chamond on 5 May, the explosion blowing his 23-ton tank off the ground and filling it with a 'column of fire'. The Schneiders were difficult for their crews to evacuate quickly because of their cramped interiors and the fact that the entire crew had to exit the tank through two small rear doors. It was easier to evacuate the St Chamond because it had more exit points but if it caught fire, the interior lights usually failed and this created further difficulties in evacuation. (However, note that at this time neither the Schneider nor any of the British tanks had interior lighting.) In battle conditions, this meant that, with both tank designs, once their tank was on fire, the crews usually were trapped and burned alive. For those Schneider crews that had placed additional petrol containers on the outside, next to the rear doors, getting out in a hurry proved impossible. Léon Dutil describes this practice as 'criminal' and it was quickly forbidden. (Interestingly, by the next year the story was circulating within the AS that it was V Armée's staff that had ordered these petrol containers to be carried but I have found no evidence that this was the case.) However, these additional petrol containers cannot account for most of the tanks that caught fire, as this inadvisable practice was by no means universal on 16 April. Tests conducted at Champlieu demonstrated that the Schneiders would not be ignited immediately when hit by an artillery shell but that such fire usually punctured the fuel tank, resulting in petrol being sprayed around the hot interior of the tank, frequently causing it to catch fire. Grenades were also a danger; in particular, the St Chamond's large flat roof proved in action to be a very dangerous grenade trap. The internal petrol tank of the Schneiders was to be moved in due course to the rear but the dangers of fire for both designs remained throughout the war.

The Struggle to Get the Tank Designs Changed

All the modifications necessary to the two tank designs were obvious to the AS personnel but these changes had to be approved by the *Comité consultatif de l'artillerie d'assaut*, which once again brought the two bodies into conflict. In the view of the AS crews, the Schneider tanks crucially needed an additional door on the left of the tank, to aid evacuation, as well as moving the interior petrol tank from the front to the rear. There were objections from Mourret to the fitting of two rear armoured interior petrol tanks, which he thought would cause the tank to overbalance whenever it was on a slope. After much debate, the *Comité* agreed to the new side door for the Schneiders but insisted that further studies on the rear fuel tanks were required before they could be approved. (The installation of the new door also required that the ammunition storage be rearranged within the tank, adding a further complication.) To speed up the process of getting the doors fitted, it was decided that the work would be undertaken at Champlieu by the AS mechanics, supervised by the factory's engineers. The Schneider factory had considerable difficulties fitting in the manufacture of the door parts to its very busy schedule and, by 8 July, only twenty-five pairs of hinges had arrived for the new doors, along with some tools and there was a further week's delay before work could commence. By this time, the *Comité* had agreed that the rear petrol tanks would be fitted and the factory began manufacturing them, although the first of these was only delivered in late August. Fortunately, moving the petrol tanks and fitting an additional door resolved another problem that had plagued the Schneiders from the first delivery in September 1916; the appalling ventilation within the tank that was a significant hazard for the crew. Again after much acrimonious debate in the *Comité*, it finally agreed to fit external exhaust pipes to address this problem but the new door and repositioned petrol tanks had largely resolved the ventilation issue, making the delivery of new extractors on 25 July 1917 somewhat irrelevant.

In relation to the St Chamond, the AS asked for the petrol tank to be armoured, as it had proved particularly vulnerable to explosions under the tank. An increase in the width of the tracks had been requested since November 1916 but only fifteen tanks out of seventy-five had the new 412mm tracks by 16 June 1917. This modification continued to be undertaken slowly and, for example, AS40 only had the larger tracks fitted to its tanks in November 1917. The St Chamond factory had devised a sloped roof, to protect against grenades, which in theory was a good idea and had received qualified support from the *Comité*. However, the new roof was so poorly implemented by the factory that the crew was left with even less outside visibility than before, that of the driver being particularly compromised. The modified roof also made access to the roof hatches dangerously narrow, thus making evacuation even more hazardous. Estienne informed the *Ministère de l'Armement* in no uncertain terms that the modified tanks should not be delivered to the army, as they were simply unusable. The ministry's response was that the modification had been notified to Estienne and the *Comité* in January and neither had made any objections to the proposals about the sloped roof. The ministry further argued that there was no time to modify the tanks. Pétain was forced to intervene; he pointed out to the minister that the *Comité* and Estienne had been assured that visibility would not be compromised by this modification, going on to say that he fully supported Estienne in his view that the tanks were unusable and that modifications needed to be made immediately, particularly to those tanks already delivered to the army.

The factory was eventually able to redesign the sloped roof on the modified tanks and replace the roofs on the unmodified ones as well as increasing the width of the tracks. Driver visibility continued to be a concern and, after tests at Champlieu on 28 June, it was agreed that the St Chamond factory would fit a newly-designed square cupola for the driver's forward position. Unfortunately, the new cupolas that arrived on 11 August still had limited visibility, which became an urgent problem as the tanks kept arriving at Cercottes in an unusable condition. The installation of the modified cupolas did not begin until 20 October and it was not until November 1917 that the modified tanks began to be delivered.

Despite the fact that Estienne had emphasised in November 1916 the importance of keeping good stocks of spares, as the tanks were in effect being tested in the field, there was always a serious shortage of spare parts, particularly in relation to the St Chamonds. Parts and tools were consistently delivered late and, for example, on 15 March 1917, out of fifty-five Schneiders in the repair-shops, thirty-four were waiting for spare parts. The situation with the St Chamonds was even worse; at the beginning of May 1917, within the two *groupes* at Champlieu, twelve tanks were out of service due to a lack of spare parts. By the end of the month, thirty out of the sixty-one St Chamonds were out of service for this reason. Estienne complained to the *Ministère de l'Armement* about this situation, pointing out that it was not possible to effectively maintain the St Chamonds that had been delivered because of the lack of spare parts. Further, he reported that only 5 per cent of the St Chamonds that had been delivered were currently operational and no combat operation could be now considered using them. He reminded the minister that, on 23 May, the latter had agreed with Pétain to reduce the number of St Chamonds to be delivered, so that more spares could be manufactured. In fact, by 12 June 1917, deliveries of the 102 St Chamonds at Cercottes to the army had been halted altogether until the spares situation could be resolved. This absurd situation could clearly not continue and, on 25 June, the *Sous-secrétariat des Fabrications* was asked by the *Ministère de l'Armement* to look for other manufacturers to make spare parts, as the St Chamond factory was at full capacity manufacturing the tanks. The situation with Schneider spares was not much better and this was never properly resolved either. Notably, on 16 November 1917, only nine Schneider *groupes*, out of sixteen, were immediately ready for action and not a single one of the St Chamond *groupes* was combat ready.

Another point of contention between Estienne and the ministry was over the issue of the SRR units and the St Chamond *char-caissons* (unarmed supply tanks). On 24 March 1917, Estienne asked GQG for six *chars-caissons* for each SRR unit and an increase in the number of SRR units, these requirements being indispensable in his view. There was considerable resistance to the latter request from Albert Thomas, as he considered that most of the SRRs' repair work could and should be done at Champlieu. (This was only resolved in the January 1918 reorganisation of the AS, which is discussed below.) The *chars-caissons* were simply standard St Chamonds with their armament removed and it appears that the factory took the easy option and prioritised them over the armed version. Dutil claims, with some justification, that the work on the *chars-caissons* was used as an excuse for the failure to deliver the combat tanks. In view of the much delayed delivery schedule of the St Chamonds, the arrival of eight *chars-caissons* at Champlieu on 27 April 1917 caused much astonishment to everybody there, which quickly turned to disappointment as they were unusable and had to be quickly sent back to the factory.

Organisation of the AS
The AS was not just in conflict with the ministry over technical issues; the organisation of the AS was the cause of much acrimonious debate between the civilian and military authorities. A major row broke out when Estienne wrote to Pétain on 12 June 1917, asking to rationalise the structure of the AS, which had been largely extemporised from the beginning. In anticipation of the arrival of large numbers of light tanks (which are discussed in Chapter 6), Estienne sensibly wanted to create a fixed base for the AS in each of the army groups. Each *Artillerie d'Assaut de Groupe d'Armées* would largely be self-contained, having its own *Centre d'Artillerie d'Assaut* with sufficient material, spares and mechanics to maintain operations in its sector. The light tanks would be organised as companies in the infantry divisions to which they would be attached to, thirty-six companies being envisaged, requiring 4,000 officers and men. So that Estienne could exercise proper oversight of material going to the front, he wanted an inspection of tanks and an inspection of automobiles created, to be under his direct command. He argued that the tank arm would be equal in size to the French air service by the end of 1917 and thus should be largely autonomous, as the air service was. He argued that the trench mortar and aviation services were organised this way and thus this change was 'indispensable' if the AS was to work efficiently.

GQG's 3 Bureau largely supported Estienne's proposals but with the caveat that definitive decisions about the light tanks, both in relation to the number to be ordered and how they would be organised, should be delayed until it was sure that they would work effectively. Pétain wrote to Albert Thomas and Paul Painlevé (the *Ministre de la Guerre*) on 20

June commending Estienne's proposals. The following month, Painlevé responded that he largely agreed with Pétain and Estienne but recommended that the inspection of automobile material should not be assigned to a DSA inspector, as the AS was a combat arm and thus should not even be partially under the authority of the DSA. As long as this continued, he said, there would be a 'complication and confusion of responsibilities'.

It took nearly a month for Thomas to respond. He declared that Estienne's recommendations were based on completely unrealistic assumptions about the number of tanks that would become available and thus his plans would result in many more cadres and repair units being raised than were necessary. Thomas wanted to maintain the DSA's control over all vehicle maintenance in the army, arguing that both the artillery and infantry had their vehicles inspected by the DSA and that the AS should be treated just like the rest of the army. In addition, he believed that it was necessary that the needs and the requests of the army in relation to the delivery of equipment should remain with the *Ministère de l'Armement*, as it was in overall charge of manufacturing.

In an attempt to resolve these disagreements, meetings were held in July and August 1917 between representatives of the *Ministère de l'Armement* and those of Pétain, including Estienne, but these largely failed to reach a consensus. With the fall of the Ribot cabinet, Albert Thomas was replaced as *Ministre de l'Armement* by Louis Loucheur. Loucheur was an industrialist who had been brought into government by Briand in 1916, partly to quieten increasing public criticism of the management of munitions production but he proved to be no more enthusiastic about the tank project than Thomas had been. For example, Loucheur wrote to Pétain about the reorganisation of the AS on 18 September 1917. Loucheur agreed to keep the four Schneider *groupements*, along with their SRRs, but stated that there should be only four St Chamond *groupements*, instead of five, arguing that by reducing their number, both personnel and material could be saved for use elsewhere. The minister insisted that there was an obligation to reduce the number of officers taken from existing units and thus only units of an 'indispensable nature' should be created. Loucheur not unreasonably argued that he was under considerable pressure to supply the rest of the army with vehicles and therefore the AS should take the minimum number necessary to operate efficiently. Of course, his view of the minimum requirements was at considerable variance with the view of GQG and the AS, this being the hub of the dispute between them.

Loucheur further argued that there should only be two AS Army Group centres, with Champlieu taking on this role for GAN. As for the new units, he believed that the St Chamond ones should be created at Cercottes, although those given material made in the Paris region (i.e. the Schneiders and Renaults) should unite personnel and material at a small camp in the region, which would be chosen so as to avoid unnecessary journeys and help maintain secrecy. This was a naked bid by Loucheur to maintain his control over AS personnel and material until units were fully formed and delivered to the army.

Loucheur's desire to maintain the authority of the *Ministère de l'Armement* over parts of the AS also intruded on the question of reorganising the AS camps in the interior (in other words, outside of the direct control of the army). Since the end of 1916, there had been two centres functioning in parallel; at Marly-le-Roi (just north of Versailles) and at Cercottes (north of the main DSA base in Orléans), both camps being run and largely staffed by the DSA. Marly supplied initial training to the personnel and was the main administration centre. Cercottes gave further instruction, uniting the crews with their tanks, before the troops moved on to Champlieu for their final training. Joffre had suggested concentrating training at the camp at Marly but Thomas pointed out that the tank crews could not be trained there with their tanks because of the lack of a suitable unloading platform at the nearby station. By contrast, Cercottes had all the requisite facilities and thus training continued to be spread between the two camps.

Initially Estienne had no authority over AS personnel in these two camps and had limited input into their training, a problem that he had alerted both Nivelle and the *Ministère de la Guerre* to in January 1917. Even after Estienne was given direct control over the movement of personnel between Marly and Cercottes and their instruction, Thomas insisted on receiving written notification of all such movements. This situation continued with minor modifications until after Loucheur became the minister. Not unreasonably, Loucheur believed that the extant organisation was the result of successive improvisations and thus could be simplified. He wanted the depot at Cercottes to receive and classify personnel, before giving them initial training, and then two instruction centres, one for tank driving and one to teach gunnery (cannons and machine guns). In order to utilise the existing installations, he argued that the depot of personnel and the tank driving school should be maintained at Marly, with the gunnery school remaining at Cercottes. The latter would provide an annexe that would act as a final instruction centre and *parc d'organisation* in the *zone des armées*. Once again, Loucheur insisted that the camps should be under his direct authority, until units were moved to Estienne's command.

When it was decided to give each AS centre a *section de parc* (light repair section), another dispute arose between the DSA and Estienne. These sections were under the control of a DSA officer, who reported to the DSA, not Estienne. The provisional instruction of 2 December 1916 relating to repairs had stated that the AS must use DSA facilities. At the beginning of 1917, the DSA had made a maintenance section (SP54) and a transport section (for material) (TM687) available to the AS at Champlieu. The issue was that the AS was simply not a priority for the DSA but, unfortunately, the DSA was determined to maintain control over all vehicle maintenance in the army and was thus unprepared to relinquish any of its control over the AS's vehicles. Although this seems a very unreasonable attitude, the DSA's position was based on what were seen as sound conclusions about efficiency that it had painfully learnt during the early part of the war. The requirement to maintain thousands of vehicles for long periods of use had not been planned well before the war, as this need was not anticipated. A central depot for all the DSA's spare parts and maintenance equipment, the *Magasin Central Automobile*, had been established in Paris, in November 1914, and this was seen as an essential part of the DSA's remarkable ability to keep large numbers of military vehicles on the road. The argument continued until the end of August 1917, when the *Ministère de l'Armement* agreed the principle of a *section technique de l'AS*, distinct from the DSA, although still under the direction of a DSA officer. The AS *sections de parc* were in operation by the end of September, immediately after authorisation from the minister. Thus, once again, the DSA had maintained its control over parts of the AS operation that would have been better served if left within direct AS control.

The arguments between the two organisations continued throughout the autumn of 1917. In the interim, Loucheur had changed his mind about Marly and closed it altogether in October 1917, giving Cercottes a triple role: depot, centre of individual instruction and the organisation's base. Instruction for AS crews in automobile theory and practice would now be undertaken at the DSA's instruction centre at nearby Orléans, with all other courses being taken at Cercottes. In a move that was probably intended to forestall any more debate, Pétain agreed to the medium tank *groupes* and SRR units continuing to be formed in the interior but he insisted that the formation of the light tank companies was made at Champlieu, in order to keep this process both secret and quick. Pétain agreed to have the individual instruction schools at Cercottes, accepting there should be only one AS centre in the interior, which had the advantage of permitting a reduction in its cadre and allow more personnel to go to the instruction unit.

A new opportunity to address these serious organisational problems came with Georges Clemenceau taking the premiership on 16 November 1917. Clemenceau came to power with considerable public support and he was determined to stamp his authority across both the government and the political bureaucracy, telling the Chamber of Deputies that his only interest was 'the war, nothing but the war'. In relation to the *Ministère de l'Armement*, Clemenceau initially wanted to reduce it to a sub-department of the *Ministère de la Guerre*. Loucheur refused to accept this change, as he did not want to compromise his original conditions for entering government; these being 'autonomy and complete power'. Clemenceau greatly valued Loucheur as a non-partisan member of the government and he was also well aware of the need for the latter's organisational talents and therefore was prepared to make a compromise; *Armement* would remain a ministry but there were significant changes made to its relationship with the AS.

Pétain told Clemenceau that the AS should be attached to the *Ministère de la Guerre*, as the most important issues concerning it were military (such as those of the organisation and command of combat units), although the tanks' manufacture and supply of parts should remain under the *Ministère de l'Armement*. Following the example of his predecessor Painlevé, Clemenceau became *Ministre de la Guerre* as well as Premier. As the *Sous-secrètaire d'État des Inventions* had been moved from the *Ministère de l'Armement* to the *Ministère de la Guerre* on 12 September 1917, Clemenceau decided to remove the influence of the *Ministère de l'Armement* from all tank issues, except those of manufacturing. In addition, there was political pressure coming from the Chamber of Deputies to create a *direction* (office) for the *artillerie d'assaut* (the deputies always being enthusiastic about any new ministry and the politicians' jobs this created). The government resisted this on the grounds of cost but eventually it was agreed that a *sous-direction de l'artillerie d'assaut* be created. This was created on 8 January 1918 under the supervision of Colonel Aubertin, who reported to the *direction d'artillerie* at the *Ministère de la Guerre*. The *sous-direction* was created for the duration of hostilities and took over responsibility for all aspects of the AS, with the exception of the manufacture of the tanks themselves and their associated spares, which remained under the control of the *Ministère de l'Armement*, as did the budget. The *sous-directeur* was also given authority, as a delegate of the *Ministre de la Guerre* (i.e. Clemenceau), to supervise aspects of the tanks' production, the most important being the establishment of quality standards. This change finally gave the AS some measure of influence over the tanks being manufactured, through the *sous-direction*, although the manufacturing process itself remained outside of AS control. Despite this reorganisation, the arguments over authority continued into the new year; for example, Aubertin was clearly angry when he wrote to Loucheur on 25 February 1918 that being 'in unison' was not the same as being 'in agreement' and that the latter was essential if the AS was to be serviced properly. He felt it necessary to remind Loucheur that the *Ministère de la Guerre* was now responsible for the tank programme, both in relation to orders for tanks and their modifications, and that the Government had decided this state of affairs. In particular, Aubertin pointed out that this situation was in order to give 'the most rapid satisfaction' to the requests of the AS commander. After this sharp exchange, it appears that Loucheur accepted that Aubertin was working under the direct authority of Clemenceau and there was considerably less friction between the ministry and the AS from this point on.

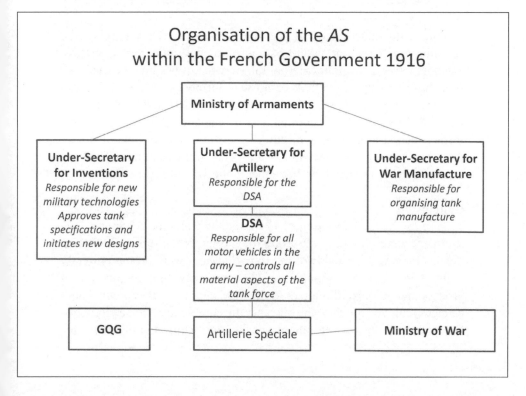

Organisation of the *AS* within the French Government 1916

Ministry of Armaments

Under-Secretary for Inventions
Responsible for new military technologies
Approves tank specifications and initiates new designs

Under-Secretary for Artillery
Responsible for the DSA

Under-Secretary for War Manufacture
Responsible for organising tank manufacture

DSA
Responsible for all motor vehicles in the army – controls all material aspects of the tank force

GQG

Artillerie Spéciale

Ministry of War

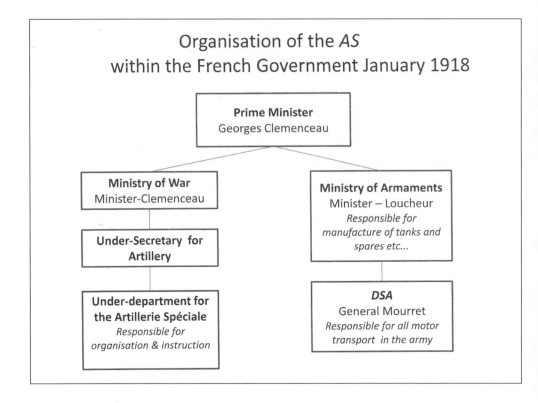

Organisation of the *AS* within the French Government January 1918

Prime Minister
Georges Clemenceau

Ministry of War
Minister-Clemenceau

Under-Secretary for Artillery

Under-department for the Artillerie Spéciale
Responsible for organisation & instruction

Ministry of Armaments
Minister – Loucheur
Responsible for manufacture of tanks and spares etc...

DSA
General Mourret
Responsible for all motor transport in the army

One immediate result of the reorganisation was clarifying the situation at Champlieu, where Estienne was now in complete control and able to run it without external interference. It became the main AS field base and the light tank camp was formed as the *Parc annexe d'organisation d'Artillerie d'assaut de Champlieu* (PAOC), functioning from 15 December 1917, commanded by Captain Petit from the DSA, former second-in-command of the AS camp at Cercottes but now under the direct command of Estienne. All aspects of the running of the base were now to be reported, by Estienne, to the *Ministre de la Guerre*.

Conclusion

To sum up, by the beginning of 1918, Estienne and the AS in the *zone d'armées* were now only reporting to, and under the direct control of, Pétain. Tank issues outside of the *zone d'armées* were brought directly under Clemenceau's supervision, leaving only the manufacturing process and associated matters to the *Ministère de l'Armement*. These changes removed much of the bureaucratic complexity that had impeded Estienne and the development of the AS; Dutil claims that this introduced 'harmony' between the various parts of the AS machine. For the first time since its inception, the AS was free of interference from the *Ministère de l'Armement* and had the full support of the *Ministère de la Guerre*. This was highly significant as it meant that the development of the AS was now entirely under the control of the army and that, for the most part, the issues connecting technology, organisation and doctrine were finally brought together. While this process had been taking place, the AS had fought an important engagement at the Battle of Malmaison in October 1917. This battle was an important part of the development of both the French army's tank tactics, as well as its more general tactical approach, and is the subject of the next chapter.

Chapter 4

'A Masterpiece of Tactics' – The Battle of Malmaison and the Tank Regulations

General Pétain had taken command of the French army at a time of great crisis and immediately took measures to respond to this by recasting to the way in which it treated its soldiers and by revising its operational and tactical methods. As part of the latter process, he accelerated the transformation already begun under Joffre's tenure as commander-in-chief from an army that was manpower-dependent to one more dependent on its material. In relation to morale, Pétain's high reputation amongst the ordinary French soldiers gave him a standing within the army that most of the other senior commanders had simply lost. However, reputation alone was insufficient to quell the widespread unrest and Pétain took a series of measures to address many of the issues that had fanned this unrest. These included keeping disciplinary action against mutineers comparatively mild, with Pétain personally approving the few executions that took place, and organising soldiers' leave in a manner that enabled troops to actually get some rest from the front, as well as addressing the issue of rations, the subject of many bitter complaints by the troops who often referred to their meat as *singe* – monkey. In relation to equipment, Pétain initiated a significant rearmament programme that would see a considerable increase in the numbers of tanks, heavy artillery and aircraft available to the French army over the following year.

Although these measures were to prove effective over time, Pétain recognised that there was also the need to modify the French army's tactical and operational approach, primarily on account of the fragile morale of the army and to restore confidence in GQG. (It was also clear that the rearmament programme that Pétain had initiated would not see fruition before the spring of 1918, with military activity needing to be maintained in the interim.) Pétain thus began to issue a series of operational and tactical instructions, starting with the keystone document, *Directive No. 1*, on 19 May 1917. This was an important statement of Pétain's operational intentions; he accepted that it was not possible to envisage, 'for the moment', a rupture of the front, followed by a strategic exploitation. Therefore the French army would undertake small-scale offensives with strictly limited objectives, the main aim of which was to cause heavy German casualties while keeping those of the French as low as possible. These operations with limited objectives would offer the opportunity to readjust the French front line by eliminating those German positions that presented the most danger, thus leaving the French in a better position to both defend against any future German offensives and permit them to launch their own in due course. There was to be a major change in French artillery methods; rather than diluting the artillery preparation by attacking the entire German position in depth, only the first line would be hit, but with overwhelming force. This approach had the advantage of allowing the French batteries to remain *in situ* throughout the operation, thus bypassing the inherent difficulties that moving the artillery forward entailed. Even more crucially, by reducing the artillery preparation, in duration but not intensity, the element of surprise could be returned to major operations, both because the enemy would expect a lengthy preparation and because the artillery and supplies needed for shorter preparations could be moved across the front more quickly. *Directive No. 1* illustrates how Pétain's operational and tactical ideas were moving towards having surprise and mobility at their centre.

These ideas were to be practised in a series of operations on various parts of the Western Front. A four-corps attack was made on 20 August at Verdun, with the dual aim of supporting the British offensive in Flanders and removing the German observation posts threatening the town of Verdun itself. The operation was very successful; it helped to begin the process of restoring faith in the ordinary soldiers that French operations could be both successful and less costly than previously, the French suffering fewer than 15,000 casualties over the five main days of the battle. It also encouraged Pétain to believe that the tactical premises of *Directive No. 1* were correct. However, another operation of this type was necessary, both to further help morale and to continue with the tactical experimentation. In May, General Paul Maistre, commander of VI Armée, had planned an attack in his sector against the Laffaux plateau (on the Chemin des Dames) but this was postponed because of the serious unrest within his army. His army-group commander, General Franchet d'Espèrey, had been pressing Pétain for permission for an operation to clear the Laffaux plateau since June and it was agreed that he and Maistre would develop a plan with this as its aim. Franchet d'Espèrey ordered Maistre to concentrate the operation on the Moulin de Laffaux, it being the key to the whole position. Initially, Pétain was only prepared to agree a minor operation on VI Armée's front but he changed his mind when he saw Maistre's plans, agreeing in late July that 'active preparation' could be undertaken for what was to become the Malmaison operation.

Planning for the Battle of Malmaison
After a discussion that took several months, primarily about how much artillery was needed for the operation, the plans for the battle were finally settled in September 1917. Maistre's army duly received the following order, which emphasised that the operation was to be one of strictly limited objectives, in line with the formulations of *Directive No. 1*. Three corps, from left to right 14, 21, 11 CA, were to attack and occupy the Laffaux plateau containing the Malmaison fort (decommissioned before the war) and the villages of Allemant, Vaudesson, Chavignon and Pargny-Filain.

The Laffaux plateau had the Ailette River running around its north and east edges, with the Oise-Aisne canal alongside. It rested on a layer of hard clay, with layers of sand over this, and was topped with a thick layer of chalk. This geology caused the plateau and surrounding area to be cut through with valleys that were long and wide, with gentle sandy slopes. There were numerous chalk quarries in the area, some as deep as twelve metres, offering varying degrees of protection for the Germans. Although some were within range of French field-artillery fire, many, such as those at Fruty and Montparnasse, were immune to all but the 400mm railway guns. The plateau was in most places over 100 metres above the surrounding terrain, thus dominating the valleys and the plain around it. Capture of it would give the French army an enfilading position over the Ailette River valley and allow effective flanking fire on the enemy positions on the eastern part of the Chemin des Dames, making it untenable for the Germans to hold. It would also remove the ability of the German artillery (largely by eliminating its observers) to fire on the French artillery positions in the Aisne valley. As it seemed likely that the Germans would feel obliged to mount a serious operation to retake this area, this would give the French, with a commanding defensive position on the plateau, the opportunity to inflict disproportionate casualties on them.

On the section of the front between Malmaison farm and Malmaison fort, where the German lines were closest to the French ones, the first objective was to be taken in one bound. The advance on either side of this would be made in two bounds, with a halt at an intermediate objective. Once the first objective had been taken across the whole front, the three corps would advance on the second objective, under the protection of a strong barrage on their front and flanks. In principle this advance would start four hours after H-hour, the exact time being determined by Maistre according to how the operation was unfolding.

Each French corps would attack in a 'square formation', with two divisions abreast and two divisions in reserve. In particular, it was essential that the quarries that littered the attack zone were methodically cleared as the area was advanced over and a detailed plan for clearing these was made by the divisions, with *Schilt* detachments (flamethrowers) being attached for this purpose. The formation of 13 DI was typical of how the French divisions organised their attack. On the right flank, in the first line there was a battalion of 109 RI reinforced with a Senegalese company and half a *génie* company, with a second battalion from 109 RI behind it in support. In the centre, there was a battalion from 21 RI in the first line, again reinforced by a Senegalese company, half a *génie* company and a flamethrower detachment, with another battalion from 21 RI in support behind them. On the left, most of 20 BCP was in the first line, similarly reinforced by a Senegalese company, half a *génie* company and a flamethrower detachment. Two companies of 20 BCP and its machine-gun company were behind them in support. The *Infanterie Divisionnaire* (ID) commander had a battalion each from 109 and 21 RI as his reserve. (The *Infanterie Divisionnaire* was the level of command that replaced brigade command in the infantry, when most of the French infantry divisions were reduced from four regiments to three, over the course of 1916–17.) The divisional reserve was 21 BCP with half a *génie* company, the divisional cavalry squadron and an infantry regiment from 170 DI.

Once the final objective was taken, the positions were to be immediately occupied and communication with the French lines established. The attack was to be supported by a dense creeping barrage, as well as by fixed and semi-fixed barrages of field and heavy artillery. The reserve divisions were not to be engaged until the end of the operation, when they would only be used to relieve the attacking divisions and occupy the ground taken. The attacking corps were to be supported on the right by 67 DI from 39 CA, which was to seize the Church at St-Berthe, and on the left by 129 DI, the left division of 14 CA, which was to occupy the first German trench line along the Bessy to Ailette ravine. Across the rest of their front, the supporting corps were to create a strong diversion, with a trench mortar barrage and trench raids, with the hope of further unsettling the German response.

The French were attacking German positions that were well thought-out and well-constructed. The German defence consisted of a first position, with three trench lines 200–300 metres apart. The German trenches were three to four metres wide and were protected by belts of barbed wire up to ten metres in depth. There was a second position between one and two kilometres behind this that consisted of only two trench lines. These contained numerous shelters but with much shallower barbed wire coverage than on the first position. (Jean Perré and other contemporary writers refers to the second position as the 'intermediate' or 'stopping' position, with the true 'second position' being on the north bank of the Ailette. As the latter German position was not attacked on 23 October, I have used the term second position to refer to what Perré calls the intermediate position for the sake of clarity.) Between the first and second positions, there were numerous machine-gun nests and several sheltered areas for the housing of reserves. The majority of the German artillery batteries were another one or two kilometres behind the second position. Around the plateau were further strong German positions on the north banks of the Ailette River and the Oise-Aisne canal.

The success of the French attack required the elimination of most of the German batteries that could fire across the plateau and the destruction of the extensive defensive positions and trench lines. To achieve this, a short but very heavy artillery preparation was ordered. How much artillery was actually be needed was the subject of a major debate amongst the French generals. The difficulty that the planners of the operation had in relation to artillery was that they wanted a shorter preparation than had been usual in previous operations (days rather than weeks) but they also needed to guarantee the destruction of most of the German positions and artillery. During discussions, it became clear that the artillery preparation, both in duration and the numbers of guns required, had to be calculated on a different basis from that of previous offensives but, naturally, this left considerable room for argument. Maistre, in particular, was most concerned that he would not have enough artillery and this caused much friction between him and both GQG and Franchet d'Espèrey. His initial request for artillery was so large that Pétain observed that it would give Maistre more artillery than I and II Armées had combined. Although Pétain made it clear that there would be limits on the extra artillery that VI Armée would receive, Maistre continued to argue for more. In September, he wrote to Franchet d'Espèrey complaining that the artillery he was to receive was based on the experience of the Somme and the Aisne and thus not sufficient for this operation, particularly in relation to heavy artillery. Franchet d'Espèrey wrote back, patiently pointing out that Maistre was not correct; the quantity of artillery to be used was based on the experience of the recent and very successful battle at Verdun in August. He also drew Maistre's attention to the fact that each of VI Armée's corps would have twice the amount of artillery that the two central corps of II Armée had been given for the Verdun operation.

In fact, a considerable amount of artillery was brought into VI Armée for this new type of artillery preparation. For example, 21 CA (at the centre of the attack) received twenty *groupes* of field artillery, thirteen *groupes* of 155C, four *groupes* of 155L, eight batteries of trench mortars, along with nine batteries of heavy artillery (from 95mm to 270mm guns). It also received two entire *groupes* of the latest high-powered artillery, the 270mm ALGP guns. The mass of artillery attached to VI Armée even included some of the brand new gigantic St Chamond 400mm railway guns, in position at Sainte-Marguerite.

It was determined that the daily artillery expenditure during the artillery preparation would be the maximum laid down by GQG in December 1916; 300 shells per gun for the 75s and 150 shells per gun for all but the heaviest artillery pieces. (In the event, the guns usually fired rather less than this; the heavy artillery regiment 6/118 RAL, equipped with 155C St Chamonds, only fired 2,928 shells with its twelve guns over the course of the preparation.) Munitions were stockpiled so that on the evening of the attack there was a reserve available of three days' worth of ammunition for the field guns and one and a half days for the heavier pieces, with a further two-day reserve in the Army depots.

We can get some indication of the sheer scale of the artillery preparation and the subsequent attack from the logistical requirements that were placed on the railway service. The French field guns needed sixty-four trainloads of ammunition, with the heavy artillery needing 180 trainloads, the trench mortars twenty trainloads, and the infantry requiring three trainloads for their rifle ammunition alone with a further six trains for their grenades. A total of 285 trains were needed to move in all the equipment required for the offensive, with an additional ten trains per day bringing in ammunition during the artillery preparation.

Between 17 and 22 October, VI Armée's artillery fired just over 1.5 million shells at the German positions, including over 200,000 gas shells, but it was not just artillery fire that the French poured onto the German defences; machine guns were also extensively used in an indirect role. However, both the French machine-gun fire and artillery preparation were hampered by very bad weather on 18 and 20–21 October, most days having only two or three hours of 'mediocre visibility'. This forced Maistre to extend the artillery preparation beyond the four days originally planned.

There were also aggressive trench raids made right up to the day of the offensive, primarily to keep field intelligence as up to date as possible. For éxample, 140 RI sent in a platoon-sized raid, in combination with 75 RI, on the morning of 22 October, capturing seven Germans and usefully discovering that the elite German 13 ID had entered the line in front of them the day before.

Of course, all of this French activity notified the enemy that an attack was imminent and, from 15 September to 15 October, seven new infantry divisions were moved into the area, as well as sixty-four artillery batteries, forty of which were heavy. This brought the German artillery in the area to a total of over 180 batteries, sixty-three being heavy. By 23 October, the Germans had six divisions in the first and second positions, from west to east; 37, 14, 13, 2 & 5 Guard, and 47 Reserve Divisions. Each front-line division held a front of between two and three kilometres in length, just behind them being three others (52, 43, 9), with another three in reserve (10, 6, 3 Bavarian). Most of these divisions had been classified by French intelligence the previous year as good but the heavy fighting in the earlier part of 1917 had significantly reduced their quality, with only 14 and 5 Guard Divisions performing well during the battle. The German artillery put down regular barrages with gas shells, both tear and toxic gas, to disrupt the French preparations but these only represented a nuisance to the French.

Pétain's August 1917 Note on Tanks

The careful planning that GQG had initiated for the infantry and artillery attack was also applied to the AS part of the operation. The AS units were to be engaged under the theoretical framework prescribed by Pétain in his 22 August 1917 note to the armies on tank use. It was accepted that the note was by necessity of a 'provisional character' and it could 'serve as a guide', since the experience gained in the April and May battles was insufficient to establish a 'firm doctrine'. From the point of view of tactics, Pétain emphasised the importance of close liaison between the tanks and the other arms. He pointed out that, as with all attacks, success required the effective neutralisation of any enemy artillery that could fire into the combat zone. To be effective, such neutralisation had to be both of the artillery itself and also of its observation posts. To achieve this, all the observation posts had to be blinded by smoke shells and the advance of the tanks was to be protected by specially-designated aircraft, acting both against enemy aircraft and directing French counter-battery fire. In the approach march, the tanks were instructed to move from cover to cover in small, dispersed groups, in stark contrast to how they had been used at Juvincourt. In most circumstances, fog or early-morning mist would be used to mask the tanks' movement on the battlefield. The problem of the tanks' mobility across wide trenches and badly-damaged ground was acknowledged and thus the note recommended that tanks generally should be used on a 'calm front' in a surprise attack on the second and third positions, after a reduced artillery preparation.

Once it was decided to include tanks in an operation, they would be attached to an infantry division, the divisional commander developing the operational plan in conjunction with the AS commanders. The latter were then to devise a plan with the relevant regimental commander and agree the tanks' plan of deployment. During combat, the tank units' senior commander was always to be stationed with the divisional commander and the *groupe* commanders were to be stationed with the regimental commanders. Tanks were ideally to be moved at night prior to combat and were to arrange their assembly positions in the cover closest to the French front lines. Reconnaissance was to continue right up to the evening before the battle. If the tanks were not to attack the first position, they were to remain in cover until signalled to move by the infantry, after the latter had made a passage for them across the battlefield or trenches, an AS liaison officer being attached to the infantry to ensure this was done correctly.

Each tank *groupe* was to enter combat in successive echelons, with one or two batteries making the initial attack, while the other batteries remained in cover until their intervention was necessary. The advance of tanks was to be covered by a creeping barrage of smoke shells, executed by the divisional artillery. Once the tanks had arrived on the enemy positions, they were to neutralise them and, once this was done, signal the infantry to advance. Pétain pointed out the danger of leaving the tanks stationary on the battlefield and they were only to do this until such time as the French infantry had occupied and consolidated the captured area. If further work was needed to allow the tanks to continue their advance (i.e. resupply of ammunition and/or petrol), they should retire to either predetermined cover or as far from the captured trench line as possible, until a new passage for them had been made and they could resume their attack. The note emphasised that it was 'indispensable' for the most thorough training to be had by the infantry if they were to co-operate effectively with the tanks. These thoroughly sensible recommendations about tank deployment were to be put to the test at Malmaison, where the theory would be applied in less than ideal circumstances.

AS Planning for the Battle

On 25 July 1917, Estienne was instructed to send an officer to GAN to make plans for a tank attack on the front of VI Armée. He chose Major Chaubès, commander of Groupement II with a wealth of experience from the Nivelle Offensive, for the task. Chaubès examined the ground between the Messy ravine and Bovettes Farm and he agreed that that a tank attack could take place, with the important proviso that certain areas where the ground was particularly broken up would have to be avoided. On 25 August, it was decided to attach five AS *groupes* to VI Armée, each *groupe* being attached to an infantry division. The *groupes* were in two *groupements*; Groupement II, comprising three Schneider *groupes* (AS8, 11 and 12), was under the command of Major Chaubès, and Groupement X, two St Chamond *groupes* (AS31 and 33), was nominally under the command of a naval officer attached to the AS; *Capitaine de frigate* de Pérrinelle. (Although de Pérrinelle's naval rank was equivalent to that of an army lieutenant colonel, he was here acting as a major. As he was attached to the AS in a technical capacity, Estienne insisted that de Pérrinelle left command of the *groupement* in combat to one of his subordinates.)

In addition, SRR1 was attached to Groupement II, SRR4 to Groupement X, both supply and repair units being under strength. AS12 was attached to 38 DI (11 CA); AS8 went to 43 DI, AS11 to 13 DI (both divisions in 21 CA), with 27 and 28 DI (both from 14 CA) receiving AS31 and AS33 respectively. The Schneider *groupes* were organised in four batteries of three tanks each, while the St Chamond *groupes* comprised fourteen tanks each, organised in four batteries, two batteries with four tanks and two batteries with three. Two Schneiders and two St Chamonds were converted into wireless-telegraphy tanks (carrying a TSF transmitter with a maximum range of twelve kilometres), not always to the pleasure of their crews. (For example, Fourier's friend Lieutenant Le Pin had his tank converted to a TSF tank, despite his 'horror' of all things scientific.) The TSF Schneiders were given to AS11 and 12, with the TSF St Chamonds going to AS31 and 33. Lieutenant Colonel Wahl took overall command of the AS units attached to VI Armée. In keeping with Pétain's note, detailed reconnaissance was made by the AS officers in VI Armée from 25 August until the day before the attack. The final plan of engagement was then agreed between the infantry commanders and the AS officers.

Considerable effort was made to ensure the tanks would avoid the difficulties moving around the battlefield encountered at Juvincourt and Berry-au-Bac. Detailed plans from *groupement* to battery level were made in connection with the approach routes, once again in close liaison with the infantry officers. In order to keep the AS as fully informed about the state of the battlefield as possible, VI Armée's 2 Bureau passed to the AS commanders new aerial photographs of the battlefront on a daily basis, which, one young AS lieutenant remembered, were the subject of 'interminable discussions'. These photographs were closely examined for changes in the ground caused by the shells from the heavy artillery, as well as checking the roads and other routes for damage.

The merits of attaching a dedicated infantry unit to the tanks in advance of the attack had been shown by the relative success of 17 BCP in the Nivelle Offensive, as had been acknowledged in Pétain's August note on tanks. In particular, it was clear that making a passage for the tanks was too difficult for troops that lacked specialised training. General Debeney, on behalf of GQG, had written in July to the commanders of GAN and GAC to canvass opinions on training troops to work and accompany the tanks, Debeney's initial thoughts being to attach some dismounted cavalry to the AS. It was subsequently agreed that two dismounted cavalry battalions would be attached to the AS, well in advance of the attack, and elements from *9* and *11 Cuirassiers à pied* moved to Champlieu on 27 August to begin training with the tanks. Five of their squadrons were to act as general *troupes d'accompagnement*, with a further three cavalrymen specifically attached to each tank as *cuirassiers d'élite*. From the former, each tank *groupe* had a section of dismounted *cuirassiers*, giving each battery around twenty men with picks and shovels, who were to advance with the first wave of infantry and prepare the way for the tanks. The *cuirassiers d'élite* were to advance with the tanks, using them as cover, helping the tank crews to identify targets, providing the observational capacity that the tanks themselves lacked.

It was realised that it was crucial for the attacking infantry to have detailed training in conjunction with the tanks. To familiarise the infantry with the tanks, fourteen infantry battalions undertook training with tanks at Champlieu between 27 August and 5 October. The battalions spent from five to seven days at Champlieu conducting daily exercises with one or two batteries of tanks, which gave the infantry an insight into both their limitations and strengths. In particular, the infantry learnt how to direct the tanks to fire on targets that were blocking them. It was also emphasised to the infantry officers that there was to be no modification made to normal infantry tactics because of the presence of the tanks. The AS officers visited the French front-line trenches to see for themselves the ground they would advance over and to familiarise the tank and infantry officers with each other.

Battlefield communications remained rudimentary; for example, the *troupes d'accompagnement* had to signal that the route was ready for the tanks by having an NCO hold up a helmet on a rifle, although in reality there was no real alternative to this. Speaking tubes were fitted to the rear of the tanks to enable the *cuirassiers d'élite* to speak to the tank crews, these giving 'great service' during the battle, it was subsequently reported. The tanks were also supplied with a white and red panel on the roof, to be used from within the tank, to call the infantry forward. The infantry were to call tanks to their aid by displaying a white panel (supplied for the purpose) or any other white object. They were then to communicate with the tanks by voice if possible or by waving objects in the direction that they wanted the tanks to attack in.

The TSF tanks were to provide communication between the relevant divisions and corps. In order that the tanks were kept in close liaison with infantry, the *groupe* commanders were to be stationed initially at the division's ID command post, connected by field telephone to their reserve battery. Each *groupe* commander was provided with one officer, one NCO, four telephonists and two runners for liaison purposes and one AS officer was attached to each division's staff as a liaison officer. Up to two field gun batteries in each division were tasked with counter anti-tank battery fire, which was to be directed by an aircraft dedicated to this task.

Considerable attention was devoted to keeping the details of the attack a secret. For example, when de Pérrinelle gave his *groupe* commanders their 'ultra-secret' orders for the attack, they were hand-written by him personally for additional security. Nonetheless the Germans were well aware that tanks might be used in the coming attack. However, the German army's success in repulsing the French tanks during the Nivelle Offensive had led OHL to believe that 'by reason of their slow and heavy movement, the tanks are excellent [artillery] targets; they are very vulnerable despite their armour. There is no place for fear if the defence is well organised; experience proves this.' This was somewhat overoptimistic as the Germans at Laffaux would discover and anti-tank defence in the Malmaison sector was largely left to indirect artillery fire; the tactic of using single field guns in forward positions had been abandoned and there were few anti-tank obstacles installed. To assure accurate indirect fire, the German artillery observation posts were carefully sited and all batteries had orders to immediately switch their fire to any tanks seen within their sector. The German infantry's only close defence against the tanks remained the mostly ineffective SmK armour-piercing round, although extra detachments of machine-gunners armed with SmK ammunition were drafted into the area before the attack, specifically to engage any tanks.

Senior AS officers were much in evidence to their troops during preparations for the attack; for example, de Pérrinelle accompanied Colonel Wahl on an inspection of Lieutenant Fourier's battery's (AS31) position on 16 October. Each AS *groupe* was given a carefully planned mission and, in keeping with the known characteristics of the two tank designs, the Schneiders were allotted to areas where a deeper advance was required, whereas the St Chamonds were sent to those parts of the front where the attack would require a shorter advance.

The Schneiders of AS12 were attached to 38 DI (on the left flank of 11 CA), the division charged with taking Malmaison Fort and advancing up to the line Chavignon–Many Farm. Its attack was to be in two phases; the first phase being to help the infantry in an attack on the edges of Bohéry and then into the trenches surrounding Malmaison fort. The tanks were ordered to pay particular attention to any German machine guns left in action after the first infantry wave had passed. They were then to help the infantry clear out the areas captured and to ward off any improvised counter-attacks. The second phase was to help the infantry capture Orme Farm, following which the tanks would support the infantry advancing to the north of the fort and ward off any counter-attacks.

AS8 (Schneiders) had a similarly-phased mission and was attached to 43 DI (on the right flank of 21 CA). The Schneiders were to help the infantry in their advance and subsequent attack on the first position. After the infantry had consolidated the first objective, the tanks were to help them advance up to the south edge of Bellecroix wood and the north slopes of the Montparnasse plateau, paying particular attention to defending the infantry's flanks.

The Schneiders of AS11, with 13 DI on the left flank of 21 CA, were to support the infantry in their advance on the first objective and then help them push forward, again paying particular attention to defending their flanks. The tanks were then to push right up to the slopes north of the plateau of la Ferme de l'Ange Gardien right up to the edge of Bellecroix wood.

The St Chamonds of AS31, attached to 27 DI on the right flank of 14 CA, were to support the infantry on the Moulin de Laffaux to Gobineaux front and take Hill 170. They were then to encircle the quarries of Fruty, which were to be neutralised during the attack by the French artillery. The tanks were not going to attack the second objective but were to help the infantry prepare for its attack, largely by guarding against any counter-attacks.

The St Chamonds of AS33, with 28 DI on the left flank of 14 CA, were to advance with the infantry along the slopes of the Allemant Ravine, helping the infantry advance guard to clear machine-gun nests and other points of resistance. Once this task was complete, the tanks were to support the new infantry advance by taking Allemant under cannon fire and guarding against any German counter-attacks from the Guerbette valley.

The French artillery preparation caused mounting concern for the AS commanders, as the battleground was becoming increasingly broken up, despite the fact that Maistre had ordered the trench artillery on 25 September to stop firing on areas where the tanks would advance. When Lieutenant Fourier and Captain Calmels (commander of AS31) reviewed aerial photographs of their sector on 19 October, they were taken aback at the extent of the artillery damage; the ground was 'chaos'. The heavy rain made the ground even worse; of particular worry to the AS was that many of the shell holes from the heavy artillery had filled with water and merged into one another, creating areas the tanks could simply not traverse.

Another officer of AS31, Captain Bruneau, was required to make a very alarming reconnaissance mission on the day before the battle started. On 22 October, Captain Calmels ordered Bruneau to make an aerial reconnaissance, which Bruneau thought 'idiotic' because of the generally poor visibility and the devastated terrain he would be flying over. However, Calmels refused to change his mind and Bruneau soon found himself and his pilot cruising at 2,000 metres over the front. Unfortunately, at this height Bruneau could see nothing except the general features of the enemy positions and he agreed with the pilot that they would descend to 800 metres. Such was the visibility that even at this height Bruneau could hardly see anything of value. However, Bruneau and his pilot were low enough for their plane to be shot at by a German anti-aircraft gun, which sent the plane into an alarming dive, the pilot only regaining control 50 metres from the ground, being shot at all the way down. Bruneau said that he only breathed out again when he got back to the French lines.

The Battle – 23 October 1917
AS11, 31 and 33 were moved from Champlieu by rail during 16 October, the units being assembled at Missy and Crouy during the night without incident. AS8 and 12 followed them by rail the next day, also without incident. The following days and nights before the attack were spent checking that their preparations were sound and making routes for the tanks to their departure positions. At midday on 22 October, Maistre set the attack for 05.45 the next day but an intercepted German radio message forced him to change his plan. This intercept indicated that German 7 Army was already alerted that the French would launch an attack the following day and had ordered its artillery to launch a counter-preparation at 05.30. Maistre quickly changed H-hour to 05.15. This had the disadvantage of increasing the amount of time that the troops would be fighting in darkness, as the sun would not rise until after 06.00, but there was no way of now avoiding this and, by 17.00, all units of VI Armée had been informed of the new start time. The bad weather continued; it rained almost continuously throughout the day, except for a brief respite in the late afternoon, and the wind remained strong all day. The rain helped further churn up the ground, already extensively damaged by artillery fire, and also made artillery observation difficult.

Once the operation commenced, the Schneider *groupes* were generally more effective than the St Chamond ones, although some of the former, such as AS12, did not have an auspicious start to the battle. By 09.15, three entire batteries of AS12 were out of action, their tanks having all ditched before engaging the Germans. One battery got to Malmaison fort, where they kept German positions under fire while the

French infantry occupied the area and dug-in. A German counter-attack from the Garenne woods (north-west of the fort) was fought off by the tanks, one tank being hit by three 77mm shells and immobilised. Unsurprisingly, 38 DI reported that the tanks of AS12 had not been of much use, other than in the destruction of a couple of machine guns. However, all the ditched tanks from AS12 were subsequently recovered and by the end of the day the *groupe* had lost ten killed and seventy-two wounded.

The four batteries of AS8 got seven out of their twelve Schneiders into action and these were of considerable assistance to the infantry advance. For example, one Schneider actually managed to catch up with the first wave of infantry, passing them and moving right up to the edge of the French creeping barrage. The infantry declined to follow the tank, despite frantic signalling from its crew for them to advance. The tank was moving rather aimlessly around 158 RI's sector when it was found by an AS liaison officer who directed it to the sector occupied by 1 and 31 BCP. It moved through the Bosseux ravine, taking under fire a number of shelters still occupied by the Germans, resulting in twenty Germans surrendering. The tank then covered the French infantry while they organised their defensive positions. It was then joined by a tank from another battery, which had actually been attempting to find the battery on the left. These two tanks contributed to seeing off a strong German counter-attack, after which they retired, one getting stuck in a shell hole on the way back.

Two tanks from the second battery of AS8 were similarly useful to the infantry, the third tank of the battery having been put out of action by a shell. While the two Schneiders advanced, one was stopped only momentarily by a shell hole but this was long enough for it to be hit by two artillery shells, which fortunately did no serious damage. The other tank had meanwhile cleared several trenches before joining the leading infantry elements at their first objective. In the course of this action, some infantry from 149 RI were able to signal to the tank commander that there was a German machine gun in action, just south-east of them. A counter-attack was organised and the tank fired one shell at the machine gun from 150 metres, putting it out of action. The tank then proceeded to fire for the next twenty minutes at various German units within range. Just after 11.00, it was joined by the other tank, which had freed itself, and both Schneiders moved to the north edge of the Chavignon plateau, where they covered the French infantry for thirty minutes, until the tanks were given the order to retire.

In regards to AS11, two tanks from its first battery took on two batteries of German 77mm guns on the south edge of Bellecroix wood, forcing the crews to abandon their guns and capturing the pieces. The tanks then split up and moved around the infantry regiment's sector mopping up the remaining machine guns. This enabled the French infantry to enter the south edges of Bellecroix wood, where the tanks covered them by fire until they received the order to retire. Schneiders from AS11 gave such effective support to the French infantry moving up the slopes west of Vaudesson that the latter were able to storm the village in less than twelve minutes.

The commander of 21 BCP directed a tank from AS11's fourth battery to attack a machine-gun nest that had halted the *chasseur* battalion. The machine-gun nest was demolished with only one tank shell and the *chasseurs* took such heart at the tank's appearance that they charged and overran the German position. The tank maintained its fire while the infantry cleared the shelters, enabling them to capture ten machine guns and 250 prisoners, including several officers. It is some indication of the confusion on the battlefield at this stage that one tank from 4 Battery/AS11 was joined by two tanks from 3 Battery and a stray St Chamond from AS31 that had entered their zone of action. The tanks continued to help the infantry advance, mainly by destroying machine-gun nests and, once the infantry were firmly entrenched in their new positions, the tanks were released to return to their assembly position.

The four batteries of AS31, totalling fourteen St Chamonds, only managed to get four tanks into action, ten ditching in holes or breaking down before being engaged. However, the St Chamonds were some help to the infantry; for example, some mounted German troops on the Grevettes plateau were dispersed by cannon fire: although these were reported as cavalry it seems more likely that they were mounted artillerymen. One French infantry regiment reported to its division that the St Chamonds had been of 'no help' to the infantry and noted that these tanks were almost useless on difficult ground.

In relation to AS33, its second battery was the most successful, despite two tanks breaking down before the battery had even got into action. The remaining two other tanks continued, successfully engaging two machine guns, capturing fifteen Germans and freeing a small group of French prisoners, before one of the tanks broke down. The fourth St Chamond carried on but was immobilised when the ground gave way underneath it while crossing a trench line. The French infantry had completely occupied their new positions by midday and two of the St

Chamonds were able to return to the assembly position under their own steam, the other two being recovered later. The other batteries of AS33 saw little action because so many of their tanks ditched in shell holes, three tanks being hit by artillery fire and one battery commander being killed. The battle had not been a happy experience for the St Chamonds; of the twenty-eight deployed, twenty-four had ditched or broken down before arriving in the combat zone.

The TSF tanks' fortunes were as mixed as those of the combat tanks. AS11's TSF tank advanced behind the combat units up to Ferme Vaurains. It continued with the advance, stopping and setting up its first transmission station at 08.20. At 09.30, it moved off and half an hour later, it set up to transmit again, in liaison with elements of 13 and 43 DI. Numerous messages had been passed from both positions and the tank retired at 17.30. It was immobilised during the return to the French lines when barbed wire got caught up in its left track, leaving it to be recovered the following evening. AS12's TSF tank left at 05.30 and advanced towards Malmaison Fort but it got stuck in a shell-hole in front of the fort. Despite this, it was able to make made several transmissions during the course of the battle and, although the reception was very weak and confused at the divisional receiver, the tanks' reception was reported as totally clear. The TSF tank with AS31 left its assembly position on time and had established communication with its division by 07.00. It continued to exchange messages with the division for the next three hours before moving back to its departure position, arriving there two hours later. AS33's TSF tank had the misfortune of having its TSF officer (who was also in command) killed by a shell while directing the tank on foot, almost immediately the battle began. The tank's second-in-command took over and moved the tank to a sheltered area, where it was again able to make contact with the infantry division. Its misfortune continued, however; the driver was killed by shrapnel from an artillery strike near the tank as it returned to its departure position. However, the TSF tanks were 'most favourably reported on' by the AS to the British and the latter were told that the tanks had conveyed 'useful information'.

Captain Bruneau left an account of the battle that allows us to see how the battle was experienced at the lowest level. In the early hours of 23 October, the tanks motors of Bruneau's battery were started at 05.50 so that they would be ready to move at 06.00, at which time the four tanks set off in a column, with Bruneau in the lead. Although he was driving the tank with his head out of the cupola, Bruneau failed to see a large shell hole in the road which almost toppled his tank over when he drove into it. However, he managed to accelerate out of the hole and advanced towards the German lines, signalling (how is not specified but presumably by flag) to his battery '*en bataille*' (in line). The three tanks moved to the right and left of Bruneau (i.e. into line) and he almost immediately lost sight of them. He then spotted German machine gun fire coming from a farm 100 metres away and he stopped the battery, to open fire with his 75mm gun. As Bruneau moved forward, he again tipped the tank into a large unseen shell hole, six metres in diameter and three metres deep, full of liquid mud. After ascertaining that he was not going to get the tank un-ditched without assistance, Bruneau dismounted the tank's machine guns and moved forward: 'We have become infantry', he said to himself. Bruneau and his crew then fought with the French infantry until the following morning when he commandeered one of his battery's other tanks, to direct it on an attack on a prepared German position in a woods. The St Chamond attacked the edges of the woods from as close as 50 metres, firing for five minutes until all fire ceased coming from the German positions. After the French infantry stormed the woods, receiving almost no fire, they captured over forty machine guns, thanks largely to Bruneau.

Final Stage of the Battle – 24 and 25 October 1917

October 24th was occupied with consolidating the conquered positions and bringing forward the French artillery. The next day saw the final phase of the operation when the French infantry pushed right up to the banks of the Ailette River. AS31 and 33 extemporised a battery each (of four tanks) out of the remnants of their units but these actually achieved very little. The battery from AS33 failed to get any of its tanks into action and it was fortunate that the French infantry that they were attached to met such little resistance. AS31's battery only got one tank to the departure position and this ditched twice over the following three hours, subsequently having to be freed by elements of the infantry that it was supporting. It did, however, eliminate a German machine gun that had completely halted the infantry's advance. The tanks took no part in the limited fighting that followed the next day and, by 26 October, French infantry were right up to the banks of the Ailette river.

Results of the Battle

We may not agree with Pierrefou's claim after the war that the Battle of Malmaison was 'a masterpiece of tactics' but it was certainly a very effective operation, fully achieving its limited goals. *Commandant* Auguste-Emile Laure, GQG liaison officer with VI Armée, arrived on 24 October at Maistre's headquarters to find the General 'very satisfied' by the success of the attack. Although there was subsequent criticism within the army that the attack at Malmaison should have been further exploited, Maistre and Pétain were in complete agreement that any such extension of the attack could have run into serious difficulties. In particular, if the operation had continued the French troops would have had serious difficulties crossing the swampy area around the Ailette river and would have then run into substantial German reserves coming from Laon. It was more important, from GQG's point of view, to have a successful but limited battle, with its immediate benefits to morale and the opportunity to experiment with tactics, than risk repeating the over-ambitious offensives of the past. Indeed, the French infantry had been extremely successful in some sectors; for example, 1 BCP (43 DI) had captured seven officers and 700 men from three different German divisions as well as eighteen artillery pieces and sixty-five machine guns, its advance elements getting as far as Chavignon. The *Régiment Infanterie Coloniale du Maroc* (RICM, part of 38 DI) had done just as well; it had captured 950 Germans while losing only ninety-one killed and 362 wounded.

The German divisions on the Laffaux front were all badly mauled in the battle; for example, German 14 ID lost the majority of its artillery and over 1,800 prisoners, leaving it with only 1,400 effectives by 26 October, and 13 ID lost a similar number of prisoners and it was reported that many of its units had surrendered *en masse* with their officers. Even German divisions that had previously fought well, such as 2 Guard ID, were overrun at Malmaison, although 5 Guard ID did put up a credible fight and only left 300 prisoners with the French.

By the time the operation was finally over on the 26th, the French in some places had advanced nearly six kilometres and had captured over 11,000 Germans, along with significant amounts of material. This had been achieved with casualties of fewer than 12,000 men, comparing very favourably with the 30,000 casualties on this ground during April and May 1917. The French gains forced the Germans to pull back to a more tenable position and, perhaps most importantly, re-established a measure of confidence in GQG within the French army. By 1 November 1917, the Germans had evacuated the whole of the Chemin-des-Dames position and retreated behind the Ailette.

Results for the AS

In relation to the tanks, the operation had been a partial tactical success. GAN 3 Bureau made a detailed report to GQG in November on the tanks' role at Malmaison which said that the overall impression in VI Armée was that the tank attack was 'satisfactory' and that the conception of employment and the tactics were generally correct. (However, the war diary of VI Armée actually states that the tanks had 'played an important role' in the battle.) The report's observations were not without caveats and it said that: 'it is necessary however to look more closely'.

The report pointed out that the tanks with 14 CA (AS31 and 33) had contributed little to the infantry they were supporting. In fact, the tank attack on this corps' front was a 'complete failure', according to the report's estimation. The tank personnel losses were not insignificant; AS33 (with its accompanying dismounted cavalry) lost seven killed, including three officers, and thirty-three wounded, including three officers. AS31 lost one killed and fifteen wounded, including five officers. The report concluded that the losses of these two *groupes* were 'out of proportion with the results obtained', a conclusion that is difficult to argue with.

By contrast, on 21 CA's front, where the tanks were employed to attack the second objective, the tanks gave effective support to the infantry and rendered 'excellent services' in the second part of the battle. Altogether, more than two-thirds of the tanks employed had broken down before arriving either at the German trenches or in the first position. If this operation had not had a limited objective and the attack had carried on, the report warned that 50 per cent of the tanks might have been lost, as in April 1917.

The report concluded that a successful tank attack could only take place after a light artillery preparation if the objectives were less than one kilometre deep, a surprising conclusion in that this is the depth that the infantry could be expected to take without support. If the objectives of a battle were to be deeper than this, with a heavier artillery preparation, then the tanks would be unable to help the infantry to conquer the first positions because of the state of the ground. They would thus have to be used, 'like artillery', to assist the infantry in the zone beyond French artillery support. To ensure the tanks' battlefield mobility, it was recommended that designated roads should receive very limited heavy artillery fire (and never with calibres larger than 155mm), which would also assist in moving supplies forward during the battle. If tanks were to be used in a surprise attack with a reduced artillery preparation, they should be employed to attack the first objectives. It pointed to the success on 21 CA's front, where the tanks had been most effective between the first and second infantry objectives.

The report determined that the essential conditions for a successful attack with tanks were as follows. There needed to be good neutralisation of the enemy artillery, which was relatively easy provided that it was a surprise attack (i.e. with an artillery preparation of short duration) and the enemy batteries' positions were known. A dense creeping barrage, possibly to be controlled via the TSF tanks, was essential, as was the necessity to avoid using tanks in areas that had been subjected to heavy artillery bombardment. An attack in depth with tanks was possible, provided that the tank units were echeloned in order to be able to mount a series of successive efforts, necessary to replace the inevitable losses that the tanks would incur. The report finished by stating that if more tanks had been available for the latter part of the battle on 23 October, then 'without doubt' the tanks could have opened the passage for the infantry right up to the Ailette, which was at that point only defended by German machine guns.

An AS analysis of the battle states that of the sixty-three tanks engaged, only twenty-one made a meaningful contribution to the battle, which, on the face of it, would seem damning. However, from the point of view of the AS, the battle's most important result was that it had restored confidence in the tanks to their crews and within the French Army. Not surprisingly, the view of the individual infantry regimental commanders was determined by the effect of the tanks in their sector. Thus the commander of the RICM felt the tanks were of no use to his regiment on 23 October but his report was the only wholly negative one. For example, Lieutenant Colonel Lardant (commander 21 RI) noted the considerable effect that the tanks had had on the morale of both the French infantry and the Germans. General Degoutte (commander, 21 CA) believed that the tanks had 'rendered great service' to his corps and that they would now be a support arm of the infantry *par excellence*. Some of the other lessons from Malmaison were rather more negative for the tanks, in that the battle confirmed many of the conditions that made tank use risky, if not pointless, as well as highlighting further problems with the tank designs.

On the mechanical front, a new problem had come to the fore; there had been significant problems with the quality of the petrol supplied to the tanks, as much of it was contaminated with Benzol, which caused either a dramatic loss of power or a complete engine failure. This was in the main a minor nuisance and does not alter the fact that most of the tanks lost had ditched in shell holes or lost tracks due to inherent design problems or because of driver error.

However, it was generally conceded that 'the ground was exceptionally awful' at Malmaison and that the tanks simply could not be expected to operate successfully in such circumstances. It now became accepted that the tanks should not operate over badly-damaged terrain, such as was found on the first German positions at Malmaison, and this was one of the most important lessons taken from the battle. It was thus established that tank employment would require ground that was not heavily damaged, which in turn implied a different approach to artillery preparation of the battle zone.

On a more positive note, the battle had shown that the tanks could suffer comparatively light casualties if, and only if, the enemy artillery was efficiently suppressed. The final casualty figures for the tank crews at Malmaison were twenty killed and sixty-two wounded, light compared with later engagements. French counter-battery work had been very effective and this is presumably why only six of the engaged tanks received direct artillery hits. Although German anti-tank guns had been placed in woods across the battlefield to provide enfilade fire, these were all neutralised by the French artillery preparation.

In particular, the tanks had been useful in eliminating those German machine-gun nests that had not been destroyed in the artillery preparation, thereby considerably reducing the French infantry's losses. On the parts of the Malmaison front where there was no tank support, infantry casualties were heavy; 64 BCP (on the Bovettes front with 66 DI) had no tanks attached and suffered severe losses. By comparison, the commander of 21 BCP drew attention to the 'relatively light losses' that his battalion had suffered, due he thought to his tank support.

To sum up, the major lesson was that getting the tanks into action close enough to the enemy was going to be difficult whenever an extensive artillery preparation had taken place. However, once they were within close range, it was clear that the Germans had limited options to counter them and the tanks could be very valuable in keeping down infantry casualties, an issue of pressing concern to Pétain. In relation to the former issue, German prisoners reported that they were very alarmed that their counter-tank preparations had been to no avail, the tanks causing 'disarray' in their ranks. In one encounter, forty Germans had surrendered to one tank.

In relation to the issue of French casualties, General Eugene Debeney drew attention to the lower percentage of overall casualties suffered at Malmaison, when compared with those on the Aisne and at Verdun in August 1917; the losses at Malmaison being 8.45 per cent on the Aisne 17.7 per cent and 18.4 per cent at Verdun (the majority of these casualties being from the infantry). The AS and GQG would use these lessons to develop their methodology for the effective use of tanks in future offensives.

The Tank Regulations
The experience gained from the Nivelle Offensive and the Battle of Malmaison was considered sufficient to enable provisional tank regulations to be issued; the *Instruction Provisoire sur l'emploi des chars d'assaut* of 29 December 1917. This was followed by the first light tank regulations; *Réglement Provisoire de manœuvre des unités de chars légers* of 10 April 1918. The *Instruction Provisoire* received one set of major modifications, in the light of the Renaults' employment and changes to the organisation of the AS, to become the *Instruction sur l'emploi des chars d'assaut* of 14 July 1918. The light tank regulations became, with minor modifications, the *Instruction Provisoire de manœuvre des unités de chars légers* of 24 June 1918. A number of other documents were issued which paraphrased the instructions and regulations, emphasising what were considered to be the most important prescriptions (see for example GAN, *Le général commandant l'AS à Monsieur le général commandant en chef,* 22 August 1918 in 16N2142). These were generally not addressed to the AS but to those who would fight with the tanks, mainly the infantry commanders. Thus the tank regulations are best considered divided into two; those dictating the actions and preparation of the tank units themselves and those regulating how the tank units were used in conjunction with the rest of the army. Initially these two parts were bundled together in one large document; the *Instruction Provisoire* of December 1917. The light tank regulations were more concerned with matters directly affecting the AS units themselves, with the general methodology of use remaining as set out in the December regulations (the light tank regulations are discussed in Chapter 6).

As the *Instruction Provisoire* of December 1917 remained the basis for tank operations throughout the rest of the war, albeit with some modifications, it is worth considering in detail. The instruction starts by defining the aim of the AS: 'The *artillerie d'assaut* acts as accompanying artillery for the infantry, immediately acting to the demands and necessities of combat.' Certain conditions were required for the tanks to be able to accomplish this mission. The ability to fight with the infantry in all terrain was considered the most important factor, with sufficiently strong armament to be able to overcome any resistance that was stopping the infantry and invulnerability to any enemy infantry weapons being the other two conditions for success. It emphasised the mechanical limitations of the medium tanks, particularly in relation to crossing broken terrain and wide trenches, the latter requiring infantry detachments to help the tanks cross them. The *Instruction* stated that light tanks were coming into service that would be less vulnerable than the medium tanks.

In relation to the organisation of the AS units, this was in line with the experiences of the year and established the *groupe* as comprising three, rather than the original four, batteries. Although the *groupe* was the technical and administrative unit, the battery remained the combat unit. A battery of four tanks would be assigned to the front of an infantry battalion in offensive operations, the infantry commander taking command of the battery during combat. Four *groupes* of Schneiders or three *groupes* of St Chamonds would constitute a *groupement*, along with an SRR unit to maintain the combat units. This combination of maintenance and combat units gave the *groupement* the ability to deploy and engage in an operation without the necessity of further support, due to the 'equilibrium' of its constituent units. The *groupements* were to be distributed between the AS centres, the army groups and the general army reserve in accordance with 22 October 1917 note.

In relation to the conditions needed for a successful tank attack, the *Instruction* was quite explicit; the best use of tanks was in an engagement where the artillery preparation 'is not complete'. If the enemy positions were subject to a heavy artillery preparation, the infantry should be able to occupy these without tank support, rendering the use of tanks 'superfluous'. The *Instruction* pointed out that a tank would be quickly immobilised crossing badly-overturned ground, with 'no profit to the infantry'. By contrast, if the artillery preparation was either short or technical issues made it less effective than normal, the use of tanks was both 'necessary' and the 'easiest' method of attacking with a reduced preparation. If the objectives of an attack did not lead to the disorganisation of the enemy artillery, then any tank breaking down on the battlefield was liable to be destroyed and this would require a judgement by the commanders as to whether this risk was justified by the potential success of the operation. Thus *coup de main* attacks against the first position were not ruled out, providing the ground was known to be suitable for tank movement. However, the deeper the objective, the better suited the operation was for tank combat, as the enemy artillery would be less effective. The *Instruction* advised that the AS 'is used-up quickly on the battlefield', requiring careful management of tank reserves by commanders. As might be expected, close liaison with the infantry and the artillery was a necessity. The tanks were to attack points of resistance, not neutralised by the preparation, that were stopping the infantry advance and also eliminate any enemy troops that appeared after the first infantry wave had passed them. The liaison necessary for this to be assured was why the AS units were commanded in battle by the infantry commanders, down to the level of battalion inclusive. However, the *Instruction* made clear that presence of the AS was not a reason to modify a general plan of engagement, which should be capable of fulfilment with or without the tanks. It was important that 'the infantry does not act as a spectator' to the AS but that they work closely together, giving mutual support. Those modifications to the general plan of engagement that tanks made necessary would also 'favour' the other arms, as they were largely concerned with neutralising the enemy artillery, as it was the most 'dangerous adversary' of the tank. The following conditions were thus essential, according to the *Instruction*; effective counter-battery fire in the preparation, arrangements for firing on enemy batteries that appeared during the battle, the blinding of enemy observation posts overlooking the battlefield, the extensive use of smoke shells in the creeping barrage and protection in the air against enemy aircraft.

These provisions obviously required considerable forward planning if they were to be implemented effectively. In relation to infantry liaison, this could not 'develop in a fruitful way on the battlefield' but required 'careful preparation' in exercises on the training grounds. Three or four combined exercises were generally considered 'sufficient' to familiarise a battalion with tank combat and enable its infantry to assist and be assisted by the tanks. The importance of this training was such that instruction centres were formed at the Army Group AS bases, which any division stationed nearby was expected to use for infantry-tank training. The tanks also needed their own immediate support infantry, as these required 'lengthy training' they could not be taken from the divisions designated for the offensive. Surprisingly, lengthy training is then defined as two or more weeks. These troops would be organised as one company of infantry per *groupement* and would be under AS command in respect of their training. In combat, they split into two groups, one forward of the tanks with the first wave of infantry to prepare the way for the tanks (the majority of the men), the other comprising three or four men who moved with the tanks to directly assist them, primarily as a liaison between the tank and 'the world outside', as well as supplying reinforcements, where necessary, for the tank crews.

Reconnaissance was considered of particular importance for a successful tank operation. The AS officer attached to each army group was expected to maintain a constant reconnaissance of the armies' fronts and organise work on the ground to enable tanks to be quickly deployed for offensive operations, in addition to advising senior commanders. Once the decision to use tanks had been made, the AS *groupements* would then be attached to either specific corps or divisions and the AS officers would work with the staffs of these units to develop a plan. The infantry and AS commanders at every planning level were expected to work closely together on both the plan and the work required to enact it. At the higher levels of command, the latter involved establishing the de-training points for the tanks and the AS units' waiting and departure positions. In the lower levels of command, clearing the tanks' routes through the front lines and finding positions for the tanks that could be easily camouflaged were of primary importance. In respect of their departure positions, the tanks needed to be as close to the front lines as possible because of their mechanical frailty but not in a position where they could be observed by the enemy.

If the tanks were to attack the first enemy position, they would leave an hour before the infantry in order to support the first waves. This movement could be accompanied by an artillery barrage to cover the noise of the tanks but this risked alerting the enemy before the attack commenced. To avoid needing this initial covering barrage, it would be necessary to have the tanks very close to the front line. However, such a barrage could be used to open larger holes in the enemy wire than the tanks could do quickly and thus remained 'advantageous'. Where tanks were to attack the enemy's second or third positions, they would set off at the same time as the infantry. The approach march had to be such that the tanks could avoid unnecessary exposure to enemy artillery and the AS units were expected to make good use of available cover from the ground and other natural features, such as woods, in their advance. Each bound should be 'made with the most speed and security possible'. Neutralising enemy observation posts and air observation was of crucial importance in the tanks' approach march, when they were most vulnerable. Increasing the proportion of smoke shells in the barrage was to occur when the tanks came into action and designated batteries were tasked with firing only on any anti-tank batteries that appeared, identified by an attached aeroplane.

Once in combat, the tanks were to precede the first waves of attacking infantry by 100 metres, just behind the barrage. The tanks were to engage enemy resistance points as they appeared, although the infantry were expected to help identify these for the tanks, it being conceded that tank crews could not always do this for themselves. Of particular importance were any intact communication trenches that were in the line of the tanks' advance, the tanks were to move closely along these in order to be able to immediately suppress any resistance from them. When the tanks had neutralised the position, they were to signal the infantry forward with a red and white panel, indicating that they should advance. (This device never worked adequately as these panels were quickly shot to pieces on the battlefield and rendered unusable.) The *Instruction* states that infantry grenadiers should use the tanks' advance to move forward themselves, using cover on the battlefield such as shell holes, and they were expected to follow the tanks as closely as possible. Because enemy positions did not always appear until after the first infantry waves had passed them, it was recommended in the *Instruction* that 'one or two tanks from each battery' should be always available to help the infantry in mopping-up operations. Once the infantry had taken control of their objectives, the tanks would cover them until they had established adequate defensive positions, which usually meant their machine guns had been installed. The tanks would then retire to a covered position, ready for a new advance if required. The tanks' engagement plan was to be designed in considerable detail by the battery and infantry battalion commanders several days before the attack. Two reserves were required; one to reinforce the front-line tanks, the other to act as a general reserve for exploitation.

To ensure that liaison was as close as possible, the AS commander was to be stationed with either the divisional or ID commander during combat and the batteries were expected to maintain constant contact with their relevant commanders. Individual tanks were instructed to keep within either voice or signal distance from the forward elements of the infantry, although the latter proved to be impossible during combat. Effective liaison on the battlefield relied on runners, although each battery commander had four pigeons and, in theory, there was a TSF tank with each *groupe*. This gave the *groupe* the equivalent of the TSF post at division and ID level. It was hoped that this would enable the battalion and divisional commanders to keep in better communication and more in touch with the combat line, which would solve the 'problem' of how to adjust the creeping barrage to events on the battlefield.

Using the AS units in a defensive battle followed the same principles. The extensive reconnaissance of the AS commander in the army groups would not only be for offensive operations but also so that AS units could be deployed 'with the maximum of speed' in counter-attacks. The *Instruction* was thus trying to institute a constant flow of plans that could be initiated quickly. However, there was little that could be done with planning to alleviate the chaos that quickly overtook offensives in the First World War, as is discussed in the following chapters.

Summary of the Tank Regulations

To sum up the regulations, the tanks were only to be used under the following conditions. There was not to be a long approach march. The battlefield should not be heavy damaged by heavy artillery fire, as this would make it impossible for the tanks to cross safely. Thus, generally, the tanks should be used when there was a reduced preparation. The attack should be in depth unless the ground was very favourable for the tanks' movement. The AS was not to fight on its own but in close liaison with the infantry. The most dangerous enemy of the AS was the artillery; to protect the tanks arrangements needed to be taken to eliminate both enemy aerial and terrestrial observation posts. The AS was, in a material sense, quickly used-up in combat and it was therefore necessary to provide sufficient tank reserves. Thus the French army entered 1918 with a well-thought out methodology for the use of tanks in offensive operations but this needed to be tested further in combat, particularly in relation to the as-yet untried light tanks.

Chapter 5

Paris in Peril –
The Battle of the Matz,
11 June 1918

The Situation of the AS in the First Half of 1918

After the autumn 1917 reorganisation of the AS, by early 1918 there were three largely autonomous AS bases; the main HQ at Champlieu and the camps at Mailly and Martigny-les-Bains. Each had a *section de parc* (201 at Champlieu, 202 at Mailly and 203 at Martigny). No longer were all the *groupements* stationed at Champlieu, which only contained the AS general reserve, under the command of Colonel Monhoven, consisting of Groupements I and III (Schneiders) and XII and XIII (St Chamonds). At Martigny-les-Bains, Lieutenant Colonel Wahl was in charge of the *AS de GAE*, comprising of Groupement II (Schneiders) and Groupement X (St Chamonds), while at Mailly Lieutenant Colonel Chédeville commanded the *AS de GAN* (this army group had previously been called GAC), which comprised of Groupement IV (Schneiders) and Groupement XI (St Chamonds). The infantry of 262 RI had been permanently attached to the AS and one battalion served with each army group and one with the reserve.

The situation for the Allies was very grave by 25 March, with General Sir Hubert Gough's British 5 Army in serious trouble. The following day, Estienne received urgent orders from GQG that all available AS units at Champlieu were to made available to GAN, with all other units evacuated to Cercottes, as Champlieu was now in potential danger of being captured by the Germans. On 29 March, Monhoven had been placed in command of the tanks attached to GAR (Fayolle) and by 12 April all the available tanks were in two large groups, one behind III Armée (Groupements III and IV initially, subsequently joined by Groupements XI and XII) and the other behind I Armée (Groupements I, II and X). At this point, Monhoven returned to acting as AS second-in-command and the two groups of tanks received a full staff and service units.

As British 5 Army was pushed back by von Hutier's troops, German attention turned to French I Armée, which was attacked in strength on 4 April at 07.30, after a three-and-a-half-hour artillery barrage. Fortunately, the French were expecting this move, having been alerted by prisoners captured the night before and the commander of I Armée, General Debeney, had organised his forces well, with the Germans getting a hot reception. There were a number of small tank engagements over the following weeks; these actions being difficult because of their impromptu nature, with little time for careful planning, and the atrocious weather that had broken over the front. For example, elements of AS4 were engaged on 5 April, supporting an infantry attack on 9 CA's front. Six Schneiders set out to join the infantry at 11.00, losing one tank which ditched before they arrived at the departure position two hours later, the tanks having benefited from the dense fog that now enveloped the battlefield. By the time they were joined by the infantry, who were half an hour late, a further tank had become immobilised crossing a small ravine. The remaining tanks had considerable difficulties crossing the battlefield and in the end only one tank got into combat. Although this tank advanced to its objective, the German artillery and machine-gun fire was so intense that the French infantry could not follow it, forcing the tank to retire to its own lines. However, German prisoners later informed the French that this one tank had caused panic in their lines and had forced them to bring an entire reserve regiment into the front line prematurely. The tank was eventually stopped by a battery of German field guns, which wounded its entire crew who were then captured.

The Battle of the Matz, 11–12 June 1918

The first large-scale use of the French tanks in 1918 was in mid-June, during the Battle of the Matz. This was an unusual battle for the AS because quite deliberately the tank regulations were abandoned due to the critical situation. On 9 June, German 18 Army, commanded by the very able tactician Oskar von Hutier, launched the Gneisenau offensive against French III Armée around Montdidier. The intention was to drive through the French positions, take Compiègne and then open up the road to Paris.

General Georges Humbert, commanding III Armée, was under the control of one of the better senior French generals, Emile Fayolle, the commander of GAR. Alerted to the forthcoming German attack by a

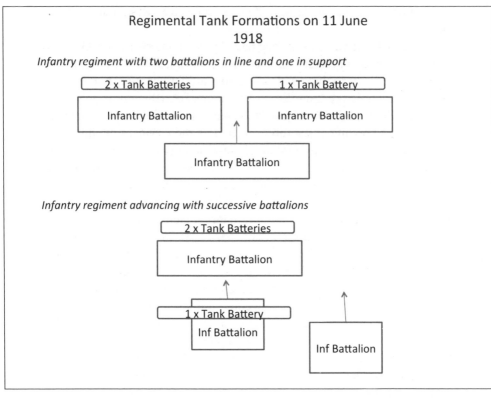

Regimental Tank Formations on 11 June 1918

Infantry regiment with two battalions in line and one in support

Infantry regiment advancing with successive battalions

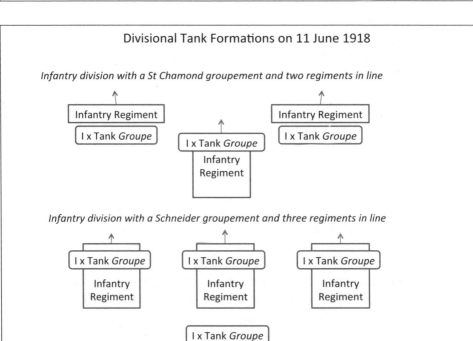

Divisional Tank Formations on 11 June 1918

Infantry division with a St Chamond groupement and two regiments in line

Infantry division with a Schneider groupement and three regiments in line

captured aviator, Humbert had pulled back his forces in order to partially absorb the anticipated attack. However, the fifteen German divisions in the first line swept through his army, capturing 8,000 French troops and advancing more than eight kilometres on the first day. The second day saw further French reverses but Fayolle had anticipated this. He had intended to allow the Germans to form a pocket, which he would then attack from two sides, but this plan was made impossible when part of the French front line collapsed, triggering a more general withdrawal. The German army was now only ten kilometres from Compiègne and Fayolle was left with little option but to strike the German advance on one flank.

General Charles Mangin was promoted from commander of 9 CA to take command of X Armée on 7 June, although initially he was only told that he had a 'new mission'. He met with Fayolle and Debeney (commander I Armée) three days later at Noailles where Fayolle confirmed that Mangin would be taking command of X Armée. However, such was the emergency, with Paris itself threatened, that Fayolle asked Mangin to first take command of a counter-attack on the German flank, which had to be carried out 'as soon as possible'. Foch put further pressure on Mangin by saying the attack should take place the following morning, although Fayolle had advised Foch that the attack would take at least two days to organise. Fayolle deferred to Foch and his order for the counter-attack, issued at 16.00 on 10 June, gave Mangin discretion as to the exact details of the attack; saying only that it must take place on 11 June and that it would be oriented according to the German positions at the time of the operation. Thus Mangin was given the shortest possible time in which to organise this intricate and delicate operation. Entirely by coincidence, on the afternoon of 10 June, Estienne was visiting Fayolle's HQ just as Pétain arrived to consult with Fayolle about the situation. Estienne departed with Mangin, when the latter left Noailles, in order to assist with the planning for the operation.

Preparations for the Battle

Groupement Mangin was formed with five infantry divisions; 48, 129, 133, 152 and 165 DIs, along with two additional regiments of field artillery and a brigade of British armoured cars. Mangin was also given one Schneider and three St Chamond *groupements*; Groupements III, X, XI, XII, all but Groupement X coming from III Armée's tank complement. The tanks were all deployed with the front-line divisions; from the left flank to the right; Groupement X was attached to 129 DI,

Groupement III to 152 DI, Groupement XII to 165 DI and Groupement XI was with 48 DI. The fifth infantry division (133 DI) was held in reserve without any tanks, along with the British armoured cars. In theory, Mangin had seventy-two batteries of field artillery and twenty-six batteries of heavy artillery available to fire on the front of his counter-attack but difficulties moving many of these into position meant that on 11 June at 10.30 (the start of the artillery preparation) there were only forty-five field artillery batteries and just over twenty heavy artillery batteries in action. However, there was some artillery support from adjacent I Armée, as well as a few high-power and super-heavy artillery pieces from GAR. Two squadrons of aircraft were attached to the four leading infantry divisions for liaison and the direction of artillery fire, with another two squadrons in an air-superiority and bombing role. Mangin issued his orders at midnight on 10 June, the attack scheduled for 10.30 but this was put back to 11.00, with the artillery preparation starting half an hour before this. The four infantry divisions in the first line would be supported to the south by 11 DI and to the north by 36 DI.

Groupement X's Preparations

On the left flank of Groupement Mangin was 129 DI (commanded by General de Corn), to which Groupement X was attached. This division had 359 RI attacking on its left with two battalions in the front line, one in support, with the *1 Groupe de Bataillon de Chasseurs* advancing on the right flank. Groupement X's commander, Major de Violet, attached AS36 to 359 RI and AS33 to the *chasseur groupe*, with two batteries supporting the flank infantry battalions and one battery with each of the centre infantry battalions. The infantry had had no opportunity to undertake any training with the tanks and many had never seen a tank before the day of the attack. However, the infantry commanders were briefed in detail by the AS officers, in particular in relation to signalling between the tanks and the infantry. De Violet, having received his orders from 129 DI's commander, issued his orders to AS33 and 36 at 23.00 on 10 June 1918. De Violet's HQ would be with the divisional HQ, where the *groupe* commanders would meet the infantry commanders at 6.30 on 11 June for a final planning meeting. De Violet drew the attention of his subordinates to the following; to be ready for counter-attacks before H-Hour and for this reason they were to liaise with the infantry commander at Tricot. He told the tank commanders to be specially alert to elements of the enemy in the dense foliage and outside of their main defensive positions. His advice was, 'In case of doubt, do not hesitate to fire the cannon.' He wanted there to be systematic tank fire on the edge of the Grand Bois near cote 100, to cover the infantry *chasseurs groupe* that was attacking the Grand Bois from the south. A tank battery was attached to the *chasseurs* to help their advance and the *groupe* commander met with the *chasseurs*' *Chef de bataillon* to co-ordinate their plans. On 11 June, the two *groupes* moved to the position of departure at 01.00, where the *groupe* commanders met with the infantry commanders and the *groupement* commander between 06.00 and 08.00. The SRR moved forward at 08.00.

Groupement X in Battle
The battery commanders of AS33 were stationed with the infantry battalion commanders and had four couriers attached from 262 RI. Two AS lieutenants were stationed with the *chasseurs*' colonel along with four couriers, the *groupe* commander moving to the ID commander's PC once the tanks had set off. At 10.00, the tanks set off, arriving with the infantry at 10.45.

The second battery of AS33, advancing to the north, moved in two lines forward of the infantry and destroyed a significant number of German machine-gun positions during its advance. The tanks cleared the plateau of its defenders and enabled the French infantry to install themselves there. The tanks were then subjected to German heavy-artillery fire from the heights of Rollot and some anti-tank pieces firing from the western edges of the Mortemer Woods. This artillery fire put the tanks out of action one by one over the course of fifteen minutes, leaving a solitary tank to continue the advance. However, the French infantry failed to follow the tank and it was eventually hit by a shell, which set fire to one of its petrol tanks. Thus all the tanks of the battery were now out of action.

The rapid advance of the first battery allowed the French infantry to push forward up to the Mery-Mortemer road, where the tanks were then taken under heavy fire by anti-tank guns, which destroyed three of them. The fourth was forced to retreat as its cannon was damaged by the German fire. Despite these setbacks, the tanks had eliminated a number of machine-gun positions and had significantly helped the infantry's advance before they were put out of action.

The third battery of AS33 advanced in the wake of the leading infantry battalion. On arriving at the Mery-Mortemer road it found all the tanks of the first battery out of action and it moved to replace them in front of the infantry. This enabled the infantry to advance several hundred metres but then a number of German anti-tank guns, including 77mm guns, at Cuvilly engaged the battery, knocking out three tanks. One AS crew managed to dismount their machine guns, which they gave to the attacking infantry. The fourth tank continued the advance but despite frantic signalling could not get the infantry to follow it, forcing it to retire. The support echelon advanced without difficulties but found no opportunity to intervene and retired. The *infanterie d'accompagnement* gave good service, particularly in relation to liaison.

AS36 was attached to 359 RI. The infantry attack formation was one battalion in the south and one battalion in the north advancing along the same axis, with a support battalion to the rear. A tank battery was attached to each of 359 RI's battalions. At 01.45, the *groupe* commander ordered the batteries to move off immediately. At 06.30, the *groupe* commander met with the regiment's commander to finalise orders. At 09.30, the *groupe* commander then met with the infantry battalion and AS battery commanders. This liaison was rushed as the infantry battalions had only just begun to detrain (at 09.45).

The first battery of AS36 was with the southern infantry battalion of 359 RI. At 10.00, the battery left the departure position and went into combat formation; two tanks in front and two behind them. Two tanks were soon hit by heavy artillery shells and caught fire, wounding the entire crew in one case. One tank was able to clear a path for the infantry through an area of German wire that the French artillery preparation had not cleared but it was then hit by a shell, wounding most of the crew. The fourth tank was immobilised crossing a road but continued to fire its cannon whenever targets appeared.

The second battery had a special mission; it was to take the village of Mortemer, one section of two tanks attacking the village frontally, while the other two flanked it from the north. The battery's tanks moved off at 11.15 in combat formation. As the battery advanced, it ran into some wounded troops from 297 RI, who asked the tanks to go and assist their infantry battalion that was halted by some German machine guns. One tank dealt with these successfully but it then became immobilised, the crew being forced to dismount and establish defensive positions around the vehicle. Another tank was hit by a shell, leaving the remaining two tanks to help the French infantry clear the German positions, in particular eliminating a small strongpoint.

The third battery was attached to the supporting battalion of 359 RI. It left its departure position at 10.15 in combat formation, joining the French infantry at 11.00. The leading tank got hit shortly after this, putting it out of action. Tank 711's commander, Lieutenant Tissot, complained in his after-action report that because the tanks had set off fifteen minutes before the French barrage began, his tank had been subjected to heavy German artillery fire. His tank was unscathed by this fire but his luck ran out at 11.15 when his tank was hit by a shell and immobilised. Tissot could see from the state of the tank that further action with it was impossible and he ordered the machine guns removed. He then attempted to reach the company commander via an infantry phone but was unable to do so and decided to retreat on foot with his crew back to Tricot, arriving there at 14.00. By contrast, Tank 739 advanced far ahead of the French infantry and ended up wandering around the plateau for half an hour without seeing any French or German troops. It was then engaged by 'violent' artillery and machine-gun fire and, lacking any support, it was ordered to retire by the battery commander. Although hit by three shells it managed to get back to the French lines, where it was clear that it could not continue without major repairs. The fourth tank (710) simply disappeared, presumed at the time to have become immobile in or near the German lines and only subsequently found when the French reoccupied the area. With the destroyed tank were found two bodies of the crew but there was no sign of the tank commander or the rest of the crew.

Major de Violet blamed the lack of effective French counter-battery fire for most of the losses of AS33. He reported that the special German anti-tank batteries had caused 'severe' losses to AS36, which had suffered nearly 40 per cent losses of material and men. The total losses for AS33 and 36 were twelve officers killed or wounded, with four missing, fifty-six other ranks killed or wounded, with forty-three men missing. The accompanying troops had lost thirty-four men but no officers. The tank losses were heavy; AS33 had lost eleven tanks and AS36 fourteen tanks, although three were subsequently recovered. Such were his groupement's losses in material, de Violet asked for light tanks to make them up.

Groupement III's Preparations

On 10 June, Groupement III, under the command of *Chef d'escadron* Lefebvre, was put on alert and immediate preparations were made to move its units. The AS crews were fully up to strength and the material was in a 'perfect' state. The *groupement* was to support 152 DI, which was attacking across a two-kilometre front in the direction of Mery-Cuvilly. Lefebvre made contact with 152 DI's commander at 20.30, at the latter's HQ at Pronleroy. One *groupe* would support 135 RI, one *groupe* would support the left battalion of 114 RI and one *groupe* was divided in the following manner; two batteries with the battalion of 114 RI attacking Mery from the south, one battery with the battalion of 114 RI flanking the right flank of the division. One *groupe* was left in reserve with 125 RI.

At 21.00 on 10 June, Lefebvre gave the *groupe* commanders their orders and the tanks moved into position at the bois de Montgerain during the night, the *groupe* commanders immediately contacting the relevant infantry commanders. At 22.00, Lefebvre went to the divisional HQ for final orders and to seek clarity from the divisional artillery commander about artillery support for the tanks. Despite his visit, Lefebvre was unable to get the assurances he wanted about the smoke barrage or about the artillery *groupes* that were supposed to be dedicated to counter anti-tank batteries. He had no better luck establishing any kind of liaison with the air service. By 03.00 on 11 June, the *groupes* were all in their departure positions, having arrived without incident. As there was much discussion about orders within the division, it was only between 08.15 and 09.00 that Lefebvre was able to give his *groupe* commanders their final instructions.

152 DI was attacking with two regiments abreast, with one in reserve. On the right AS15 was supporting 114 RI, which had one infantry battalion in the first line, with two batteries of tanks, and one battalion in support with one tank battery. In the centre, a battalion of 114 RI with AS10 was attacking Mery. On the left, 135 RI was attacking with its battalions in column, supported by AS1, with two tank batteries with the front infantry battalion, one battery with the support battalion. AS6 was held in reserve with 125 RI. The forward elements of the infantry were to be near Mery by 11.00. The AS batteries were to advance in front of the infantry, with three tanks in the first line and one in support. The *groupement* commander was to be stationed with the divisional commander, with the *groupement*'s second in command placed with the ID commander. The latter was keep in touch with the *groupement* commander by motorcycle or bicycle. Each *groupe* had half a company from 262 RI, who were tasked with making paths for the tanks over the Estrees-Mondidier railway, something they did very effectively.

Groupement III's Battle

On 11 June, the French infantry advance unfolded as planned and they crossed the railway at 10.00. AS10 made contact with the infantry battalion holding the last houses of Mery, the Germans occupying the majority of the village. One tank battery attacked up the principal street with the infantry, destroying machine guns as they advanced, as well as taking a number of prisoners. Clearing the village took nearly an hour because of the sheer weight of German machine-gun fire. Two tank batteries advanced into the village from the south while the third one flanked the village and entered into it from the north. By midday, all three batteries had fought their way through to the eastern part of Mery. On the right of AS10, AS15 advanced between the south edges of Mery, meeting little resistance. On the left, AS1 reached the Mery Chapel before it met much resistance but it was then hit by a sharp bombardment that left two tanks immobilised, one tank falling into an unseen hole and the other being hit by a shell. The support battery reinforced the first line. The tanks stopped two 'tentative' counter-attacks coming from the north-east. The infantry coordinated well with the tanks and were able to indicate to them the numerous enemy machine-gun positions.

As the tanks passed the Mery-Courcelles road, they came under heavy artillery fire from the bois de Merlier and north-west of the woods. The advance of the French infantry became more difficult and slowed to a halt around midday. The tanks continued to attack newly-identified machine-gun positions but all the tanks with the centre battalion of 114 RI were successively hit by direct artillery fire, some tanks quickly catching fire. The only tanks to escape destruction from this fire were those waiting under camouflage by the Mery-Ressons road. On the right, the advance was less difficult but lively resistance was encountered from the edges of Belloy and Val-Laploye woods and several tanks were hit by a small-calibre gun. After repulsing a German counter-attack, the tanks resumed their advance but as soon as they crossed over the raised Ressons-Mery road they came under heavy direct artillery fire, which destroyed more tanks. By 13.30, all of the tanks of AS1, AS10 and AS6 were out of action and only AS15 was able to continue the struggle with five Schneiders. These supported elements of 114 RI in an attack on the village of Cuvilly and the tanks then saw off a German counter-attack from Lataule. The fighting was over by 19.00 and the tanks were ordered to retire. On the night of 11 June, Lefebvre agreed with the divisional commander that his *groupement* would be retired from the operation, except for a battery that remained at Mery to support an infantry attack on 13 June. From 11 to 13 June, the *groupement* had left thirty-one tanks on the battlefield and had lost forty-one officers and 109 men, with 262 RI losing fifty men.

Groupement XII's Preparations

Groupement XII, under the command of *Chef de bataillon* Azais, was attached to 165 DI (commanded by General Caron). This division was advancing with two infantry regiments in the first line (287 and 154 RI) and one (155 RI) in reserve.

On 10 June, at 16.30, Azais received an order to move his *groupement* that night and an hour later the order to move was given verbally by AS III Army commander to Azais. Azais met with General Caron, who briefed him on the situation and gave him his orders. Azais in turn gave his orders to his *groupe* commanders at 21.00 on 10 June; AS37 and AS39 were attached to 287 RI, 154 RI having AS38 attached, leaving no tanks with the reserve regiment. AS37 would be attacking with 287 RI north of the edges of Belloy and the west edge of Lataule, AS39 attacking, with 287 RI, the south edges of Belloy and bois de Lataule, AS38 was attacking west of Belloy with 154 RI. The *groupe* commanders were told that it was imperative in an operation so quickly planned to keep in close contact with the regimental commanders. The liaison with the infantry colonels was thus good but the liaison further down the line (i.e. between the tank batteries and the infantry battalions) was organised too hastily to be efficient. The lack of the normal *infanterie d'accompagnement* for the tanks had a serious effect on tank-infantry liaison, the batteries having too few crew to do the liaison work themselves. In the event, most of the battery commanders spent the entire engagement on foot, continually moving between the tanks and the French infantry. AS37 would advance two batteries with the leading infantry waves, with one battery moving with the support infantry battalion, ready to support the other tank batteries if necessary. AS39 had the same formation but AS38 would be advancing with all of its batteries in the front infantry line.

Groupement XII's Battle

On 11 June, Groupement XII's three *groupes* set off at 11.00 in two columns; in the north was AS37 followed by AS39, with AS38 making up the southern column. The French infantry had jumped off at 11.00 but was almost immediately stopped by heavy German resistance and the former had to wait for the tanks. This took some time and most of the tanks only caught up with the French infantry around 13.00.

The leading battery of AS37's column only lost one tank in the initial advance, which broke its tracks crossing a railway line, leaving three tanks in action. Two deployed in front of their objective but the third saw some Schneiders from Groupement III in action in its zone and the tank commander decided to join them attacking the west edge of the village. The magneto of the battery commander's tank failed, requiring a tense thirty minutes to fix, although the tank continued firing during this time. The tank that had joined the Schneiders now found itself alone with no idea where the rest of its battery was and, as it could not find the battery, it attached itself to the adjoining battery from AS37. The tank that had broken its track on the railway was repaired in time for it to rejoin the action but it was hit when it entered the combat zone, catching fire almost immediately.

The adjacent battery reached the French infantry a little earlier than the others because the infantry had been stopped mere metres from Belloy. Seeing the Schneiders and the St Chamonds from AS37 in action to the north of the village, the battery commander decided to manoeuvre around to the south of the village. As the battery moved forward, it encountered serious resistance from the western edge of the village, which it cleared before continuing its advance. However, just before Belloy, one tank was hit by a shell and immobilised as its tracks were badly damaged. The other three tanks moved to a position where they could cover the north-east edge of the village with fire, which they did for an hour and a half. The battery was retired around 17.00, with one tank destroyed by a shell as they moved back to the French lines.

The final battery from AS37 was following in the wake of the other batteries. As it advanced, one tank broke down, leaving only three tanks to continue. The battery was then ordered to support the fierce struggle now going on for Belloy. Its three tanks engaged and destroyed numerous machine-gun positions around the village, helping the French infantry to advance. One tank received a hit which destroyed its gun; the crew dismounted with their machine guns and took up defensive positions around their tank. Another tank was hit by a shell and caught fire, leaving only four tanks remaining of the eleven from the battery that had gone into combat.

AS39 was following AS37 and its tanks had a similar experience, although only one tank broke down with a minor engine problem that was quickly fixed. Two of its batteries arrived just after 13.00 at a ravine west of Belloy to find the French infantry completely pinned down by German machine gun fire. The tank batteries cleared the area of enemy machine-gun positions and then destroyed a German counter-attack that was launched shortly after this. However, in mid-afternoon two tanks were hit by shells and temporarily immobilised. The batteries were retired on the orders of Azais at 18.15. Of the eleven tanks from AS39 engaged, ten remained in working order by the early evening.

AS38's batteries were operating with 154 RI against the Bauchemont and Garenne farms as well as the Bout and Genlis woods. The tanks only arrived at the regimental HQ after noon and they were immediately directed to join the infantry that was held up in front of the farms. While assisting the French infantry, one tank broke down after frying its electric motor and another ditched in a shell hole. In fact, all three batteries were reduced to half strength by mid-afternoon, largely due to breakdowns although several tanks were hit by German artillery fire and destroyed. The *groupe* was withdrawn as evening fell, with five tanks still in operation out of twelve engaged.

Captain Bruneau, who we have seen fighting at Malmaison, was now in charge of Groupement XII's AS38 (with twelve St Chamonds), the *groupe* being known as 'the Crocodiles'. Having spent the night under camouflaged positions near St Martin-aux-Bois, Bruneau's *groupe* set off as planned, advancing in column across the Ménévillers plain quite easily. Bruneau thought the noise from the French barrage was 'infernal'. Although the German artillery had reacted strongly to the French advance, the tanks were not hit and Bruneau deployed his three batteries facing the objective (i.e. in line) behind a line of French infantry that were unable to advance further. At Bruneau's signal, the line of tanks moved forward in line at full speed towards the Bois de Belloy. One battery advanced into the south-west corner of the woods, destroying a German machine gun and allowing the infantry to enter the woods. Heavy fighting then commenced, the Germans putting up serious resistance but seemingly unable to stop the tanks. However, a single German field gun then opened fire and in several minutes four tanks were immobilised, although the woods were captured despite this setback. The battery on the left attacked Lataule village but only one tank got into the village, where it got stuck against a wall and was subsequently captured by the Germans. Bruneau stopped for an hour to regroup the tanks of his *groupe* but he was only able to find two combat ready tanks. *Commandant* Azais ordered Bruneau to stand down and for his tanks to remain in place as the infantry could not advance any further. During the night, a 'rapid' salvage operation was mounted and six tanks were recovered, the *groupe* then returning to St Martin-aux-Bois.

AS37 had six officers wounded, one man killed and twenty wounded, with four missing. AS38 lost two officers wounded and one missing, three men were killed with eleven wounded and eight missing. AS39 had one officer killed, one wounded, with one man killed, eight wounded and one missing. SRR 107 had no casualties in this engagement. There was thus a total of sixty-nine casualties, although this included twelve lightly wounded who did not need hospitalisation. The material losses had been high; AS37 lost six tanks destroyed, out of twelve engaged, AS38 had four tanks destroyed, with one missing, although AS39 got off rather more lightly with ten tanks getting back to the assembly position, out of the twelve engaged. with three tanks having been hit by shells. AS37 had fired 169 shells and used eighty-four machine-gun belts, AS38 had fired ninety-four shells and thirty-seven machine-gun belts with AS39 using 174 shells and fifty-six machine-gun belts.

Groupement XI's Preparations

Groupement XI, under the command of *Chef de bataillon* Herlaut, was attached to 48 DI (commanded by General Prax), which was attacking with three infantry regiments, divided between two brigades, with one regiment on the left flank (95 Brigade, two battalions in the front line, one in support) and two regiments on the right flank (96 Brigade, three battalions in the front line, one in support) and one regiment in reserve (*1 Zouaves*). Two batteries of AS34 were attached to 95 Brigade to support the two front-line battalions, with one battery going to 96 Brigade along with the three batteries of AS35, a battery with each front-line infantry battalion.

On 9 June, Groupement XI, was alerted that it was to move to an intermediate destination at Moyenneville, where the unit would wait for further orders before being moved into the Mery-Lataule region for an operation. On the evening of 10 June, Herlaut was instructed to contact General Prax to receive his orders for the operation. During the course of the night, Herlaut assisted in the drawing up of the division's operation orders and he insisted on a number of conditions required by the tank regulations; close liaison between the tanks and the attacking infantry, with mutually-agreed procedures for it. The *groupe* commanders were to ensure that these conditions were reflected in the infantry's orders but the rapidity with which the operation was mounted meant that in practice it was almost impossible for these conditions to be met.

Despite Herlaut's efforts, liaison prior to the battle between the infantry commanders of the division and the AS officers simply did not happen. The infantry brigade commanders only reached their headquarters at around 09.00 on 11 June and their infantry regiments were detrained so late in the morning that they had to immediately move off to their departure positions. This left no time for effective planning and the AS *groupe* commanders were obliged to order their subordinates to offer support to whatever infantry units were in their zone of action. This did not get better during the battle; in 96 Brigade, for example, liaison was carried out during combat between the infantry battalion commanders and the tank battery commanders but this was described by a participant as 'always precarious'. However, 48 DI managed to ensure some liaison during the battle because the tanks had been given the same axis of advance as the infantry they were supporting. The late arrival of many of 48 DI's units meant that this division would jump off half an hour later than the other French divisions in the attack.

Groupement XI's Battle

On 11 June, the tanks were all in position between 03.00 and 05.00. AS34's first battery was supporting the right-hand battalion of the first infantry line, the *9 Tirailleurs*, and we will look at this battery's action in detail. The battery successfully crossed the railway in a column at 11.00 and then deployed into battle formation; three tanks in the front with one tank 100 metres to the rear, with the infantry 200 metres behind them. One tank (62.495) cleared a number of enemy machine-gun positions, despite receiving on one occasion heavy fire from a 77mm battery, and got as far as 200 metres from village before its motor started playing up, forcing the crew to abandon their mission. Tank 62.526 engaged a 'large number' of German machine guns, destroying them with its main gun, before it was hit with a shell, which damaged its oil reservoir, ending its action for the day. Tank 62.516 cleared some machine-gun positions around the slopes east of Neufvy ravine, which had stopped the infantry's advance, allowing the latter to move forward. The tank was then fired at by a small-calibre anti-tank gun, receiving several hits which failed to penetrate its armour. However, the rear machine gun was damaged which suggest the tank was initially fired on from the rear. Three shells fired from the tank silenced the gun and the tank resumed its advance. The tank then engaged some machine-gun positions at Garenne farm, which had stopped the French infantry, but the tank's other machine guns were knocked out by enemy fire. The crew became concerned about the state of the tank's engine and decided to move to the resupply position, where it arrived at 19.30, despite coming under fire from German heavy artillery. The tank and its crew had been in combat for over six hours and fired eighteen shells and used five machine-gun belts. As it set off, tank 62.538 almost immediately engaged a small group of Germans, dispersing them, and then destroyed a machine gun that fired on it. It then intercepted a party of over twenty retreating Germans and captured them. After handing over its prisoners to some passing French infantry, the tank continued forward, destroying a number of machine guns as it went. When it became apparent that the infantry were not following the tank, its commander decided to withdraw his vehicle. On the way back to the French lines, the tank came across a demolished 77mm battery and killed the survivors with its machine guns. By late afternoon, the tank was partially immobilised by a broken magneto and it limped back to the resupply position, only arriving at midnight. The battery had fired in total fifty-four shells and nineteen machine-gun belts and most of its crews had been in combat for more than five hours.

The second battery, 400 metres north of the first, had a similar experience, the tanks crossing the battlefield destroying German machine-gun positions as they came upon them. One of its tanks, number 62.408, had a particularly eventful day. It began by destroying several machine-gun positions, with several isolated machine guns being dealt with by its *infanterie d'accompagnement*. The tank continued to clear out the area, despite being attacked by some German machine guns firing armour-piercing ammunition. It captured around twenty prisoners who were handed over to the French infantry just as elements of 2 RMZT arrived and asked the tanks to engage some machine-gun positions around St. Maur and Lataule. Tank fire quickly silenced the enemy machine guns but the tank was now running out of petrol, which was worrying for the crew as the French infantry had not caught up with them. Fortunately the troops of 2 RMZT arrived in time and the tank covered them as they established themselves in the captured position. The tank retired to the resupply position at 16.45, having been in combat for over four hours. By contrast, tank 62.490 only lasted in combat for twenty minutes. As it advanced it was hit by a burst of three shells; one which hit the rear but did no damage, one which hit the left side of the tank and set it on fire, the third striking the front of the tank, wounding the driver (who was second-in-command of the tank), the gunner and the forward machine-gunner. Although the tank commander was hit as he left the tank, he and his crew eventually made it back to the French lines, despite having to run through an artillery barrage on the way. The tank, however, was totally destroyed, although it managed to fire six shells and use five machine-gun belts during its brief time in combat. Herlaut ordered the *groupe* at

19.30 to return to the waiting position and resupply themselves there. This was done over the course of the night.

AS35, under the command of Captain Adrien Balland (from AS34), had four batteries, which included one from AS34, and was supporting 96 Brigade. Preparations for the attack were haphazard as the AS officers were unable to plan anything with the brigade commander, as he did not arrive at his forward HQ until 09.00. Balland gave the following orders; two batteries were to support the infantry battalion on the right, one battery would support the centre battalion and the battery from AS34 would go with battalion on the left.

The first battery set off in column and then deployed, receiving orders from the infantry battalion commander and the tanks and infantry initially advancing together. However, the tanks soon found themselves largely without infantry support, causing some difficulties. St Chamond 62.532 from the first battery of AS35 was actually subjected to a close assault by German troops armed with grenades, which the crew fought off with their pistols, demonstrating how close the attackers got to the tanks. They had only got so near because the French infantry had not followed the tank's advance. The tank then moved to a position at the edge of a nearby ravine where it spent over an hour firing at the 'swarms' of German infantry crossing the *route nationale 35*. The extent of this tank's fire can be gauged by the fact that it fired more shells than any other bar one on 11 June, sixty-one being used, along with six machine-gun belts. (Tank 62.512 from the fourth battery of AS34 fired seventy shells during five hours of nearly continuous combat before being destroyed by a shell, while just outside St. Maur.)

By contrast, tank 62.550 from the same battery had a rather easier time of it. Although it took a number of German machine-gun positions under fire, this fire gave an 'uncertain result' as they were well hidden. As the tank advanced to a firing position on the crest, its fan belt broke, which required the tank to halt while this was repaired. Despite this delay, there was no sign of the French infantry when the repair was finished and the tank turned back to shelter in the ravine at Neufvy. The tank had only fired two shells and used one machine-gun belt. Tank 62.631 had all of its machine guns put out of action during a fierce fire-fight with some German machine guns positioned along the *route nationale 17*, having to repulse a counter-attack by some German infantry with its main gun. It was then fired on by an anti-tank gun that allegedly fired more than sixty shells at it in quick succession, forcing the tank to retire back to the French infantry. When it became clear that the infantry advance was over, the tank retired to the ravine at Neufvy to join the rest of AS35.

The second battery, engaged to the left of the first battery, moved forward in column, with two tanks breaking down almost immediately. The others continued and were heavily engaged around *route nationale 17* and the Garenne Farm. The experience of the tank crews was similar; for example, both 62.588 and 62.541 engaged and destroyed a number of German machine guns that were troubling the French infantry, one tank firing on a position from only 15 metres away. One of the tanks that had broken down at the departure position was eventually fixed but by this time the rest of the battery was out of sight. The tank commander could see the tanks of AS34 at the side of Garenne Farm and moved to support them, making a south-east movement around the farm. As it manoeuvred, the tank fired on several machine guns and a group of German infantry retreating to the east of the farm. The tank finally retired with AS34 to the ravine at Neufvy. Interestingly, the tank had fired no shells but had used six machine-gun belts.

The third battery initially advanced with just three tanks, a tank breaking down at the departure position, requiring repairs that were ultimately unsuccessful. The battery deployed after leaving the Neufvy ravine and advanced towards cote 110, the objective. While crossing a narrow-gauge railway, one of the tanks broke its tracks, ending its part in the battle. Another tank was destroyed by a shell before getting into the fight but tank 62.691 was heavily engaged supporting some French infantry near *route nationale 17*. Here it destroyed several machine guns and disrupted a counter-attack, killing over a dozen Germans. The tank was forced to retire after it was shelled with gas and retired to the edges of the bois de Perimont. The rest of the battery retired at 18.30 to the Pres farm.

The fourth battery, attached from AS34, moved out in column and deployed into a single line after crossing a small road near to cote 98. One tank broke down at the departure position, ceasing its part in the action, and another was hit by a shell and destroyed during the initial part of the advance. The remaining two tanks then went on to engage entrenched German infantry, strongly occupying slopes south of the bois de Belloy, that were firing on the flanks of 96 Brigade. Around 21.30, the batteries of AS35 were together at the Pres farm (the resupply position), from where they were then moved to a resupply position further back from the front.

All the tanks of AS32, under Captain Walch, were attached to *1 Zouaves* in reserve, with the intention of using both to push through the forward elements of the division when the divisional objectives were taken and advance to a provisional objective. *1 Zouaves* would thus jump off at 14.00, with the infantry advancing behind the tanks. AS32 set off at 14.00, as planned, and advanced with the *Zouaves* to continue the division's attack. Only one tank broke down during operations, the infantry-tank combat only being suspended at 20.30 when the *Zouaves* were ordered to stand down, the tanks being retired to an assembly position, losing one tank which broke one of its tracks.

The operation had been very effective but also costly. 95 Brigade had taken Garenne Farm and cote 117 but its infantry had been caught by deadly long-range machine-gun fire from around the bois de Lataule and cotes 110–109, one company of *9 Tirailleurs* losing three officers and ninety-one men (out of 174 officers and men) to this fire. 96 Brigade had a similar experience, although its infantry had also suffered from artillery fire directed at the tanks.

There were many stories of outstanding individual bravery in the AS during the Battle of the Matz, of which one will have to suffice. Lieutenant Fernand Orens, born in 1891 and originally from the *5 Régiment de dragons*, was a Schneider commander in 3 Battery/AS15 (Groupement III). Orens and his battery were advancing west of Belloy with the reserve battalion of 114 RI. When the infantry were stalled in front of Belloy, the tank battery received heavy artillery fire and two tanks were hit, including that of Orens, both catching fire immediately. Orens was very seriously wounded in the eyes but insisted on continuing in combat and a tank from the reserve was brought up for him. He then participated in the battery's attack on Cuvilly and helped see off the German counter-attack from Lataule. However, shortly afterwards, his second tank was hit by German artillery fire and set on fire, requiring the crew to evacuate the vehicle. Even the alarming experience of having two tanks knocked out in such a short period did not stop Orens; he spent the rest of the battle riding in one of the battery's other tanks. Commended by General Mangin after this battle for his conduct, Lieutenant Orens was to be killed on the first day of the Battle of Soissons in July 1918.

The Battle Continues, 12 and 13 June

Although the attack on 11 June had been a striking success, the battle was not entirely over and, on 12 and 13 June, further smaller attacks were made. During the evening of 11 June, Herlaut received notice that Groupement XI would be supporting 2 RMZT (48 DI) in an attack on cote 109 the following morning. Herlaut agreed with Prax that they would use two batteries from AS32, issuing orders to them at 02.00. The batteries arrived at the departure position in good time but it had been changed without notifying them, requiring a journey of nearly two hours to get to the new position. Unsurprisingly, two tanks broke down during the move to the new departure position, leaving only three tanks in each battery. The tanks jumped off with the infantry at 09.05.

The tank battery on the right advanced on a 200-metre front with two tanks forward of the first line of infantry and one in the second. The two forward tanks destroyed various German machine guns that they encountered but they then ran into a field-gun battery, which resulted in one being hit and set on fire. The other moved off, engaging several more machine guns and a small-calibre anti-tank gun before being hit in turn by two artillery shells, again catching fire, both tanks being out of action within thirty minutes of entering action. The reserve tank came up but it only lasted another twenty minutes before being hit by artillery fire and set on fire.

The battery on the left moved in the same formation as that on the right but ran into difficulties almost immediately as its area was covered in dense wheat-fields that made seeing the German machine-gun positions almost impossible, except at very close range. In one tank the forward machine-gunner was seriously wounded by machine-gun fire, requiring the tank to return temporarily to the French lines before resuming its advance and another tank's engine temporarily caught fire. However, the tanks were successful in clearing out the Germans from the wheat fields, eventually finding a trench line with numerous machine-gun posts, which it attacked, killing or dispersing the crews. The French infantry moved up at the urging of the battery commander and occupied these positions, one tank going on to seize part of the trench and capturing over thirty prisoners, along with several machine guns and a small-calibre anti-tank gun. All the battery's tanks were still operational by the time the infantry were installed in their newly captured positions, at which time the tanks retired. Over the course of 12 June, the troops of 48 DI had captured four field-guns, three howitzers, ten machine guns and taken 251 prisoners.

Although the French counter-attack was officially over on 13 June, Mangin ordered a series of small operations to consolidate the front line. The only tanks in action would be one battery from Groupement III, which was used to support 152 DI in a small operation to occupy the bois du Merlier. Such was the state of Groupement III, that Lefebvre was only able to organise a *batterie de marche* from AS10 to support the French infantry. Although there was no time for reconnaissance by the AS officers, this was mitigated by the fact that the area was well known to them and that their task was relatively simple, to eliminate a group of German machine guns positioned to the south-east of the bois du Merlier. The operation did not begin well for the three tanks in the battery as they were hit by artillery as they moved to the departure position. This knocked-out one tank and also wounded the commanders of the other two, requiring replacements to be rushed in before the tanks could resume their move to the departure position. This was difficult as the tanks found themselves moving through heavy German counter-battery fire, which included a large proportion of gas shells. This delayed the tanks so much that by the time they got to the combat zone, the French infantry had already occupied the bois du Merlier. However, the German positions south-east of the woods had not been attacked and the two tanks moved forward to engage them, accompanied by some French grenadiers. The Germans rapidly evacuated their positions when the tanks advanced on them and the area was soon cleared of enemy troops. While the French infantry installed themselves in the newly-occupied positions, the tanks chased the Germans up the Mortemer-Belloy road, only retiring when there was no-one left to fire at. One tank became immobilised after being hit by a shell on the return to the resupply position, although the other returned without incident. The Battle of the Matz was now over and the German army turned its attention to an attack on X Armée, on the right flank of III Armée.

Conclusion

Although the Battle of the Matz was costly, particularly for the tanks, it was a crucial success for the hard-pressed French army. In three days, the French had pushed the Germans back three kilometres, across a front of eight, and, as it was clear that the German offensive could not continue, they were able to assume a defensive posture on 13 June. The Germans had lost large numbers of machine guns, taken heavy casualties to their infantry and all the divisions engaged were now in a state of some disorder. Mangin's divisions had captured nearly 600 prisoners, from five different divisions, as well as a great deal of equipment. French infantry losses for the battle were heavy; Groupement Mangin had taken over 11,000 casualties (this figure including those men reported missing) by the evening of 13 June. The cost for the AS was also very high; sixty-nine tanks were lost out of 144 and out of the 2,313 men who had gone into action, there were 389 casualties, including sixty-three dead. These casualties were not evenly distributed among the AS units, with some *groupes* being sorely tested. For example, Groupement X had lost nineteen St Chamonds of its twenty-four. By contrast, Groupement XI lost only four of its thirty-six tanks. Roughly three-quarters of the tanks lost were hit by direct fire, usually from field guns, the others succumbing to indirect heavy artillery fire. On the evening of 11 June, Mangin had assigned one *groupe* of field artillery from each division to the protection of the tanks but this was simply too late to have any affect as the operation was in effect over the next day. Mangin and the French army learnt this lesson about tank support well; in the large-scale offensive at Soissons on 18 July the tanks were amply covered by dedicated artillery. Such was the attrition caused by the Matz operation that Groupement III was thereafter forced to reorganise into three batteries per *groupe*, with only two tanks in each battery. However, it needs to be remembered that the tanks had been engaged on a battlefield with an astonishing weight of German fire on it. This can be illustrated by how many of Groupement XI's St Chamonds' weapons were damaged by small arms and artillery fire on 11 June; six main guns were put out of action along with twenty-eight machine guns. Jean Perré makes the interesting point that the Battle of the Matz was a stunning strategic success because of the speed of planning and mounting the operation but that it was this very speed that caused great tactical difficulties.

GAN circulated a note about the battle to all the senior French commanders within two weeks of its close. It stated that the counter-attack executed on III Army's front had been mounted in conditions of exceptional rapidity but that 'in the current circumstances, operations of this type will occur frequently'. The note was issued with the aim of informing senior commanders about the employment of tanks before and during the attack.

It drew the commanders' attention to the following information. If the tanks were to support the infantry, they in turn needed support from the artillery. Specifically, this support required senior commanders to ensure that a strong counter-battery plan was in place, in addition to using smoke shells to blind known enemy observation posts and using aircraft to direct fire against anti-tank batteries. The infantry needed to be reminded that they were the principal arm because only they could occupy ground: the tanks were there only to assist the infantry and their presence did not allow infantry tactics to change (i.e. fire and movement). The note pointed out that Mangin had instructed his infantry to plan their attack as though there was no tank support. The infantry needed to be trained to recognise and exploit the opportunities offered by the tanks, as these opportunities would be 'infrequent'. The infantry's security depended on the speed at which they could occupy and consolidate the terrain which the tanks had freed while the enemy was still reeling from the tank attack. It should be a point of honour for the infantry never to leave any tanks in the hands of the enemy. They should be trained to fire on any French tank being closely assaulted by German infantry, provided that armour-piercing cartridges were not used. The note also mentioned that aircraft should be used to give to the overall commander constant information on the positions of both the tanks and the infantry. The note mentioned that all of these observations were in line with the tank regulations, in particular the prescriptions of the *Instruction Provisoire* of 29 December 1917. The note finished by reminding senior commanders that their infantry would be frequently engaged with tanks and it was therefore important that commanders and all their officers knew and understood the principles of tank employment.

AS Reflections on the Battle
Although it was generally accepted that the Battle of the Matz had been conducted as an emergency operation, with the deviation from good practice that this required, the AS commanders nonetheless sought to learn lessons. The nature of the ground for the operation had meant that tanks' departure positions were much further back than was ideal but the lack of cover further forward and the daylight jump-off time made this unavoidable. However, this meant that the tanks often did not catch up with the infantry until nearly two hours after the latter had set off in their attack. This is an example of where the prescriptions of the tank regulations would have been implemented if the situation had not been so critical. Despite this, once the tanks had caught up and passed the French infantry, they had a significant effect on the fighting, largely due to their fire, although on a number of occasions their appearance alone was enough to demoralise the German defenders. However, by this point most of the French infantry, having been fighting for over two hours, was in serious disarray, which prevented it from getting the most benefit from the tanks. There had been an additional problem caused when some of the St Chamond and Schneider units had ended up in the same position on the battlefield, giving the German artillery a particularly

dense set of targets. Groupement III had lost many tanks when they took a position on the crest of Mery-Belloy to fire on the German defenders at Belloy but this, again, was unavoidable due to the exigencies of the battle.

On Groupement III's front, the tanks were hit by a considerable weight of armour-piercing small-arms fire and direct artillery fire had been very effective. Fortunately for the AS crews, the German artillerymen generally had set their fuses too short, which caused the shells to explode on contact with the tanks' exterior, rather than penetrating inside, resulting in damage to the tank but fewer crew casualties. Some tanks had received accurate direct fire from small-calibre artillery, probably 57mm, which had in all cases rendered the tanks *hors de combat*.

There were various other miscellaneous problems. Groupement XI reported that the panels fitted to the tanks to call the infantry were not a success; the cables operating the panels received so much small-arms and shell fire that they became 'close to unusable'. Herlaut recommended that, as a matter of urgency, another system would have to be devised. On the other hand, the new periscope had been 'very useful' to the tank commanders and Herlaut thought that there should be two allotted to each tank in case of damage. He reported that communication within the tanks continued to be very difficult because of the sheer noise in the interior.

As might be expected, the St Chamonds had been sorely tested by the battle, particularly as many of the tanks were well overdue for a major service, most of the tanks' motors having been run for over eighty hours without major maintenance. This resulted in a number of seized engines, as well as several broken generators, largely caused by the crews' inexperience in regular maintenance, according to Azais. Interestingly, there were not many issues with the St Chamonds' tracks but this was probably due to the relatively good terrain that had been fought over. The *chars-caissons* were reported to have given the 'very best service', transporting petrol and giving assistance in un-ditching immobilised tanks.

Groupement XII's conclusions were that the tanks had been essential in helping the French infantry in taking Belloy, a key part of the battle. The provisions of the tank regulations had been reinforced by the experience of the battle. The large number of German machine guns on the battlefield required the tanks to be used *en masse* and the front of 200 metres per battery had proved effective. It was clear from later stages of the battle that the tanks must operate at least in batteries, never individually, and it was a requirement for the AS to be fighting with infantry divisions that had an adequate understanding of tank combat and their part in it.

Although the Battle of the Matz had been a very tough experience for the AS crews, they had certainly impressed their enemy. German prisoners told the French that the tanks had inflicted 'grave' losses and had caused 'great terror'. A captured major told some officers of Groupement III; 'It is not men you have in your tanks, they're much more than that!'

Chapter 6

Engine of Victory –
The Renault Light Tank

Although the design and manufacture of the medium tanks required considerable resources, French industry and the military continued to examine a variety of other projects connected with armoured vehicles and their equipment. Some projects proved beyond the capabilities of the time; for example, a small remotely-controlled electric tracked vehicle (1.5 metres long), packed with 70 kilograms of explosive, was tested in the summer of 1916. As with the German Goliath demolition vehicle of the Second World War, this vehicle would have been driven into an enemy position and then detonated but the prototype failed as it could not climb even a gentle slope and the idea was abandoned. Of possibly greater potential utility were the investigations into giving the tanks some form of smoke-generating capability but it proved difficult to find ways to do this efficiently and the main line of research used acid to generate the smoke. Although this was tested using modified light tanks, it was of limited success as the smoke generators could only cover a couple of tanks at a time and this for a very limited period. As there were also obvious dangers in transporting acid around a battlefield, this idea was abandoned and the tanks had to rely on artillery support for smoke cover. However, there were two projects that received the most attention and activity but which had startlingly different outcomes; the heavy tanks and the light tanks. The heavy tank project failed to get a single French heavy tank onto the battlefield during the war (and thus will not be discussed here) but, by contrast, the revolutionary light tank design became a crucial component of the success of the AS.

Genesis of the Light Tank
Although Heinz Guderian claims in *Achtung-Panzer!* that Estienne realised shortly before the Nivelle Offensive that the two current designs of tank 'were far too cumbersome' and then devised the idea of a light

tank, work on the light tank design had actually begun much earlier than this. Although the documentary evidence does not allow us to state definitively when Estienne began thinking of a light tank, it appears to have germinated in his mind around the time of his visit to the British tank factory at Lincoln at the end of June 1916. While there, he saw that the British tanks were going to be considerably heavier than the French designs and, as an artilleryman, he was used to the concept of different classes of artillery. He quickly saw that the combination of the heavy British tanks and the French mediums would give a tank force much more flexibility in combat. Further consideration led him to see that a light tank could fulfil a number of roles; reconnaissance, direct support of the infantry and as a commander's tank. When Estienne met the great French industrialist Louis Renault in July 1916, they discussed the idea of a light tank, armed with a machine gun. Renault had refused to participate in the initial tank programme because he was too busy but he had subsequently become interested in armoured vehicles, his factory being involved in some preliminary tank studies with another factory. There is some dispute as to how Estienne and Renault's conversation went, with some of Renault's supporters claiming that Estienne was initially opposed to Renault's plans for a light tank, but the meeting ended with Renault agreeing to make a preliminary study and mock-up of the light tank. Estienne's initial specifications were for a tank weighing no more than four tonnes, with a machine gun in a turret and a two-man crew, capable of up to twelve kilometres per hour. When Estienne approached Mourret at the DSA to formalise the arrangement with Renault, Mourret informed him that the DSA would not be ordering any further combat tanks. Despite this setback, Louis Renault's interest in the project was such that he continued to work on the prototype, even without an official order.

Estienne was forced to bypass Mourret and the DSA to keep the light tank project alive and he wrote directly to Joffre, in November 1916, stating that a two-man light tank could be produced, which could be of use to the AS as a command tank and as a special support unit for infantry divisions engaged in offensives. He pointed out that the production of light tanks should be easier for French industry than any of the proposed heavy tank designs and that Renault's studies meant that production could be implemented quickly. Joffre agreed with Estienne and wrote to Albert Thomas asking for an order to be made for 1,000 light tanks but Thomas replied that the order would be made only if a working prototype could be demonstrated satisfactorily to the ministry.

A prototype light tank was shown to the *Comité consultative* at the Renault factory at Billancourt on 30 December 1916 and was the subject of a heated debate. There were numerous objections from members of the committee, which centred on doubts about its size, which called into question the very necessity of a light tank in the first place. Mourret was the first to voice his concerns; he stated that, while he had no objection in principle to a machine-gun armed tank, the Renault was far too small to be of any use and was too lightly armed, having only one machine gun. (Later in the meeting he argued for the manufacture of more armoured cars instead of the light tanks, it not being a coincidence that the DSA operated all the armoured cars in the army.) Estienne responded that the light tank could be a decisive method of bringing mobile machine guns to the front line, reminding the *Comité* that the decision to develop a light tank had already been made by Joffre. Renault told the *Comité* that he had made the tank as light as possible in order to enable rapid manufacture. Renault was challenged over the power of the motor but his counter-argument was that using an existing standard car engine would speed up manufacture. There was concerns about the Renault's armour until Renault pointed out that the light tank would have the same thickness of armour as the St Chamond, Rimailho himself testifying that this would be sufficient protection against direct 37mm gunfire. There was one concern raised that would prove to be accurate, interestingly made by Rimailho, and that was in relation to the difficulties of manufacturing the turret. After a vote (seven in favour, three against), the *Comité* agreed to an initial order of between 100 and 200 light tanks.

During January and February 1917, the ministry's concerns about the manufacture of the medium tanks led it to strenuously oppose the Renault being manufactured, which appeared to be entirely unreasonable to most in the AS. However, the ministry had good grounds for concern as the French were by this stage of the war running into serious difficulties with the lack of raw materials, in particular steel plate, most of which had to be imported. There were further delays when Nivelle became commander-in-chief and decided to give priority to artillery tractors, a position that Thomas supported with enthusiasm. This is a good illustration of how genuinely difficult questions about resources for the French army were complicated by prejudices within the civilian bureaucracy.

However, as the light tank project developed, it became clear the Renaults would have a significant operational advantage over the existing medium tanks as, unlike the latter, the Renaults could be transported on lorries or light trailers, as well as by train. By using road transport, the light tanks could be rapidly transported and concentrated on any part of the front for both offensives and counter-attacks, without tying up valuable space on the rail network, increasingly needed for the requirements of the artillery. In addition, the Renaults used existing ammunition, which was taken from the infantry and not the more resource-pressed artillery, and required a crew of only two, manpower rapidly becoming scarce and thus at a premium. On a tactical level, the abilities of the light tank in relation to battlefield mobility, being able to go where the French medium and British heavy tanks could not, was yet another advantage.

Another row broke out when Estienne used his initiative and arranged for the Renault prototype to be taken to Champlieu, where the tank could be tested on ground more similar to the battlefield than at Marly. (The Marly test track was designed to give initial instruction to drivers and thus did not have the difficult terrain that might be found on the battlefield. Champlieu, by contrast, was built on an area already broken up and fought over. Louis Renault was also able to test the light tank across barbed wire and slopes of varying degrees there.) Although Renault and his tank were only at Champlieu for a day, Thomas was absolutely furious about the trip and he accused Estienne of over-stepping his authority and, disgracefully, suggested that there was some form of financial collusion between Estienne and Renault. Estienne responded that he was simply trying to help Renault make progress with the design and that he had no intention of bypassing the *Comité*. Indeed, he had informed both Breton and the DSA of the proposed test and the test itself had been very useful on a technical level. After further tests on the Renault before the *Comité* at Champlieu on 9 and 10 April, Nivelle was persuaded to reverse his earlier decision and give priority to tank production, in particular he recommended concentrating resources on the existing Schneider design and machine gun-armed light tanks.

It was not long before another problem arose but this time it was from within the AS. After further testing at Marly of the light tank, the base commander, *Commandant* d'Alincourt (a DSA officer), made a coruscating report on what he saw as the tank's failings. D'Alincourt declared that effective machine-gun fire from the light tank was impossible and, in any case, the gunner would suffocate in the turret from engine fumes whenever the tank was stationary. In addition, he thought the turret gunner would be isolated 'both materially and morally', creating 'irredeemable problems'. For these reasons, he recommended that the turret should be redesigned to take two crewmen, a redesign that would have involved changing the entire tank. Unsurprisingly, the ministry seized upon this report as an excuse to suspend production and Thomas wrote to Pétain on 1 May 1917 demanding a redesign of the tank. By the time Pétain received this, Thomas was already on his way to Russia on a government mission to the Kerensky government. There was thus no-one in the ministry with the authority to change his decision and the long journey to Russia via Scotland and Norway made communication with Thomas difficult.

Fortunately, Thomas' behaviour caused outrage within the *Comité*, which if anything strengthened the support there for the light tank. It was a matter of 'great astonishment that the minister has so abruptly suspended production', wrote Estienne. Another important opponent of the tank then had a change of heart. Mourret had commissioned the *Directeur de la section technique du Service Automobile* to undertake a series of tests on a two-kilometre obstacle course, over which a Renault had been driven continuously for seven hours, only stopping when its drive-sprocket broke. On 5 May, he reported to the *Comité* that, from an automobile point of view, the tank was ready and was 'very superior' to the existing medium tanks. As can be imagined, Mourret's former opposition to the light tank gave his positive report considerable weight within the *Comité* and, after representations from the *Comité* and Pétain, it was agreed that a Renault tank would be sent to Champlieu for further tests.

These tests took place over three days, in front of delegates from the *Comité* but this time with the addition of a commission of seven AS combat veterans who had fought on 16 April. The test destroyed the final traces of opposition within the *Comité*. It was unanimously agreed that the Renault was a real improvement over the current tank designs and it recommended that it should be adopted, with intensive construction beginning immediately. These results went to the *Comité* on 10 May and it was agreed to order 1,150 Renault light tanks. Pétain's appointment as commander-in-chief fortuitously coincided with this test and he immediately asked for 2,000 Renaults to be ordered, although the ministry only agreed to increase the order to 1,000 light tanks. Estienne continued to press for more light tanks to be ordered at every opportunity and, in September 1917, Pétain placed an order for a further 2,500 Renaults, to be delivered by the spring of 1918.

The size of these orders presented the ministry with a new and difficult manufacturing problem, as there had already been a considerable delay in the deliveries of medium tanks. The light tanks were not to be made at the same factories as the medium tanks but the large number ordered would still require a considerable amount of steel plate that had to come from the UK or the US, as this was unavailable in France. The shortage of steel in France had already created serous delays to the delivery of the medium tanks and the need for more steel for the light tanks was to exacerbate this issue. By January 1917, the manufacture of 75mm shells was entirely dependent on steel from abroad, as France simply could not produce enough. Although a complex agreement was made between France, the UK and the US for the importation of steel into France, steel continued to be in short supply throughout 1917, putting much pressure on the minister in relation to priorities.

In addition, it quickly became clear that the Renault factory would not be able to deal with an order of this size, Estienne suggesting as early as July 1917 that the US should be asked to manufacture light tanks to alleviate the burden on French industry, a good example of his foresight. (GQG and the minister agreed in November 1917 that the US would be asked to construct 1,200 light tanks but this project never came to fruition, the first two US-manufactured Renaults arriving in France just after the armistice.) Other French manufacturers (Berliet, SOMUA and Delaunay-Belleville) were brought in to help with manufacture but this failed to speed-up deliveries significantly. By October 1917, only 114 light tanks had been manufactured and the majority of these were not delivered to the army until the following year; by December 1917 the army had only thirty-one un-armoured Renaults available, for training only.

When Albert Thomas was replaced as minister by Louis Loucheur, the latter initially proved just as resistant to prioritising light tank manufacture as his predecessor had been. Loucheur's enthusiasm for a heavy tank design from Schneider, the CA3, led to resources being diverted to the Schneider factory and away from the Renault factory, causing much disgust within the AS. Léon Dutil referred rather pointedly to the CA3 as 'the tank that the interior wanted to construct, long after the combatants stopped wanting it'. Despite strenuous opposition from the army, resources continued to be diverted to the CA3, adding to the delay in Renault deliveries. Loucheur told Pétain in late October that the extra Renaults ordered in September 1917 (bringing the total order to 3,650 light tanks) would not be delivered, promising only that it was 'probable' that 1000 Renaults would be available by 31 March 1918, deliveries thereafter being projected at 400 to 500 per month. Pétain responded that Estienne and the *Comité* had advised him that the proposed Schneider CA3 would not be available by August 1918 and thus manufacturing should be concentrated on the Renaults. After some very bad-tempered correspondence between

Loucheur, Pétain and Estienne, it was agreed to abandon the CA3.

However, the slow delivery of light tanks continued to be a concern for the army. Pétain wrote a sharp letter to Loucheur in December insisting that a 'great effort' be made over the winter to manufacture the light tanks but he just received more promises that could not be kept, Loucheur replying that there would be 850 Renaults in service by 1 April 1918. The ministry continued to deliver tanks that were simply unfit to be used; by 21 March 1918, the army only had one Renault in 'a state to go into combat'. A further 234 light tanks were manufactured in March but only 225 of these were delivered, all of which needed 'complete revision' by workers from the factory before they could be used. As with the situation with the medium tanks, the feeling within the AS was that the main aim of the ministry was to deliver the greatest number of tanks, regardless of their serviceability.

To be fair to the ministry, there were a number of issues with the Renault tank that were caused by the design itself rather than because of bureaucratic delays. The most intractable initial problem was in manufacturing the one-piece cast turret, which proved so difficult that it was necessary to change the entire turret design to one made from riveted steel plates (known as the omnibus turret). The *Paul Girod* factory, which manufactured the turrets for the light tank, was eventually able to successfully produce a two-piece cast turret that was fitted to later Renaults. Each of the light tank factories according to Maurice Constantin-Weyer, assistant to the commander of 19 BCL from August 1918, produced tanks with different defects; for example, the SOMUA-made tanks had weak clutches whereas on the Delaunay-Belleville tanks the control levers frequently broke. The Berliet tanks were all so badly manufactured that it became necessary to group them together in one company within 19 BCL. (Interestingly, most of the problems, bar the general one with the Berliet tanks, were fixed within the light tank battalion's own workshop.) However, the most persistent problem with the Renault design was with its engine, in particular the fan-belts and the pumps. The regulations concerning revving the engine had been changed, from a maximum of 1,500 rpm to 1,650 rpm, to gain more speed for the tank. The Renault factory had insisted that the engine could support the additional strain caused by this rpm but in the field this proved to be incorrect. A number of other technical difficulties arose; for example, there were 225 light tanks at Cercottes waiting for replacement drive-sprockets on 5 October 1918. As with the medium tanks, there was also a continuing problem with spares; as late as 5 November 1918, Aubertin was complaining to the CAMA that there were insufficient spare parts available for AS370 and three other Renault companies had no rail disembarking ramps.

There was increasing friction about the delay in getting the light tanks into action. For example, Loucheur told Poincaré (1 April 1918) that the light tanks were ready but that Estienne and the other AS officers were 'hesitant' to use them, 'under a variety of pretexts'. However, by July 1918 there were over 1,000 light tanks in service with combat units, which considering the delivery record of the medium tanks is a quite impressive effort from the ministry. The delivery figures show that Loucheur significantly increased the production of light tanks as time went on, although not at the speed wished by the AS. In fact, by the second half of 1918, there was an increasing disparity between the number of Renaults delivered and those in combat units, largely because the AS could not train crews fast enough.

The Light Tank Regulations

In order to account for the differences between the medium tanks and the light ones, a provisional set of regulations for the light tanks were issued in April 1918. This document is unsurprisingly similar to the *Instruction* of December 1917, the only changes made were to account for the differences in combat, organisation and maintenance between the Renaults and the medium tanks. In particular, the light tanks would be acting more closely with the infantry.

Unlike with the medium tanks, the technical and administrative unit for the Renault tanks was the company, composed of three identical combat sections, a resupply and repair unit and a TSF tank. The combat sections, to be commanded by a lieutenant or *sous-lieutenant*, would have six combat tanks; one gun tank for the section chief, two half-sections each comprising a gun tank, a machine-gun tank and a 75mm gun tank, the latter of which did not enter service during the war. The resupply unit had five replacement tanks (three with guns, two with machine guns), plus three re-supply tanks (two with guns, one with machine gun). The company's effectives would be 115 men, including five officers, fifteen *sous-officiers* and eighteen *brigadiers*. Until the introduction of the 75mm tank, sections would have five tanks and be commanded by an officer in a gun tank and comprised of two *demi-sections* (half-sections) of two tanks, each *demi-section* having a gun tank and a machine-gun tank. There were only two section formations laid down by the regulations, whether the tanks were moving or stationary; in column or in line ('in battle').

Tank regiments would usually consist of three light tank battalions, along with a number of medium or heavy tank *groupements*, the Renault battalions consisting of three companies and a staff. The battalion staff would consist of a major with three assistants; a tactical assistant, who was second in command of the battalion during combat and assisted in planning, a technical assistant charged with dealing with material and the resupply of fuel and spares, and a *sous-officier* dealing with administration.

The regulations emphasised the importance of training. It was an important principle for the light tanks in contrast with the medium ones that, as there were only two crewmen, they had to be interchangeable, with all light tank crew personnel receiving individual instruction in driving. In relation to the driver/mechanics, their instruction was to 'inculcate confidence' in their machine, as well as their ability to repair it. The regulations state that 'one well maintained and well driven tank is worth four others'.

Considerable attention was paid in the regulations to the preparation of light tank engagements, which mainly follow the general principles laid down in the *Instruction* of 27 December 1917; the light tanks should participate in offensive actions that were either 'regularly mounted' (i.e. with adequate planning and preparation) or in operations that were rather more *ad hoc*, such as the second phase of an offensive or repelling counter-attacks. In the latter case, it was of particular importance to make sure that there were AS officers attached at every level, to take account of the more fluid nature of such operations, so that the tanks would be engaged 'in the best possible conditions'. As per the *Instruction*, there was to be a detailed reconnaissance made by the AS officers at every level. Once this had been made, an engagement plan for the AS units was developed in conjunction with the infantry commanders. The light tank units were instructed to train with the infantry units that they were to be attached to, something that was rather easier to recommend than implement.

In relation to combat, the section was to be the main tactical unit and it 'should never be divided'. The section would have a front of 200 metres and would normally be in battle formation, with the machine-gun tanks on the flanks and slightly to the rear of the gun tanks. In combat, the section was to be under the orders of the infantry battalion that it was attached to but it could be asked to fight with several successive waves of infantry. The section would advance in the midst of the infantry, moving beyond them to attack any resistance that appeared, as well as covering the flanks. The regulations are very emphatic that the section was never to '*cavalier seul*' (go it alone, i.e. without infantry support) but should always fight in close liaison with the infantry.

In principle, a tank company was to be attached to an infantry regiment, normally deployed in depth, to accommodate losses and enable continuity of action. The leading tank sections would be attached to the first-line infantry, with the supporting tank section either being attached to the infantry in the second line or forming a reserve for the AS company commander. The company's support unit was divided in two; an advanced element which served as a breakdown crew and for un-ditching tanks on the battlefield, with the main SRR element consisting of the unit's recovery tanks, spare parts and supply ingredients, carried on trailers. Each company was thus well equipped to maintain its tanks, except for major damage or major component failure.

In June 1918, Pétain issued a note for infantry officers on the employment of the light tanks which summarised the relevant parts of the *Réglement*. He wrote that the light tanks' purpose was to fight in the ranks of the infantry and it was expected that the tanks would be a useful tool for the infantry, clearing strongpoints, such as machine-gun nests, as well as fighting off counter-attacks. He reminded the infantry officers that they should not modify their tactics because tanks were attached and battalion commanders were instructed never to divide their tank sections or use them on a front wider than 600 metres. Pétain ordered that a light tank section was never to be used in isolation; it was only there to support the infantry. The light tank section was normally to be with the forward elements of the infantry, only advancing beyond them when attacking a strongpoint or stopping counter-attacks. There were no arrangements for efficiently signalling between the tanks and the infantry, the only method mentioned in Pétain's note was for the infantry to fire in the general direction of points of resistance, which the tanks would take as a signal to attack. The tanks would often be able to push forward of the infantry but 'their actions are in vain if not supported properly by the infantry'. There was an important prescription attached to the end of Pétain's note; he said that the light tanks were only to be used *en masse* (that is one battalion per infantry division) in properly-organised offensives and that any derogation from this rule must be reported immediately to Pétain.

Pétain gave the Renault crews further instructions emphasising the points of 'extreme importance' from the regulations; in particular, both section and tank commanders were reminded again never to *cavalier seul*. The section commanders were reminded never to divide their sections and always to remain behind the infantry until resistance was encountered, which they should engage without waiting for orders. They were never to fire on the move; 'efficient fire [i.e. stationary], [being] the quickest means of advancing'. This was a prescription that would be changed as experience would show that stationary fire was not always the best tactic.

In June, it was decided that the *Instruction Provisoire* was in need of revision because of the coming introduction into service of the light and heavy tanks and the formation of the tank regiments. In addition, GQG believed that experience had demonstrated that a number of principles on tank use could now be fixed more precisely. The changes ranged from added emphasis, such as adding to the preamble about the aim of tank combat a reminder that 'movement is the most powerful mode of action for the tanks', to more detailed instructions about moving the tanks from front to front. Most importantly, a part of the resume was changed; from stating 'the AS should only be used *en masse* and with a precise aim', it was changed to read, 'the AS should only be used *en masse* in regularly mounted offensives'. Thus the French army had a well-thought out methodology for the use of tanks but this needed to be tested further in combat, particularly in relation to the untried light tanks.

One of the leaders of the British tank corps, H. J. Elles, said that the employment of British tanks during the war had been 'one long conflict between policy and expediency'. Policy dictated that tank operations should only be undertaken in well-planned operations with a mass of tanks but expediency meant that tanks had often to be used in unsuitable conditions. This epitomises the situation of the AS during the first half of 1918. As can be seen, the intention of GQG was only to use tanks in organised offensive actions, not in defensive operations. Indeed, both the *Instruction* and the light tank regulations gave only a paragraph to the use of tanks in a defensive battle. However, expediency was now a driving factor in the war and the French army was forced by necessity to debut the light tank during the desperate defensive battles against the German spring offensives. We will now look at this operation in detail to see how the regulations were in line with the actual experience of tank combat and illustrate certain parts of the regulations not already discussed.

The Renault Tank in Action
On 31 May 1918, the Renaults were thrown into a counter-attack against German 7 Army, which was making alarming progress south-west of Soissons and thus in the general direction of Paris. GQG had ordered

that all combat troops were to be thrown into the battle to stop the Germans entering the forest of Villers-Cotterets, 'whatever the cost'. 1 CA was to organise a local counter-attack with 35 DI taking the main role, supported on its right by the Moroccan Division (DM), with the aim of relieving pressure on 11 CA. As 1 CA had been engaged in heavy fighting over the previous two days, the corps was given two Renault companies from 2 BCL to stiffen it.

2 BCL was at Champlieu on the evening of 29 May, when it received orders to join 1 CA and, the following day, it was given a mixture of various lorries, tractors and trailers to transport the battalion. The sheer variety of vehicles complicated the move, as many were unfamiliar to the AS crews, making loading and unloading both difficult and slow. To add to their difficulties, the AS crews had to manoeuvre their vehicles through the very narrow roads of the Forêt de Retz and by 09.00 on 31 May only six of nine tank sections had arrived at Saint-Pierre-Aigle and Dommiers. Difficulties were further compounded because the majority of 1 CA's troops were late in arriving at the staging areas, having made a forced march from the Compiègne region. Arriving at the Forêt de Retz, the AS officers saw French troops milling around without any officers and numerous civilians leaving the area, both of which 'gave the impression of a certain disarray'. AS305 was expecting to join 33 RI in a counter-attack but the infantry arrived in considerable disorder, after a forty-mile overnight forced march, long after the tanks had assembled. However, the situation was urgent enough for General Lacapelle (commander, 1 CA) to decide to attack with what he had available; three sections from AS305, two from AS304 and one section from AS306 (to be used together), along with two *tirailleur* regiments. AS304/306 (hereafter AS304) was attached to *4 Tirailleurs* on the left flank, with AS305 attached to *7 Tirailleurs* on the right. There was much confusion in the issuing of orders, the corps' orders being changed three times, and final deployments were only agreed an hour before the attack was to begin. This left the AS and *tirailleur* commanders no time at all to make contact and little time for the tank officers to make their own plans.

In relation to the approach march, contrary to regulations but necessary in the circumstances, a long column of tanks was formed nearly two kilometres from the front in open terrain. This column proceeded to advance three kilometres, under a 'splendid sun' and in full view of two German observation balloons. For some reason, this did not bring down any artillery fire, section commander Lieutenant Aubert (AS304) noting that the approach march was 'very different' to those he had experienced in 1917, which had been made under an 'inferno' of shells. By 13.05, the companies had passed through the French lines and for the first time came under directed artillery fire, making any potential liaison with the infantry 'impossible to establish'.

This artillery fire was to prove a mixed blessing for AS305; such was its intensity that two German aircraft that had been attacking the tanks were forced to break off. Although the artillery fire was heavy, no tanks were hit and AS305 only lost one tank during the advance and this was an accident; it ran into a hidden bank and caught fire. The tank company advanced nearly 400 metres through wheat fields until they came to a clearing, where they encountered a large group of Germans in the process of preparing an assault. The Germans could only see the tank turrets and several of them waved at the tanks, presumably thinking they were German. A number of the Germans were wearing French trenchcoats, which confused some of the tank crews and made them hesitant to fire. It seems that both the Germans and the French realised they were in the presence of the enemy at about the same time; as the Germans went to man their machine guns, the AS crews gunned them down; the 37mm shells blowing men and material 'into the air'. The Germans retreated in disorder, initially to the nearby GMP trenches, a former French fortified position, and then to some wooded ravines that the tanks could not follow them into. It was now early afternoon and the tanks retired to find some infantry to occupy the GMP trenches, suffering from heavy artillery fire in the process. Eventually, some *chasseurs* from the adjoining division came up and occupied the trenches, allowing the tanks to retire, one tank ditching on the way back. The official reports state that AS305 was followed by the troops of *7 Tirailleurs* but AS officers reported later that they never saw more than three or four *tirailleurs* together during the entire engagement. Nonetheless, the *7 Tirailleurs* did eventually take their objectives in the Chazelle ravine and AS305 had cleared the immediate area of machine guns and a number of 37mm guns.

The attack of the composite company of AS304/306 was even less well supported by the French infantry. 35 DI's attack was supposed to jump off at 12.00 but this was postponed to 14.00 and 2 BCL's commander only found out at 13.05 that the attack was delayed, by which time AS304 was already in action. *4 Tirailleurs* had specific orders not go into action until 35 DI began its attack and thus AS304 went into combat with no infantry support at all.

The tanks of AS304 had set off for the departure position at 11.45 and advanced through wheat fields, with good going except for a number of steep banks that required careful crossing. We can look at the experience of Lieutenant Aubert's Renault section in detail as he wrote an article on the engagement for *La Revue d'infanterie*, in addition to his official after-action report.

Aubert's section got across no man's land without seeing much enemy activity, although the tanks fired several times 'without any precise targets'. This was contrary to the tank regulations but, if nothing else, it appears to have boosted the crews' confidence. The tanks moved into combat formation once they passed the French lines and then crossed several hundred metres of wheat-fields, before finding themselves on 'bare, uncultivated ground', where they were subjected to heavy fire from a German machine gun only fifty metres away. Aubert immediately fired on the machine gun, using five shells, and then he ran over the German position with his tank. It was now clear to him that the section was on the main German line but there was no sign whatsoever of the French infantry (*4 Tirailleurs*), who had not advanced further than the last wheat-field (in other words the last piece of cover). Aubert was forced to leave his section in order to find the infantry, whom he found but then encountered a new problem. Aubert discovered that, for the infantry, 'it was by no means easy to approach the tanks' as 'bullets ricocheting off the armour created a most unpleasant zone all around us'. This is a good example of how difficult in practice it was for the tanks to communicate with the infantry on the battlefield as the regulations dictated. Aubert had no success in persuading the infantry to advance and he returned to his section. In the interim, the section had been active; some tanks found cover and were firing, others moved in a figure-of-eight pattern to make themselves a difficult target. (I can find no reference to this latter tactic in any official documents and it appears to have been developed by the AS crews themselves.) The section then resumed its advance, the tanks firing at any position they thought fire had come from, the second time in the engagement that the tanks had fired at unseen targets, contrary to the regulations. This tactic appears to have been developed by the Renault crews themselves and would later became part of standard practice. This is a good example of tactical innovation that was developed from the bottom up, rather than from the top through the tank regulations. Problems with the infantry support continued; they 'merely watched us draw away from them', Aubert said.

As the advance continued, Aubert's tank was engaged by an anti-tank gun from 600 metres away, which the other tanks of his section had not seen, as it had not fired previously. Aubert fired at the anti-tank gun without stopping his tank, taking cover behind a bush and eliminating the German gun with numerous shells. Aubert believed his success against this gun was the result of his 'firing immediately through reflex'. When Aubert arrived at the section's final objective, just by a ravine, he could see the wrecked German gun, 'probably a 77mm', with its dead crew around it. As his section came over the ravine's crest, the tanks were able to fire on a group of retreating Germans, 'engulfing them'. The tanks held their position and had a long wait for the infantry to arrive, the latter only turning up after nightfall, at which point the tanks returned to their assembly position without incident.

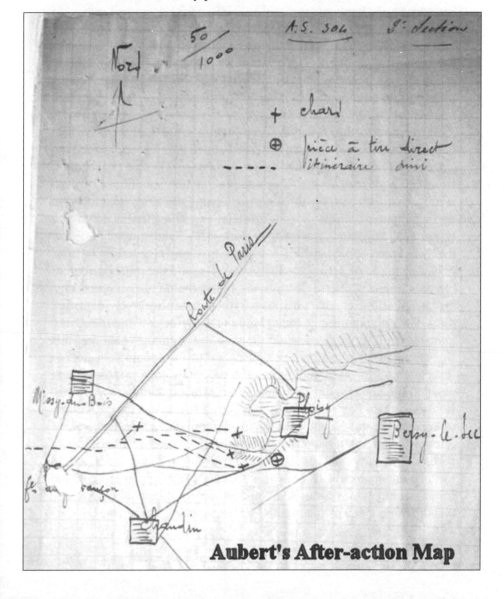

Aubert's After-action Map

Results of Chaudun

What became later known as the 'Charge at Chaudun' had been a mixed success for the French army but a great success for the Renault tank design. This was despite the fact that their first engagement had been in 'the most unfavourable conditions', particularly in relation to the poor state of their infantry support. The engagement was a considerable boost for morale in the AS; it had left the light tank crews 'full of confidence and joy' about their success. The tanks had been beaten off, eventually, by the Germans but the offensive capacity of two German divisions had been 'crippled' and it seems that the first appearance of the light tanks had caused real panic in their ranks. The Renault design had proved to be very effective; one report stated that 'the material worked well' and the tanks' speed on the battlefield impressed everybody. Only five tanks had been permanently lost out of the thirty-one that had gone into action and the Renaults' armour appeared capable of stopping all but direct hits from artillery, although a number of injuries were sustained through fragments penetrating the view ports.

In relation to the Renault's firepower, it is instructive to look at Aubert's experience. The two observed targets he engaged were at the extremes of range; one at fifty metres and one at 600 metres. The light tank regulations stated that 'in principle' the gun should not be used at more than 200 metres, although fire beyond this range was allowed against enemy machine guns or artillery, as well as troops deploying *en masse*. The gunner was only to fire 'wisely' and was reminded of the by now well-established tank mantra, that 'movement was the most powerful mode of action for the tanks'. Despite the prescriptions of the regulations, Aubert's section had fired on a number of occasions against possible enemy positions, rather than positively-identified ones. The regulations stated that both the machine gun and the 37mm gun were only to be fired while the tank was stationary and that this fire should usually be aimed fire, firing on the move being considered 'exceptional'. As discussed, Aubert did not halt to engage the anti-tank gun that fired on him but continued firing, while moving to seek cover. It is also notable that there is little reported fire by the entire section, rather than the individual tank; the regulations stated that it was 'in all circumstances' better to concentrate together the fire of the entire section. The regulations explained that concentrated tank fire was used to force enemy troops to ground, impeding their firepower while the French infantry moved up and attacked them. Of course, on 31 May this did not happen as the infantry failed to follow the tanks.

The emphasis on aimed fire was largely due to concerns about the limited amount of ammunition that could be carried in the light tanks, particularly for the 37mm gun; 'precision and economy are [thus] essential' said the regulations. In practice, the Renaults could carry more than enough ammunition for combat and I have found very few documented cases when tanks ran out of ammunition during a battle. For example, Aubert had fired twenty-six shells in total on 31 May; around five on the first machine gun, four or five on the second and third, with the remainder fired on the anti-tank gun. This is in sharp contrast to the other two gun tanks in his section, one of which only fired eight shells, with the other not firing at all during the entire engagement. The machine-gun tank in Aubert's section had fired thirteen belts (with ninety-six rounds in each belt, thus a total of 1,248 rounds). The other sections of his light tank battalion used more ammunition; on average fifty 37mm shells or fifteen machine-gun belts were used. The ammunition consumption for the battalion in this battle was actually comparatively high for this period, as the average consumption of ammunition by individual Renaults in combat between 31 May and 28 June was thirty-four shells or seven machine-gun belts, although it is worth noting that the Renaults throughout the war expended more ammunition in combat than did the medium tanks. Towards the end of the war, Estienne asked the commander of a machine-gun Renault, who had won the *Croix de guerre* for destroying a number of enemy machine guns on 26 September 1918, how much ammunition he had fired that day; the reply was no more than one belt.

Casualties in the light tank crews had been relatively light; the six tank sections lost only three killed, six seriously wounded and two missing. There was, however, an ominous portent of what was to come; the comparatively heavy losses in officers. Of the six section commanders, three were hit by enemy fire; one being killed, one wounded and the third only narrowly escaping injury as a shell went through the tail of his tank. In total, seven of the casualties had been tank commanders. The implications of this were not realised at the time, probably because the operation had been mounted so rapidly that high casualties were expected. However, the large-scale battles in July and September would confirm that the Renault tank units would suffer heavier personnel losses than material ones, the reverse being the case with the medium tank units. In particular, the tank commanders were considerably more exposed than their drivers, being higher up in the turret, and thus they took more casualties. This could have serious implications for command and control on the battlefield; towards the end of the 31 May action, the tank section on the left of AS304 had lost its commander and a *demi-section* commander, thereby leaving three tanks without leadership. It is notable that Aubert spent more time trying to find and then liaise with the infantry than he did actually directing his section in combat, although his *demi-section* commanders seem to have managed without him.

Under the tank regulations, the *demi-section* commanders had the theoretically simple task of following the section commander's tank and orders, as well as keeping their machine-gun tanks in line with the gun tanks. It was just as well that these tasks were so elementary, as battlefield control was rudimentary and relied entirely on simple flag signals, of which there were only three; 'Do as I do', 'Column formation' and 'Battle formation', each requiring the section commander to wave his flag in a different manner. The *demi-section* commander thus had to pay attention to his commander's tank was doing and be near enough to see a flag being waved, the regulation distance between tanks in combat being at most fifty metres. In relation to 31 May 1918, probably because the day was clear and there was comparatively light artillery fire, there is little mention in the first-hand accounts of flag use; for example, Aubert only mentions flags being used once as a company halt signal.

Two key areas required by the regulations for a successful tank operation were missing on 31 May; infantry support and an early morning start, to take advantage of low visibility. In relation to the latter, it is probably only that the advance was through dense wheat fields, their height compensating for the high daylight visibility, which prevented disaster. In relation to the infantry, the heavy casualties that the Moroccan *tirailleurs* had sustained in the previous days' fighting, particularly in officers, meant that liaison was always going to be difficult and shortage of time made it impossible. The tank regulations required that the AS command structure be integrated with that of the infantry during combat but on 31 May there was no such integration, again because of the constraints of time. Even at the lowest level, communication between the tanks and the infantry was non-existent; one section commander reported that he had 'no liaison' with the infantry before the battle and language difficulties with the Moroccan troops meant that communication was 'impossible' during it. At least in the case of AS305, the tanks were able to cover the infantry installation, as envisaged by the regulations, when the latter finally arrived.

Boudon's Fight

An even more startling illustration of the effectiveness of the Renaults occurred on 3 June 1918, again in the Chaudun area. It is particularly interesting as it was mounted in great haste and unfolded almost entirely in contradiction to the regulations but it demonstrates the power of the light tank.

On 30 May, AS Lieutenant Charles Boudon and his section from AS309 were moved from Champlieu to positions in the forest of Villers-Cotterets, part of the positioning of 2 and 3 BCLs in a defensive posture in the forest. During the course of 1 and 2 June, the two tank battalions were moved up to support the infantry defending the edges of the forest. Such was the concern about the state of the infantry that the tanks were deployed by section on the front line in order that they could immediately engage any German attacks, 3 BCL being divided between two infantry divisions. Dividing the tank battalion in this manner was contrary to the tank regulations and 3 BCL's commander, *Commandant* Péraldi, complained about the situation to his immediate superior, Lieutenant Colonel Maurice Velpry. Velpry, however, believed that the serious situation justified having the tanks more exposed and fragmented than was normally desirable.

On the early morning of 3 June, Boudon was woken up by a German artillery barrage, quickly followed by French counter-battery fire, which alerted him to the fact that the nearby French lines were under serious attack (his tank section being positioned on the Hautwison road, south of Fleury). The French positions were being assaulted by German 28 ID, with 111 Reserve Jäger Regiment on its right and 110 Reserve Jäger Regiment on the left flank. After alerting his tank officers, Boudon located an infantry officer and told him to regroup his men and follow Boudon's tanks, as they were going to counter-attack the Germans. Driving out of the forest onto the plateau, the tanks almost immediately ran into German infantry hiding in the rye just 50 metres away. The sight of the tanks appears to have unnerved the Germans, most of whom then fled, the remnants being rounded up by the French infantry. The tanks then advanced with the infantry behind them up to the Vouty-Corcy road and it was at this point that Boudon became separated from his section. He set off to attack the Saint-Paul farm but was followed by only one of his tanks; his *demi-section* commander, *Maréchal de Logis* Bellavoine, and the other two tanks of the section lost sight of Boudon's tank in the mist and smoke. Bellavoine continued his advance with the two remaining tanks of the section to the south of Saint-Paul farm. After fighting off three German battalions, the tanks began to receive artillery fire that was clearly aimed at them and they slowly retired out of the battle. Bellavoine reported that there were so many abandoned German machine guns on the battlefield that he thought it would be difficult for the French infantry to recover them all.

While Bellavoine was leading the section, Boudon had continued his advance, without apparently realising for some time that he only had one tank from his section with him. Despite this tank breaking down and being left for later recovery, Boudon continued to advance around the Saint-Paul farm area, where he was joined by a Renault that had been separated from another section. After fighting their way past the farm, Boudon received a serious eye injury when his tank was attacked by a German aircraft. His driver, *Maréchal de Logis* Célestin Belabre, had been forced to drive with his viewport closed due the weight of fire that had been directed at the tank, relying on Boudon for directions, and with Boudon's sight now impaired, it is perhaps not surprising that the tank soon became immobilised after driving into some tree roots. (After the war, Estienne told Boudon that it had taken two tractors to pull the tank free.) While Boudon was getting out of the tank to see if it could be freed, he was seized by German infantry and made a prisoner, along with his driver. Boudon was taken to a German first aid post where he estimated there were over 300 casualties, all the result of tank fire. Two of the German regiments had lost over 500 officers and men that day and 28 Division took two days to restore to combat readiness. Thus five light tanks had reduced a German division to complete disorder in less than three hours. The French losses were four missing (including Boudon and his driver), two killed and two wounded, with two tanks left in German-held territory. Of course, this was an unusual incident but we might wonder what impact there would have been if the ordered, but not delivered, 1,000 Renaults had been available at this date.

However, none of this was known to the French until after the war. As far as was known at 501 RAS HQ, there had been serious losses suffered with an uncertain impact on the Germans. In particular, there was considerable concern about the two missing light tanks; aerial searches failed to identify where they were, making them unrecoverable and very possibly in the hands of the Germans. Boudon, the internal AS report said, had charged ahead of his section 'like a cavalryman', disobeying his specific orders and the light tank regulations. It is worth remembering that Boudon's unit had only been formed on 29 May and thus all concerned were somewhat inexperienced, but Boudon was thirty-six years old in 1918 and thus certainly not a hot-headed youth.

These engagements illustrate how effective the light tanks could be in small operations. Although the Renault was designed as an offensive weapon, it had worked well in a series of mostly improvised counter-attacks. This is in sharp contrast to the fate of the medium tanks used in the counter-attack at Mery-Courcelles on 11 June as described in the previous chapter. However, the real test of the Renaults was to be their use *en masse*, as per the regulations, in a large-scale offensive. Pétain's methodology for such a large scale offensive was being devised during the initial fighting by the Renaults and its implementation is the subject of the following chapter.

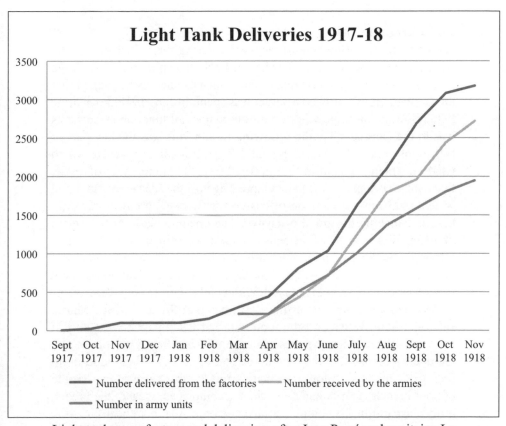

Light tank manufacture and deliveries, after Jean Perré and capitaine Le Gouest, 'Chars et statistique: Les constructions et les pertes', *La Revue d'infanterie*, July 1935, pp. 75–113.

Chapter 7

'The Greatest Day Since the Marne' – The Battle of Soissons, July 1918

The Marne Salient

As the German spring offensives were entering their final stages, the Allied commander-in-chief, Ferdinand Foch, began to plan for a large offensive against the Germans, to take place as soon as he judged that the German army's offensive power was spent. In June 1918, Foch drew Pétain's attention to how important the major rail junction at Soissons was to the Germans. By the following month, this was the key part of the supply chain for German 9 and 7 Armies all the way down to Chateau Thierry. Pétain in turn notified Fayolle, commander of GAR, that a major offensive was to be planned against the Marne salient. Foch waited until the last German offensive finally petered out in mid-July before launching his grand offensive. The opening battle of this series of offensives was to be at Soissons and we will now look at this important but largely unknown battle. As the majority of AS units were on X Armée's front, this will be considered in most detail, although there is a discussion of the parts played by the tanks with IX and VI Armée.

German attention was primarily directed at the east of the Marne salient, where Reims and the mountains of Champagne were still in French hands, leaving the western edge of the salient vulnerable. The Germans assumed that they would be alerted to any Allied build-up in plenty of time to shift forces to that part of the front as past experience of poor French security had given them a complacent view of the French army's capabilities, a complacency that would cost them dear.

Planning for the Battle of Soissons

The commander of X Armée, Charles Mangin, submitted his preliminary plans to Fayolle on 20 June, these being almost immediately approved and the long process of assembling X Armée in the Forêt de Retz began. Mangin's army was made up of specially-chosen French divisions, as well as two large US divisions. In the front line, the French had some of their best units; for example, 38 DI had in its ranks the most decorated regiment in the entire French army, the *Régiment Infanterie Coloniale du Maroc* (RICM). It is indicative of French manpower shortages by this stage in the war that in this regiment one entire battalion was made up of troops from Madagascar, while a third of the troops in the other two battalions were from Somalia. The Moroccan Division was another elite unit, including in its regiments the Foreign Legion *régiment de marche* (RMLE) and a battalion of Russians. The US divisions were fairly inexperienced but this was offset to some extent by their large size; each US division being nearly the size of a French corps with 28,000 men, which included over 12,000 men in the infantry companies.

Much effort went into creating an effective army reserve; the *2e Corps de cavalerie* (2 CC) was attached to X Armée for this purpose, along with two infantry *groupements*, transported on lorries, one a mix of French and US battalions, the other with two French battalions. Three 75mm *groupes* were attached from 20 CA and two *groupes* from 30 CA were also incorporated into the reserve, although they were to begin the battle firing in the opening barrage, then limbering-up and joining the reserve. 2 CC also received a dedicated fighter squadron.

The German positions

Facing X Armée was German 9 Army, consisting of ten infantry divisions, which were in varying states of combat readiness. Only three of these divisions were rated as first class by French intelligence, with only two of those in the front line. 9 Army had a further five divisions in reserve, of which 6 Division was rated by the French as 'one of the best German shock divisions'. The other available divisions were of variable quality; 28 and 3 Reserve Divisions were considered mediocre formations, while 34 Division was considered good but very under-strength. Some of the German units were divisions in name only; 47 Reserve Division had only forty to fifty men in each company. Adding to the German defenders' difficulties was the fact that their heavy artillery was being moved north for the planned Hagen Offensive and was thus in short supply when the Marne salient was attacked. The German troops on the Soissons front had not had enough time to fortify their positions in more than a rudimentary fashion and the trench lines werc very weak compared to the heavily-fortified positions on other parts of the Western Front. However, the Germans were amply provided with machine guns and were expert at positioning them in interlocking fields of fire.

The terrain that the Allies were advancing over was in most places good going for tanks, as it was not broken up by shell holes and had comparatively gentle slopes onto the numerous plateaux. However, there were a series of large ravines across the battlefield, with steep slopes that were heavily overgrown with vegetation. These were impassable to the tanks and, providing good covered positions for defenders, would prove difficult for the infantry to assault without support. Mangin ordered his troops to 'avoid the ravines' but this was simply not possible because the ravines covered a number of crucial areas on the battlefield. In addition, the small hamlets and villages in the area were all built of stone and thus easily turned into very strong defensive positions. The frontage for X Armée was approximately two kilometres per division, with the German divisions having to cover from four to five kilometres each.

Tank plans

As previously discussed, Estienne and GQG were now confident that a large-scale attack could be made without an artillery preparation, with the tanks used *en masse*. At Soissons, the tanks would go forward with the first wave of infantry, just as an intensive artillery barrage was unleashed. Estienne had a theoretical total of 540 Renaults and 240 medium tanks available on 17 July 1918, although inevitably breakdowns would prevent many of these participating on 18 July. As envisaged in the tank regulations, the original planning was for the light tanks to accompany each front-line infantry division but there were simply too few Renaults available and they became the army reserve, to come into action only when the medium tank units were exhausted or for the exploitation of success. As there would be no artillery preparation, the tanks were ordered to advance ahead of the infantry. As per the regulations, the tanks were tasked with neutralising enemy machine guns and any strongpoints not destroyed by artillery fire. The operation's jump-off time of 04.35 was chosen so that the tanks could get into action in semi-darkness, in line with the tank regulations. In addition to the normal counter-battery fire and efforts to blind the known German artillery observation posts, there were a large number of smoke shells added to the barrage. In each infantry division, a *groupe* of field guns was tasked with only undertaking counter-battery fire on anti-tank guns, which would be signalled by a dedicated reconnaissance plane.

Mangin was a general who was never happy with the resources given to him and he was not in agreement with the number of tanks X Armée had been allotted. He wrote to Fayolle on 12 July, complaining that a 'great number' of these were not ready for combat and he demanded another tank regiment for the coming offensive. Fayolle passed Mangin's request for more tanks to GAN, rather than argue with Mangin, but they were firmly told that there were no more available for X Armée, which had 'sufficient tanks' for its operation.

At midnight on 13 July, Lieutenant Colonel Chédeville (commander, 2 AS Brigade) received orders from Pétain to take command of and transport a number of *groupements* and battalions to X Armée's front. The majority of tank units were moved by rail, although some were transported by heavy artillery tractors and some had to travel under their own steam. Although this movement was done at great speed, it was for the most part successful, despite many tank units arriving at their destination nearly twelve hours late.

The following morning saw Chédeville's arrival and installation at X Armée HQ. That evening, he met his *groupement* and battalion commanders, allotting each AS officer a part of the army's front to study but without giving them any details of the offensive at all. The AS officers set off the next morning to make their preparations, which included a study of the routes into combat, the set-off positions for day or night, the first objectives where the tanks could be employed, the holding and fallback positions. They would meet again for orders from Chédeville at 16.00 on 15 July. While his officers were thus occupied, Chédeville was organising with his staff the necessary liaisons with the infantry and artillery, as well as sorting out supplies and replenishments.

X Armée's plans

The main thrust from X Armée was to be by two of its corps; 20 and 30 CA. General Berdoulat commanding 20 CA had 276 field guns, ninety-six howitzers, seventy-six heavy guns and fifty aircraft available. 20 CA was to have three divisions in the first line and two in the second line; 1 US Division, the DM, 2 US Division in first line, 58 and 87 DI in the second. 30 CA was commanded by General Penet and had 216 field-guns, seventy-two howitzers, forty heavy guns and fifty aircraft. 30 CA was to have two divisions in the first line and two divisions in the second; 48 and 38 DI in first line, 9 and 1 DI in the second. 11 CA was to have two divisions in the first line and one in the second; 128 and 41 DI in the first line, 5 DI in the second. 1 CA was to have three divisions in the first line, with one in the second; 72, 11, 153 DI in the first line, 69 DI in the second. After examining how the infantry formations had been organised, on the evening of 15 July Chédeville presented to Mangin his proposals for the use of the tanks in the offensive.

AS plans for the battle

As the main attack corps, 20 CA was given the most tanks, under the overall command of *Commandant* Velpry (commander, 501 RAS). There were four *groupements* in the corps; Groupement XII, under *Commandant* Azais, consisting of two *groupes*, each having nine tanks in three batteries, and one *groupe* of twelve tanks in three batteries, Groupement XI, under *Commandant* Herlaut, had five *groupes* of three batteries, each with three to four tanks. Both of these were to be attached to US 2 Division. Groupement IV, under *Commandant* Chanoine, had four *groupes* of twelve tanks each, in three batteries, and this was attached to the DM. Groupement I, under Captain de Blic, had four *groupes* of twelve tanks each, in three batteries, and was attached to 1 US Division.

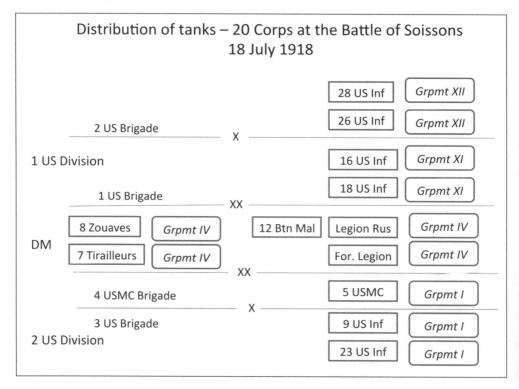

Distribution of tanks – 20 Corps at the Battle of Soissons
18 July 1918

The original plan had Groupement XI acting as the reserve for 2 US Division, with 1 and 3 BCL following the DM and US 1 Division respectively. However, this had to be changed when it became clear that Groupement XI would only be able to field three weak *groupes*, rather than five, and, in consequence, Groupements XI and XII were merged under the command of *Commandant* Herlaut and attached to US 1 Division, with Groupement I moved to US 2 Division. Mangin ordered the AS units in the army reserve to 'be pushed as far forward as the situation permits' but they were only to be deployed when the tanks on the front line were exhausted. Various concerns about the readiness of some tank units meant that another change was made; on 17 July, the reserve became 1 BCL, which would follow US 1 Division, 3 BCL, following 48 DI, with Herlaut's *groupement de marche* following the DM.

The corps on the flanks of 20 CA were also allotted tanks; 1 CA received Groupement III, which it was specified had to be used with the division adjacent to 20 CA, 153 DI. The significant losses that Groupement III had suffered at Méry-Courcelles in June had not been made up and it could only field three *groupes* of nine tanks each, organised in three batteries. *Chef d'escadron* Lefebvre, commander of Groupement III, arrived to start planning at 1 CA HQ on 15 July.

30 CA received Groupement X, under *Commandant* de Violet, which was intended to be attached to the division flanking 20 CA. It consisted of one *groupe* of twelve tanks, in three batteries, and two *groupes* of nine tanks each, in three batteries. Although the *groupement* was originally attached in its entirety to 38 DI, adjacent to the right flank of 20 CA, it was decided after examining the ground that the majority of tanks would go with 48 DI. 38 DI's zone had particularly bad terrain for the tanks, the ground being badly broken up with a railway crossing the zone diagonally. The corps front was very compressed (roughly 2.5 kilometres) and it was decided that 20 CA's flank would be sufficiently protected if 48 DI made a successful attack. Therefore, one *groupe* of twelve St Chamonds went to 48 DI (on the right) and another *groupe* with nine St Chamonds was put behind it. The last *groupe* went to 38 DI on the left, its mission was to clear the successive small ravines that went north to south in Savière. This is a good example of the fact that when the provisions of the tank regulations were not appropriate, the AS commanders were flexible enough to vary them to suit the situation.

For all tactical matters, as per the regulations, the AS units were to take orders from the infantry commanders of the units they were attached to. For general supply, the AS units would be included in the infantry supply chain but in relation to the special tank supply requirements, petrol, oil and special ammunition, these were to be supplied from within the AS, under the control of Chédeville.

The AS Tactical Deployments

On 1 CA's front, the tanks were attached to 153 DI; AS15 went to the regiment on the right, 1 TM (Moroccan infantry), which was the closest to the principal attack; AS1 was split between the other two regiments (two batteries to the one in the centre and one to the regiment on the left). The third *groupe* was in reserve; two batteries from AS6 acted as the ID commander's reserve, with the third battery serving as the divisional reserve. The tanks attached to the infantry were to advance with the leading wave of infantry.

On 20 CA's front, Groupement XII was attached to the left brigade of US 1 Division, with Groupement XI going to the right US brigade. From each *groupement*, a *groupe* was given to the infantry regiments to support their battalions in the first line, the third *groupes* being held in reserve.

Groupement IV gave a *groupe* to each regiment in the DM, except for the RMLE because the legionnaires were advancing into a wood and they were given only two tank batteries, the third being attached to the brigade in the second infantry wave.

Groupement I had two *groupes* with each brigade of US 2 Division, one in the first wave, one in reserve. Thus each US regiment had half a tank *groupe* attached, configured as two forward batteries and one in reserve. It was quite contrary to the regulations to split a *groupe* between two infantry regiments like this but it was felt that it was of paramount importance to keep a reserve *groupe* in each brigade, thus supplying a potential exploitation force but also covering the division's flanks.

Thus each of 20 CA's infantry battalions in the first wave had a *groupe* of tanks attached to it, with the exception of US 2 Division. Each tank battery contributed two or three tanks to advance in front of the infantry, with one tank per battery held in reserve with the infantry's reserve company. The infantry battalions of the second wave had one *groupe* each, thus giving theoretically every division in 20 CA three lines of tanks. Of course, it did not work quite so smoothly in practice, largely due to delays in the tanks arriving at the departure position and the confusion of the battlefield, as is discussed below. On 30 CA's front, the larger of the St Chamond *groupes* was to advance over the bridge at Longpont, after the *1 Zouaves* had reached the Violaine crest, with the other *groupe* one kilometre behind in support.

In keeping with Pétain's *Directive No 5*, security measures for the Soissons operation were maintained at the highest level. However, such tight security was a double-edged sword, as it meant that commanders at all levels only received their orders at the very last minute. Although Allied security was a complete success in the sense that the Germans were completely surprised by the attack, the measures taken to keep it a secret had serious effects on the organisation of the offensive. Most infantry division commanders received their final orders to move into line less than ten hours before the attack, which forced units to travel at night with all the subsequent disorder that entailed. US 1 Division arrived in 20 CA's zone on 17 July, only to be immediately told that they would be attacking at 04.35 the next morning. The entire 2 CC, in another example, was moved three times between 8 and 15 July, starting its journey north-west of Beauvais without any idea of where it was going to end up. After a two-day march around VI Armée's zone, its commander General Robillot was ordered to report to Mangin on 14 July. Most of the tank units did not arrive in their assembly positions until the afternoon of 17 July, at which stage only the AS battalion and *groupement* commanders knew where and when they would be fighting.

Among the AS crews and junior officers, nothing was at all known about what was being planned. It was clear that an offensive would take place imminently but 'of the intentions of the command, we knew nothing', said tank commander Lieutenant Chenu. On the afternoon of 17 July, Chenu and the other officers of his battery (AS5) were told by their captain that they would be taking part in an 'immense battle' to take the Soissons to Paris road. The captain would not give them a definite answer as to whether the attack would be the next day. In fact, Chenu and the other tank commanders were only told that the attack was starting five minutes before it commenced. He queried the order with his captain and asked why their artillery had not started a preparation. To his considerable surprise, he was told that 'the method has changed' and that there would be no preparation. Chenu was only reassured when the enormous barrage began; 'Suddenly the forest entirely exploded. We were stupefied.'

The Battle of Soissons
18 July 1918
Unknown to Chenu, the offensive had actually started forty-five minutes earlier when an artillery barrage opened on VI Armée's front at 04.00, followed by one in IX Armée's zone at 05.00. These opening barrages

made it difficult for the Germans to ascertain where the main French effort would be taking place.

When the attack began on X Armée's front, visibility was limited to 'a few yards', due to the morning mist and the heavy smoke barrage. Visibility was so limited that, for example, the soldiers of 1 RI were forced to march to their jump-off positions holding the jacket of the man in front. However, for the most part the mist and smoke helped the infantry overwhelm the initial German positions and it may well have been a major factor in the weakness and, more importantly, the slow response of the German artillery to the Allied attack. The initial German defensive barrage largely missed the forward French and US battalions, although it did hit the rear battalions in the forward divisions, in some cases causing significant casualties.

On 1 CA's front, the infantry advance was initially very easy, despite a German artillery barrage that fell on the French front line just prior to the jump off. The infantry of 153 and 72 DI advanced nearly six kilometres in the first few hours of the attack but this rate of advance quickly slowed down and by 11.00 the infantry attack was stopped on the plateau west of the Saconin ravine. Groupement III helped the infantry move forward several hundred metres but with heavy losses; fourteen tanks out of twenty-six were out of action by the end of the day and personnel losses were seven killed and thirty-seven wounded. However, forty-two officers and 2,074 men were captured from German 241 Division, which was forced to withdraw in disorder through the Aisne valley back towards Soissons. 11 Bavarian Division was 'wrecked' by the attack but was able to hold onto the ridge west of Vauxbuin, as it was reinforced in the afternoon and then not attacked until the next morning. Even the units without tank support in 1 CA did well; for example, 418 RI took 905 prisoners and captured sixteen field guns, advancing just over seven kilometers in a couple of hours. The attack was not entirely successful. 153 DI was not able to eliminate a series of machine-gun nests on its right, which were able to lay down heavy enfilading fire on US 2 Brigade/1 Division as it advanced, on the left of 20 CA's zone.

On 20 CA's front, US 1 Division made good progress from the start. The defenders were taken completely by surprise and a number of German officers were captured only partially clothed. The first objective was taken easily and it was not until the Missy ravine was reached (just after 07.00) that the US infantry encountered their first serious resistance, the fighting then becoming heavy. On US 2 Brigade's front,

Groupement XII only got twenty-three tanks to the departure point where the St Chamonds of AS38 and AS39 joined the American infantry in front of Missy-aux-Bois and together they took the village. The tanks subsequently broke up a counter-attack coming from the farm at Cravançon. US 2 Brigade was unable to continue forward after this, due to the enfilading machine-gun fire from 153 DI's zone to the north. Only four medium tanks got back to the re-supply position, eleven tanks being destroyed by artillery fire.

Groupement XI (with US 1 Brigade) only got eight tanks from AS35 into position on time to advance with the US infantry, after a difficult seven-kilometre drive from its waiting position. It had lost one tank to a breakdown by the time it passed the US infantry's jump-off point. AS32, with nine tanks, did not arrive at the front line until 05.30, as did AS34, with twelve tanks. Despite their late arrival, the tanks helped the infantry take all their objectives before midday, although of the twenty-seven tanks engaged, seven were destroyed by enemy artillery. US 1 Division captured approximately 2,000 prisoners and thirty field guns during the day.

On the DM's front, Groupement IV's tanks had good departure positions and those with the first French brigade moved out of their final cover only 800 metres from the front line, escorting their infantry a short distance to the intermediate objective. The tanks helped take Dommiers and Glaux Farm, although three tanks were put out of action 'in several minutes' by a 77mm field-gun battery. This German battery had the misfortune to be facing the *Légion* infantry, who stormed the position, bayoneting the crews and capturing the guns. The second French brigade and its tanks passed through the first brigade to the intermediate objective as envisaged and reached the edges of Chazelles and l'Echelle without difficulty, although neither village was taken until the evening. By the end of the day, German 42 Division had lost 1,400 prisoners, most of whom were taken by the DM. Groupement IV had significant losses; of forty-nine Schneiders engaged, seventeen were destroyed and fifteen damaged, with twenty-nine officers and men killed and fifty wounded.

On the front of US 2 Division, the infantry advanced so quickly that AS9 took over five hours to catch up with them, arriving with nine tanks, three having broken down. In fact, the US infantry had moved so fast that it had overrun all of German 42 Division's artillery by 08.30. Because of the speed of the advance, some of the US troops had no contact with the tanks at all during this period of the battle; for example, Captain Speer, commanding US 1 Battalion/9 US Infantry, did not see any tanks in action during the entire morning. Forty-five tanks from Groupement I had left their departure positions and only one was destroyed by enemy artillery, although eleven Schneiders had various mechanical problems that prevented them from coming into action. The *groupement* had fired nearly 500 shells during the day, although AS9 and 2 had expended no ammunition whatsoever.

On 30 CA's front, the tanks of Groupement X had to cross the bridge at Longpont in single file and then advance over the steep slopes of the ravine, before crossing the railway. AS31 and AS33 assisted the infantry of 48 DI and 38 DI to achieve their objectives; the village of Villers-Hélon and a series of small ravines respectively, after which the *groupes* retired. The reserve *groupe* (AS36) went into action at 16.30 in support of two infantry regiments from 48 DI that were advancing on Mauloy woods; the woods were taken but the French infantry were too exhausted to advance any further due to heavy German artillery and machine-gun fire. Thirty-four tanks from Groupement X had gone into action, of which eight were *hors de combat* by the evening of 18 July.

The army reserve that had been so carefully assembled barely got into action. At 07.15, Mangin had ordered 2 CC to advance and prepare to move through the Allied infantry, to attack the rear of the enemy. The cavalry corps took two hours to get moving and, after some confusion amongst the divisional columns in the forest, 4 DC arrived at Saint-Pierre-Aigle at 10.50, with 2 and 6 DCs arriving in position shortly after. Around 11.00, Mangin personally ordered Robillot (commander, 2 CC), who was at his forward HQ, to advance the cavalry to support the infantry. Robillot only had two telephones available to send orders to his widely-dispersed corps and it took until 13.00 for his orders to reach one of his divisions, although Robillot himself had delayed matters by initially objecting to Mangin's orders. Despite this activity, by 14.00, the cavalry reserve was still nowhere near the front line; 4 DC had only just arrived at Dommiers, 6 DC was west of Vertefeuille and 2 DC was at Coeuvres. However, as the cavalry was inching forward, it became clear that the front line was not as far forward as had been thought.

The motorised infantry battalions of the army reserve left Mortefontaine and Vivières, around 13.00, and headed towards Chaudun and Vierzy, while the attached artillery *groupes* were ordered to limber up and join the cavalry. However, by 17.00 the motorised infantry had only got as far as Montgobert, because of the heavy congestion on the roads. It was now clear to Mangin that most of the army reserve would not get into action before nightfall and he stood down its infantry and artillery components, returning them to their parent formations. The dismounted cavalry finally got into action an hour later, along with the divisional armoured cars, in an attack between Vierzy and Tigny.

At 07.25, the three light tank battalions were released by Mangin to 20 and 30 CA but the corps commanders had the same instructions as previously; the light tanks were not to be used until the medium ones were spent. Both 1 and 2 BCL were south of Vivières and were thus attached to 20 CA, with 3 BCL attached to 30 CA. At 18.00, 1 BCL, which had been waiting in reserve at Vertefeuille farm during the day, was ordered forward. However, both the AS and the officers decided they needed more time to prepare and a delay ensued. Just over an hour later, when the Renault tanks advanced, they were subject to so much German fire that the accompanying American infantry were obliged to run across the battlefield to keep in front of the tanks. However, the tanks were reported to have been 'a great deal of assistance' to the US infantry by eliminating machine-gun nests that impeded the latter. 1 BCL lost no tanks during the attack and only six officers and men were wounded. In all, the advance had moved another three kilometres, stopping just before Villemontoire and Tigny. 3 BCL had considerable difficulty moving forward through the heavy traffic jams in the roads through the forest and it then had to compete for space with the rear elements of 30 CA, moving out of Longpont. It was not until the early evening that AS309 from 3 BCL arrived to support 38 DI, although it did not get into action, the other companies being held in reserve. 2 BCL only got one section into action at 20.00, losing three of the fifteen tanks engaged. Thus the light tank battalions, through no fault of their own, contributed little to that day's fighting.

As the day wore on, both infantry and tank units were detached from each other and the fighting increasingly took place on a smaller and smaller scale. For example, shortly after leaving their front line, a company from US 16 Infantry got separated from the rest of its battalion due to the smoke and mist. As the mist lifted, the company was pinned down by heavy German machine-gun fire, coming from a small hill on the western edge of the Missy-aux-Bois Ravine. Four French tanks appeared and they were able to make contact with the US infantry commander. After he had identified the machine-gun positions for the tanks, they moved into the ravine and cleared out the German troops, allowing the US infantry to continue their advance.

The small-scale and improvised attacks that characterised the fighting of the afternoon and evening of 18 July were costly for the tanks, particularly when compared to the morning attacks. For example, on the Moroccan Division's front, a series of attacks were made on the l'Echelle ravine by small units of tanks, supporting the *8 Zouaves*. The first attack by a battery of four tanks was repulsed, for the loss of two tanks by artillery fire. Four hours later, nine tanks were brought up and another attack took place but this was equally unsuccessful, four tanks being lost to artillery fire. AS306 made a final attack with the infantry at 20.00, once again to no avail, although fortunately casualties were light, only one tank being lost and its crew wounded. In all of these cases, the attack failed because the infantry was unable to maintain its forward momentum, which was the result of there being too few tanks now available to replace the weight of artillery support that had been available for the morning attack. Indeed, seven tanks were lost in the afternoon for no discernible advantage, in stark contrast to the success of the morning's fighting. Contrary to the requirements of the tank regulations, in each of the attacks on the l'Echelle Ravine, the tanks were required to make a long approach march in the open that alerted the Germans. By attacking piecemeal with the tanks, rather than the regulation *en masse*, the French had allowed the German artillery to concentrate its fire on each successive attack, causing heavy losses to both the tanks and infantry.

It can thus be seen that the initial tank attack on 18 July had been very successful but this success had waned as the day progressed. On 18 July, out of the 226 tanks engaged, sixty-one were destroyed by artillery, with 290 personnel being put out of action, representing nearly 25 per cent of the AS troops in combat. There had been considerable delays in getting into action those tanks that were not in the first infantry wave. For example, with 1 US Division, fifty-three tanks got to their departure positions but only twenty went into action with the first wave of infantry, despite a surprisingly low number of breakdowns (most of the tanks had run into shell holes and became immobilised). The initial wave of the attack needed to be as strong as possible to gain the tactical surprise (more properly 'shock') required by *Directive No. 5* and the French army arguably failed here to get the maximum effect from its armour. Much of the support received by the AS had been weak; De Blic, Groupement I commander, complained that the artillery of US 2 Division had failed to use any smoke shells in either its barrages or the counter-battery fire made on both 18 and 19 July. However, most of the infantry attacks had been very successful; the *Légion* had overrun the German positions in front of it and taken large numbers of prisoners in under two hours, even though the legionnaires were left behind by the creeping barrage when they stopped to eliminate machine-gun positions. This was at some cost to the *Légion*, it losing 420 casualties, including fourteen officers.

During the night of 18 July, the tanks regrouped. The tank crews were fully employed making repairs and conducting routine maintenance, as well as recovering immobilised tanks, where possible. Such had been the tank losses on the first day, Chenu wrote; 'a *groupement* becomes a *groupe*, a *groupe* a battery. After tomorrow, if any remain, a tank will call itself a *groupe*.' These losses, however, have to be balanced against the overall success of the operation; the Allied armies' 'tactical surprise was complete' on 18 July, according to one German army group war-diary. This success, said the German diary, was primarily due to the French tanks as they were employed 'in numbers never known before and much better developed technically' than previously. The diary admitted that the defence was 'effective only in spots' against the tanks, which often meant that the German infantry rather unsurprisingly 'lost their nerve'.

19 July

Pétain and Fayolle arrived to see Mangin at X Armée HQ around 18.00 on the 18th, with the former declaring that the operation had been a 'great success'. Mangin did not hesitate to ask for more troops to continue the offensive but Pétain told him that there none available. Mangin pressed Pétain hard, arguing that they were all on the verge of 'decisive results', which would be jeopardised if the attack did not continue at the same pace. However, Pétain was not to be moved and he left Mangin without promising any reinforcements. After sending a message to Foch complaining about Pétain, Mangin ordered a new attack to start at 04.00 on 19 July, with the objectives remaining those set for the previous day. Mangin was well aware that this was a major error, as there were now fewer tanks and less infantry to attack positions that had not been taken with more of both the previous day. Pétain clearly should have moved troops to Mangin from other armies' fronts but this was not in keeping with his conservative approach and Mangin was left to slog it out without significant reinforcements. From the point of view of the AS, 19 July was to mainly follow the pattern of the afternoon of 18 July; that is disorganised and un-coordinated attacks with diminishing results.

For example, 20 CA resumed its attack with US 1 Division and a small *groupement de marche* of six tanks from RAS 501. The tanks took heavy losses; five tanks were knocked-out and the US infantry only managed to advance 400 metres. An attack by Groupement I in conjunction with US 2 Division ran into even worse problems. The *groupement*'s commander, de Blic, insisted the attack commence at 04.00, in order to keep the tanks in semi-darkness for as long as possible, in accordance with the tank regulations. The decision was taken to cancel the attack just after the tanks assembled at the jump-off position and the tanks began to disperse from their departure positions. However, when de Blic arrived at the divisional headquarters, he was astonished to discover that the attack had been rescheduled for 07.00. At the last moment, the time of the attack was changed again (to 08.30) but this was not communicated to all the tank *groupes*. Two of AS9's tanks set off at 07.00, not having been informed of the change of plan and they had to be hurriedly returned to their departure position when news came through of their new orders. None of the *groupes* was able to get back into position on time and the Germans were now alerted by the noise of the tanks to an imminent attack. Unsurprisingly, the French tanks and US infantry met with heavy artillery fire as soon as they began their attack, made worse by the lack of a smoke screen due to the US artillery running out of smoke shells. It was contrary to the tank regulations to make such attack in daylight and without smoke cover and many of the tanks were put out of action quickly. For example, AS2 lost only one tank prior to reaching its departure position and then five tanks were lost in forty-five minutes to artillery fire. This left the *groupe* with only two tanks, which duly advanced on Tigny and took German positions there under fire. The results were unclear and the tanks returned to their supply positions at 13.00, taking no further part in the fighting that day. AS9 was forced to make a precipitous advance because the US troops set off too early and the *groupe* came under direct fire after advancing 1,800 metres, losing seven of its eight tanks in just thirty minutes. These tank losses were fruitless as, by the end of the day, most of the Allied infantry had been pushed back to their original front line. There were some minor successes; eight tanks from Groupement IV supported a successful attack on Charentigny, losing two tanks but clearing the village.

In 30 CA's zone, a similarly disorganised tank attack took place. AS309 was ordered to support the right brigade of 38 DI but it was then switched to support 4 Moroccan Brigade on the left, causing considerable confusion. The Renault crews of AS309 had the unnerving experience of seeing the leading companies of 4 RMZT, having become lost exiting a ravine, line up in an attack formation facing the tanks.

A Renault gun-armed light tank in US Army service, demonstrating its manoeuvrability.

Schneiders detraining. Note the cross-hatch camouflage, used to disguise the tank's viewports.

A late-model Schneider, with appliqué armour, on manoeuvres with French infantry.

An early-model St Chamond with the flat roof and 75mm Rimailho gun.

A St Chamond moving through a destroyed French village.

A late-model St Chamond, without the driver's cupola but with the sloped roof, being used to raise war bonds in the interior of France.

A machine-gun Renault undertaking testing, probably at Champlieu.

Interior of a
Schneider tank.

Interior of a St
Chamond.

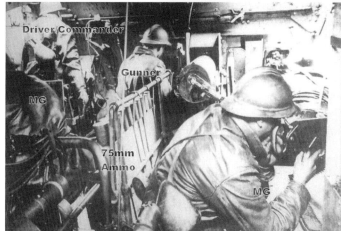

Two US tank crewmen
in their Renault tank.
Note the thickness of
the Renault's armour
and also how cramped
it was for the crew.

Renaults moving to the front line, being filmed by the French Army photographic service.

A group of post-war Renault gun tanks.

Renault tanks in US Army service.

A Renault Company moving to the front in Northern France – note the TSF (Wireless Telegraphy) Tank and the AS motorcycle.

A good picture of a machine-gun Renault in Spanish service during the Rif War in the 1920s.

One of the many remaining Great War Renault gun tanks still in existence, this one being at Les Invalides in Paris.

Assuming that they were about to be attacked by a considerable number of German infantry, the tanks opened fire, killing a number of their compatriots before the situation was clarified.

At 08.00, 48 DI mounted a two-regiment attack, with a tank section from AS307 supporting each regiment. One tank section arrived so late that it missed the infantry attack altogether but the other section gave some effective support, although the infantry took 'severe losses', which prevented the ground taken by the tanks from being held. Two attempts were made to take the village of Blanzy, which was only taken on the second attempt thanks to the help of eleven St Chamonds from AS31, although the majority of the tanks were rendered *hors de combat* during the engagement.

1 CA remained in a defensive posture during 19 July, as it had pushed far enough forward the previous day to bring Soissons under French artillery fire, and it only made some minor attacks with Groupement III, the *groupement* nonetheless losing six tanks.

The tank attacks on 19 July had been mounted so hastily that numerous mistakes had been made, particularly in relation to co-ordination with the infantry, but this for the most part appears largely inevitable by virtue of the nature of the operations that day. Matters were no better for the infantry; on the night of 18 July, 365 RI had marched eight kilometres to get to its jump-off position, for an attack at 04.45. The battalions only reached their jump-off positions at 04.00 and did not have time to establish any kind of liaison with their adjoining units. This resulted in the leading battalions advancing across each other and only a prompt change of plan by one of the battalion commanders restored some semblance of order to the regimental attack.

July 19th was a costly day for the AS; of the 105 tanks that went into combat, fifty were destroyed by enemy artillery, with 129 men out of action, a casualty rate of nearly 22 per cent. It was now clear that the battle had turned into one of attrition and 2 CC, except for 6 DC (dismounted), was moved out of X Armée that night.

20 July

The next day saw a further series of small-scale attacks, the tanks remaining attached to the higher formations as before. For example, Groupement III, on 1 CA's front, managed to get only one battery of three Schneiders into action in the afternoon. At the jump-off position, the tanks came under intense fire from German machine guns; there were so many of these that the tanks could not suppress them all. This resulted in two tank commanders being wounded along with their crews; another tank was hit by a shell as it tried to move forward, this being the only tank of the three that was put out of action. The infantry took heavy losses and were forced to retreat back to their departure position. The tanks with 20 CA were largely inactive; only one small action with ten Renaults from AS305 took place and was not successful; six of the tanks were left on the battlefield, three of which were destroyed. It was a similar story on 30 CA's front, where several small-scale tank attacks were made over the course of the day but with never more than a section of light tanks or three batteries of medium tanks at one time. None was successful; although the tanks inflicted losses on the Germans and pushed them back, the French infantry were unable to exploit this.

These examples all demonstrate why the tank regulations advised against such small-scale attacks; there were simply not enough tanks available in these operations to overcome the opposition, which only resulted in heavy losses for few or no gains. This was another costly day for the AS; out of thirty-two tanks engaged (twenty Renaults, three Schneiders and nine St Chamonds), seventeen were destroyed by enemy artillery, although only one man was killed and eight wounded.

21 July

On the 21st, the recipe continued of asking the AS to try and take objectives it had failed to take previously, now with even less equipment and exhausted crews. For example, Groupement III could only field two batteries of three Schneiders each but was given the same objective as the previous day. Unsurprisingly, this attack was no more successful than the previous one had been and 50 per cent of the tanks were lost, along with twenty-five officers and men who were killed or wounded. At least 1 and 2 BCLs were able to go into action as entire battalions, which enabled them to make good progress in an attack that was rendered irrelevant by the inability of the French infantry to follow them. It should be noted that the operations of 20 and 30 CA were not co-ordinated at all on 21 July, resulting in small-scale infantry and tank attacks being made across the front at various times during the day, to little or no effect.

German large-calibre anti-tank rifles (firing 13mm armour-piercing rounds), with a crew of two, appeared in the front line, although they were no more than a nuisance at this time. A total of 110 tanks had gone into combat on 21 July (eighty-eight Renaults, twenty-two Schneiders), of which twenty-six were destroyed, with fifty-eight casualties.

22–23 July

On 22 July, it became evident that the enemy had been substantially reinforced and that the battle had changed in character. The tank units were all placed in the army reserve to regroup for a large-scale action on 23 July, except for three St Chamonds from Groupement X which participated in a successful infantry attack on Plessier-Huleu. That evening, it was clear to Mangin's staff that the tank units had been seriously eroded by the small-scale attacks of the previous days, with little to show for it. The next attack on 23 July would at least have better protection for the tanks; X Armée's orders for 23 July reminded commanders to use 'a great number of smoke shells' in conjunction with the tanks. The main role was for 30 CA, with support on its flanks from 20 and 11 CA. By this stage of the battle, nearly all the French infantry had been involved in intensive fighting for several days and they were disorganised and depleted; for example, the third battalion of 418 RI had lost all its officers, except the adjutant, and was reduced to just forty-five men. Although more tanks would be in action on 23 July than on the previous two days, there was no question of it being an attack *en masse* as there were simply not enough tanks left.

Such had been the attrition of the medium tank units, 20 CA was forced to use a *groupement de marche* of medium tanks, formed from what remained of Groupements I, IV, XI and XII (a mixture of St Chamonds and Schneiders), thirty-four tanks in all. The French infantry had considerable difficulty advancing due to the weight of enemy machine-gun fire and they were unable to take or even significantly weaken the German resistance around Tigny. This was the main objective so the operation cannot be considered a success, wasting both men and tanks. There was even less success on 30 CA's front, where neither the Renaults nor the St Chamonds made any progress against the German positions.

The lack of success at this stage persuaded Mangin not to engage the reserve tanks. Of the eighty-five tanks engaged on 23 July, thirty-nine were destroyed; twenty Renaults, two Schneiders and seventeen St Chamonds, with 128 men wounded. Although the attack had been well planned, its failure was in stark contrast to the success of 18 July. The Franco-Americans were now up against a German defence that was well prepared and equipped, both in terms of the defensive positions themselves and available artillery.

After six days of combat, the tank units of X Armée were exhausted and they were all moved into the army reserve on the evening of 23 July.

As a post-war AS examination of the battle says; 'X Armée's tanks had been given the order to fight to the last tank and man; they had completed this mission.' On 25 July, all the AS units in GAR and GAC were placed under the direct command of GQG and ordered to move as quickly as possible by rail to new positions, in order to regroup.

Results of the Battle
Although the Battle of Soissons was a great tactical and strategic success for the Allies, striking a blow to the German army that it never recovered from, it illustrates a number of inherent problems with Great War offensive operations. A key problem at Soissons for the Allies was that the German defence, already skilfully handled, got easier as the Germans retreated towards their rear positions. In relation to the AS, the German anti-tank defences had rapidly responded to the success of the tanks; within days, additional batteries were dedicated to anti-tank work, as were extra aircraft. German gunner Herbert Sulzbach wrote on 23 July; 'Our batteries now have to specialise in close-quarters work, including anti-tank shooting and defence against infantry assaults.' The constant danger to the tanks from hidden German field guns that the battle had revealed would be a feature of all further French tank actions in the war. The Renaults were found to be particularly useful for attacking machine-gun positions in woods, something that had always been difficult for infantry and largely impossible for the medium tanks.

Another factor was that the German reserves could be moved to the front much faster than those of the Allies. Although the thunderstorm on 17/18 July had helped mask preparations for the offensive, it subsequently wrecked the roads, causing chaos behind the French lines. One French participant in the battle described the roads as 'veritable rivers'. By comparison, German reserves could be rushed to the front faster. 51 Reserve ID moved eleven kilometres in under four hours, for example, which is a sharp contrast to the time it took the Renault battalions to get into action on 18 July; for example, 2 BCL received orders to move at 8.00 but it did not get into action for twelve hours having moved less than fourteen kilometres.

As anticipated in the tank regulations, tank units became weaker every day due to sheer mechanical wastage. A key question about the battle after the war was whether there should have been a bigger tank reserve with X Armée. Guderian argues that the distribution of tanks within the Soissons offensive should have been better, his criticism being twofold; he maintains that all of the French tanks should have been concentrated in X Armée and that too many tanks were placed in the rear and reserve positions of X Armée. In relation to the first point, there were a considerable number of tanks attached to IX, V and VI Armées, so it is worth considering their employment during the battle.

502 RAS was split between V Armée and IX Armée on 19 July in the expectation of a general German retreat from the Marne salient. V Armée received 4 and 6 BCLs, with IX Armée receiving 5 BCL and four Schneider batteries from Groupement II. It was almost immediately decided to return the tanks to the army reserve but this order failed to get through to the AS units on IX Armée's front. The tanks launched an attack against German positions that, unknown to the French, had been evacuated the previous night. There were no casualties, except for an unfortunate NCO whose arm was driven over by a tank. Other smaller tank engagements took place after this on both armies' fronts, which resulted in few gains and significant losses. The three light tank battalions had twenty-five Renaults destroyed by artillery, with another eleven badly damaged but repairable. The operations that the tanks undertook for V and IX Armées were not essential and therefore these tanks could probably have been used more effectively with either X Armée.

The situation regarding the tanks with VI Armée was similar. *Chef de battalion* Michel, commander of 503 RAS, took overall command of VI Armée's tank force. By 16 July, Groupement XIII only had one of three *groupes* ready for combat which Michel thought sufficient 'from a tactical point of view,' due to the 'density of light tanks'. There was only one company from 9 BCL could be disembarked on the army's front in time to join in operations on 18 July and thus VI Armée had at its disposal two battalions and a company of light tanks and one St Chamond *groupe*. For the duration of the Battle of Soissons, 503 RAS never had fewer than 125 Renaults in a combat-ready state and yet these were only used in small-scale engagements. Only around a quarter of the Renaults available to 503 RAS were used from 18 to 27 July. For example, AS319 was only engaged on two days during this period, the rest of the time being in reserve and AS322 had a similar experience. Personnel casualties were accordingly light; of approximately fifty officers and 1,000 men engaged, eleven officers and men were killed, with sixty-one seriously wounded. However, material losses were far from negligible; twelve tanks were 'definitely out of service,' of which ten were hit by direct fire from 77mm guns or minenwerfers, with forty-six seriously damaged, seven of which had been hit by direct artillery fire. As with IX Armée's tanks, with the benefit of hindsight it is appears that these tanks could have been better used with X Armée. However, although the main thrust of the offensive was on X Armée's front, maintaining pressure on the Germans on the other parts of the front was thought necessary for the success of X Armée. Therefore it is not surprising that GQG thought it prudent to give a tank element to all the armies on the Marne front. It is also necessary to understand that the tanks were seen by Pétain and GQG as a key element in keeping infantry losses to acceptable levels. It thus made sense to have tanks in with all the attacking infantry divisions, even those where the fighting was not as intense.

In relation to the positioning of the tanks within the attack formations, Guderian's criticism is better founded, although he is exaggerating when he says that the tanks in the rear lines were 'completely ineffective'. As discussed, in the initial attack, both the tanks in the rear infantry waves and the tanks in the reserve had difficulty getting into action. It would thus seem correct to suggest that the tanks in the attacking divisions should have all been concentrated in the first wave of infantry. However, it is more difficult to see how the tank reserve might have been better positioned. We have seen that Mangin ordered it as far forward as was considered practical but Guderian believed that it should been even further forward. The problem with his suggestion is that the further forward the tank reserve was, the more exposed it would be to being hit by a German barrage. The Forêt de Retz was an ideal position for the tank assembly area, as it gave extensive cover for both waiting and then moving the tanks in comparative secrecy, it being out of range of all but German super-heavy artillery. By its very nature, the tank reserve was going to be immobile for the first part of the battle, until it was clear where it should be used, and it therefore needed to be well protected during this period of vulnerability. In addition, Guderian seems to underestimate the inevitable bottlenecks that the limited road network on the Soissons front produced, given the large number of troops and equipment that needed to move along it. The only main road, the *route nationale* from Soissons to Villers-Cotterêts (and then to Paris) crossed the battlefield diagonally and was therefore little use for transportation. The other roads, although crossing the battlefield west to east and thus being along the axis of advance, were minor and thus not suited for the large amount of military traffic that was required, as well as being vulnerable to the effects of bad weather. This problem with the road network was compounded by the fact that it was necessary for some of the divisions from both X and VI Armées to cross the Savières River, which ran parallel to the *route nationale* for much of the battlefield. This created further transportation problems, as has been discussed. Guderian also suggests that the Renault battalions should have been moved forward as one unit, reinforcing the most successful division, rather than being split into separate battalions following different divisions. This was have provided the theoretical ideal of the tank attack *en masse* but would have run up against the same problems with the roads that bedevilled the other tank operations. There is no reason to believe that the three Renault battalions moving along the same axis would not have produced an even worse traffic jam, with its associated delays. As the light tank battalions only just got into action anyway on 18 July, it seems likely that moving the Renault battalions together behind only one division would have created chaos, which would have probably stopped the tanks from participating in the battle at all.

To have taken any of the steps that Guderian suggests would have required taking a considerable risk, something that the French planners avoided. The issue of risk is the key to understanding French planning for this battle and those that followed it, as well as what where the tanks fitted into this conception. By this stage of the war, French commanders were well aware of the fragile nature of their troops and were, not unreasonably, very risk-averse. French military planning was therefore centred around avoiding or minimising risk, even if taking a risk might produce better results. It was also clear that infantry casualties would be high, even in a successful operation, and it was of the highest priority to ensure the initial attack was successful, without taking undue risks. It was therefore seen as more prudent to keep a tank reserve in both the attacking divisions and the attacking army that was not committed until its success was to all intents and purposes guaranteed. However, Guderian has a good point in relation to some of the departure points set for the French tanks, in relation to the infantry that they were supporting. For example, on 18 July the departure position for Groupement XI was over a kilometre behind their infantry, making it difficult for tanks that could only move at walking pace to catch up, whereas Groupement XII was only several hundred metres behind its infantry.

Soissons and the Tank Regulations
Soissons raised a number of issues connected with the tank regulations, although these were to do with their implementation rather than any

issues with their prescriptions. Tank officers were taught after the war that one of the key mistakes made during the Battle of Soissons was that the tank units had often been used piecemeal, with weakened infantry units, in insufficiently planned ('improvised') attacks. Although it was conceded that it was 'tempting' for commanders to use every means at their disposal to increase their success, it was erroneous to believe that small-scale tank attacks, unsupported by artillery and with depleted and exhausted infantry, would ever be successful against enemy positions that had already resisted a full scale tank attack. However, getting this message across to the infantry commanders, desperate to limit their casualties, was to remain a problem for the rest of the war.

This issue was compounded by the state of the infantry formations after the initial phase of combat operations. The infantry took such heavy casualties initially that their combat strength was quickly reduced, something that tank support could not make up for. This rapid depletion of the infantry can be gauged by the casualties suffered by the RMLE; 780 men were lost over just three days of combat at Soissons. This is an example when both training and regulations had little influence; the infantry knew they should be following the tanks but just decided they could not or would not.

The Note on Tank Use of 9 September 1918

Pétain and Estienne were very dissatisfied by the way that the tank units had been used during July and August and decided that the Army commanders needed reminding of the important points from the tank regulations. They subsequently issued a *Note* to the Army commanders on 9 September 1918. This begins by pointing out that the important prescriptions of the Instruction of 14 July 1918 in relations to tanks had been 'often forgotten in the last battles', giving 'poor results'. The *Note* summarised the essential lessons for tank employment as had been laid down by the regulations issued since December 1917.

As per the *Instruction* of 14 July, the tanks were only to be used *en masse*. It had been 'clearly established' by recent tank operations that using under-strength tank units gave 'no results', as did using weakened infantry units with the tanks. Under-strength tank units were unable to overcome all the enemy machine guns and would also attract concentrated artillery fire, to the detriment of accompanying infantry. Weakened infantry units were unable to occupy any positions captured by the tanks, making the whole effort 'in vain.' To avoid using depleted tank units, infantry commanders were reminded that it was necessary for tank reserves to be held at army, divisional and regimental level, in order to maintain a continuous tank presence during the battle.

Protecting the tanks against 'their most dangerous enemy' (artillery) was an 'indispensable condition' for successful tank actions. This required mounting tank attacks in the early morning, covered by mist, and this was to be 'scrupulously observed'. It was noted that the tanks had incurred serious losses from enemy anti-tank batteries that revealed themselves after combat began; this was to be considered 'one of the most difficult problems [now] posed'. The solution was to be found in the *Instruction* of 14 July; the use of smoke shells to blind enemy observation posts and a dedicated artillery *groupe* to engage anti-tank batteries, directed by aircraft were all essential. The *Note* clearly states that 'these conditions must be accepted' (emphasis in the original) by the infantry and artillery officers. This reflected numerous complaints made by AS officers after Soissons that some of the divisional commanders had reassigned the artillery given to them for tank protection. Another common complaint was that there was resistance in some of the artillery batteries to stockpiling smoke shells, which had to replace explosive rounds in the limited storage space available, meaning that smoke shells were often not available to cover the tanks. A minor AS operation in August had demonstrated the advantage of using smoke shells in a box barrage in addition to the creeping barrage; this had given the infantry and tanks an area to work in that was obscured from outside but within which they had good visibility for combat.

It remained to be seen if this recapitulation of the regulations was sufficient to prevent the problems seen in July and August from being repeated during subsequent operations.

Chapter 8

With the Americans: From Cantigny to the Meuse-Argonne, 1918

The French tanks would not only serve the French army but also the nascent US army on the Western Front, an experience that would sometimes prove very challenging for the French military in general and for the tank officers in particular. The welcome arrival of the US into the war on the Allied side was not without difficulties as, rather like the BEF in 1914, the US Army was in no state to engage in large-scale modern warfare, being both small in size and un-equipped with the latest weapons, particularly heavy artillery and tanks. The problems the US Army faced were not made easier by Pershing's determination to keep his army as autonomous as possible. However, to begin with the Americans were forced to rely on British and French expertise and equipment, particularly in relation to tank warfare. The French supplied and helped train the emerging US Tank Corps, mainly armed with French-made light tanks, and by necessity the French army had to supply AS units to bolster the Americans on a number of occasions. The first French tank engagement fighting with the US army would be in May 1918 at Cantigny, north-west of Montdidier.

Cantigny
On 12 May, General Eugene Debeney, commander of French 1 Armée, was informed that US Major General Robert Bullard, commander of US 1 Division, wanted to conduct a surprise attack on the German-held village of Cantigny. US 1 Division was under the command of French X CA, part of 1 Armée, along with 60 and 162 DIs. The US division was very large compared to British and French infantry divisions (almost twice the size) and its troops enthusiastic but these advantages were

offset by their comparative inexperience. For example, on 3 May 1918 the Germans subjected US 18 Infantry to an intensive gas bombardment that caused over 500 casualties and it was noted by Bullard on 8 May that during its time on the front his division was taking casualties that were two to four times as great as those of the adjacent French divisions.

As it was essential from their point of view for the US operation to be a success, the French lavishly supported what was to all intents and purposes a large-scale trench raid with tanks and a considerable amount of artillery, including some super-heavy artillery (240mm and 280mm guns). The French also supplied a *Schilt* (flamethrower) company.

Cantigny was a modest village surrounded by woods and orchards on the slope of gentle crest that formed a small salient in the US held part of the front. Although the village was heavily fortified, the Americans held a commanding position from which to attack it and the village itself was in a position that made German observation and reinforcement difficult. It was thus ideal for a limited objective attack as, with sufficient Allied artillery, the village could be isolated during the operation and the Germans prevented from reinforcing it.

The three-day artillery barrage commenced on the 25 May, there being nearly twenty French and US Artillery *groupes* firing on a front of only 1,600 metres. Although the French were prepared to attach a tank *groupement* to the US attack, close analysis of the battlefield by Groupement I's commander, *Chef d'escadron* de Forsanz, showed that the approach to Cantigny from the south was not suitable for tanks because of the numerous sunken roads that crossed that part of the front. It was therefore decided that only AS5 (commanded by Captain Noscereau with thirteen Schneiders in three batteries) from Groupement I would support the US infantry attack from the west into the village and from the north as an outflanking move.

US 28 Infantry was tasked with the attack and to prepare for the operation it was taken out of the line on 6 May, only returning on the night of 26 May. To assist the tanks, half a company of 262 RI was brought in to act as *infanterie d'accompagnement* and, on 21 May, twelve US soldiers who spoke French were attached to AS5. The latter would be used as liaison officers during the attack, allowing for one with each tank battery and each US infantry company, as well as with the overall tank and infantry commanders. The infantry and tank commanders thus had some considerable time to prepare their operation, which offset some of the disadvantages caused by the inexperience of the US troops.

US 28 Division would be attacking Cantigny with three battalions; one from the south without tank support, one (battalion B) attacking the centre and north with tank support, the remaining battalion covering the left flank of the operation.

The tanks left their assembly position late on the evening of 27 May, arriving at their waiting position at 03.30 the following day. At 05.50, they were at the departure position. They set off into combat at 06.40, covered by the smoke barrage and a significant amount of dust that had been thrown into the air by the intensive shelling. The tanks were further favoured by a mist that covered much of the battlefield.

On the right flank, 1 Battery/AS5, commanded by Lieutenant Mainardy, was supporting company 1B from US 28 Infantry's attack on the western edges of Cantigny, guarding the left flank of the American infantry, and, if necessary, providing enfilading fire on the south of the village. Once these tasks had been completed, the tanks were to move into a reserve position north-west of the village. Just prior to setting off, Mainardy received an order to send one of his tanks to 2 Battery/AS5, as a replacement for a damaged tank, leaving him with three tanks. The battery's entry into combat was not auspicious, as the clutch burnt out on Lieutenant Rouillot's tank, meaning Mainardy now had only half his battery available. Rouillot and his crew dismounted their machine guns and joined the American infantry in their advance, only returning to their tank when the objective had been taken. Mainardy's two other tanks advanced towards Cantigny, where they caused panic amongst the German infantry, one tank dispersed several groups of them without firing, leaving the Germans so disordered that they were easily captured by the advancing American infantry. The tank then took up an over-watch position covering the south of the village until the American infantry had reached their objective, the tank then moving into the reserve position to the north-west of the village. The remaining tank (which Mainardy was riding in) destroyed a machine-gun position covering the Plessier-Cantigny road and then advanced to the north-west rallying point.

In the centre, 2 Battery/AS5, commanded by Lieutenant Chenu, was advancing in front of the American infantry towards the north-west corner of the village, containing a cemetery, where it would neutralise the orchards that offered effective cover for any German defenders. *Sous-Lieutenant* d'Anterroches's tank got into a fight with a fortified position in a house situated just outside of the village, which the tank easily won, the German defenders having no anti-tank weapons.

Unfortunately, the tank subsequently got stuck in a shell hole, bringing its part in the operation to an end. Lieutenant Charrier and his tank had been attached from 1 Battery and he was given the task of entering the orchards and clearing them. In the orchards the tank encountered a German machine gun that was brushed aside with cannon fire. As the orchards were now clear, Charrier decided to investigate the sounds of intensive fire coming from the north of their position and they advanced in the direction of the Lalval woods. There he found a dug-in German machine gun in a partial trench line that covered the road into Cantigny and, after the tank destroyed the machine gun, the American infantry were able to came forward and take numerous prisoners. The tank remained to cover the infantry as they installed themselves in the area.

The only AS fatality at Cantigny, one which exemplifies the *esprit de corps* of the men of the AS, was in 2 Battery's area. One of the AS liaison officers serving with the US infantry, Lieutenant Blancot, was killed while helping direct fire from Lieutenant Dechamps' tank (with battery commander Lieutenant Chenu aboard). A group of Germans with a machine gun had taken cover behind a thick hedge along the side of the Lalval road and were all-but-invisible to the tank crew. As their fire was stopping the US infantry from advancing, it was vital that they were flushed out of this position. Blancot rushed up and began firing at the Germans with his revolver to alert the tank crew to the former's position. The Germans returned his fire and he was shot in the head and killed instantly. The enraged Chenu and his AS crew subjected the Germans to withering fire from their machine guns and cannon, then crashed their tank through the hedge, which allowed the US infantry to move forward and bayonet the remaining Germans. Chenu felt that the twenty Germans that he and the Americans left dead behind the hedge were sufficient revenge for his friend Lieutenant Blancot. The tank continued the advance up to the objective and then remained to cover the American infantry as they installed themselves in the position.

The other tank in this section, commanded by Lieutenant Gigot, was following thirty metres closely behind Deschamps' tank but slightly to the left. The American infantry advanced so quickly that the tank could not keep up with them and by the time the former were at the edge of the cemetery the tank was some way behind. This was fortunate, however, as the tank spotted a group of German infantry trying to outflank the US infantry and the tank dispersed them with two shots from its cannon. After it caught up with Chenu and Dubois' tanks, it advanced to the objective, destroying at least three German machine guns on the way. The tank reported that it seen large numbers of German dead.

3 Battery/AS5, commanded by Lieutenant de Compiègne, was advancing in front of the American infantry to clear the route of all opposition and then cover the area north of the village, in anticipation of German counter-attacks. The first section, with the battery commander, advanced along the northern edges of Cantigny. The lead tank, commanded by Lieutenant Dubois, reached the cemetery without receiving any fire but once it moved forward it was engaged by several hidden German machine guns, one in a silo, that were dispatched with cannon and machine-gun fire from the tank. As the American infantry were organising the captured area, the tank fired on the exit to a ravine situated to the north-east with its cannon and used machine gun fire on the edges of both Lalval and Framicourt woods. This is an example of the increasing use by the AS of neutralisation fire, rather than strictly firing at identified targets as per the tank regulations. Lieutenant Rousset's tank, with de Compiègne aboard, followed Dubois' tank up to the cemetery but then moved round the south side of this landmark. Although there were no Germans in the cemetery, the tank received heavy fire from the orchards as it came forward, requiring it to stop and return fire. The tank then continued its advance along the Lalval road, eliminating a number of German resistance points as it went. Once the US infantry had caught up with the tank, it remained to cover them, firing on a German machine gun that revealed itself by opening fire on the Allied troops. The other section of 3 Battery/AS5 had much the same objectives as the other section but the two tanks advanced to the north of the cemetery. With Lieutenant Rousset's tank in the lead, Rousset and Lieutenant David's tanks successfully engaged several German machine guns before stopping to protect the US infantry as they dug in. While there, Rousset fired on the edges of the ravine and the trench line in front of his tank to prevent any enemy counter-attacks from developing in these positions. As David's tank moved forward it got stuck in a shell hole, which took its crew fifteen minutes of frantic activity to get it moving again. However, there was no German artillery fire to worry about and the tank was able to move to the reserve position without incident.

The *groupe* commander, Captain Noscereau, and his tank followed the route taken by 2 Battery. Noscereau was able to successfully intervene a number of times during the battle, as he made sure he was always in a position that gave good observation of the battlefield. For example, he decided that 2 Battery had the most onerous task and thus moved the tank from 1 Battery, as has been mentioned. He placed his tank in an over-watch position while the US infantry dug in and only recalled the *groupe*'s tanks when he was sure that the infantry had finished their work.

The tanks had on average covered twenty-eight kilometres from departure to return, most having been in combat for just over an hour. Noscereau observed in his report that the approach march to the departure position had been too long and had put some strain on the tanks' engines. However, all the *groupe*'s tanks had returned from combat. The tanks had fired on average twelve shells and used eight machine-gun belts. None of the tanks had been hit by artillery fire and the infantry fire that they had received had only damaged the paintwork. Strangely enough, the early German reports alleged that the French tanks attacking Cantigny had been 'shot to pieces', which was not correct as only one tank was left temporally on the battlefield. The newly-issued periscope had a universally good reception and was clearly very effective. Blancot was the only AS man killed that day, although one tank crewman was badly injured by mustard gas, with their *infanterie d'accompagnement* having two men wounded. Two of the US liaison officers were also wounded.

A prisoner told his American captors on 27 May that the Germans were aware that there would be an attack on Cantigny but that the troops had been told that it would be easy to repel as they would only be fighting Americans. This extraordinarily lax German attitude to the coming attack on Cantigny was such that, according to prisoners' statements after the battle, there were no preparations made by 272 Reserve Infantry regiment for a counter-attack if the village was lost. The fact that the German artillery reacted so weakly to the US attack also demonstrates their lack of preparation. In addition, the Americans were surprised at the physical state of the captured Germans, one US officer describing them as looking 'hollow-cheeked, wan and underfed'.

The Germans lost 255 prisoners, including an artillery officer with maps detailing their artillery positions in the area, and had at least 1,000 killed and over 500 wounded during the two days of fighting at Cantigny, in addition to a large amount of equipment captured by the Americans. Both German 271 and 272 IRs were left incapable of further offensive action. Such was the surprise of the attack that the US infantry found many unopened cases containing ammunition and machine guns in the captured positions at Cantigny. The Americans estimated that three entire German companies in Cantigny itself had been completely destroyed, a US report grimly noting that there had been very few prisoners taken in the village. German 26 Reserve Corps reported that its men had been demoralised by the appearance of the French tanks, which they had never seen before.

The Cantigny operation had thus been an unqualified success for the Allies. Although the French tank officers and their American counterparts had got along well and thus fought together effectively in the Cantigny operation, the AS officers were to find their subsequent experiences working with the Americans to be much less harmonious. However, after Cantigny it would be the autumn of 1918 before the officers and men of the AS fought with the US army again, although as might be expected the AS was deeply involved in assisting the training of the US army tank crews using the French-supplied light tanks.

The St Mihiel Salient and the Battle of Meuse-Argonne
On 30 August, Foch unveiled to Pershing and Pétain his plans for an offensive across the entire Western Front. The BEF, supported by the left flank of the French army, was to continue its attacks in the direction of Cambrai and St Quentin, the centre of the French army was to continue pushing the Germans along the Aisne and the American Army, supported by the right of the French army, was to push in the general direction of Mézières. The Germans would thus find themselves pressed both from the west and the south. In particular, the French saw Mézières as a key objective, the capture of which would severely interfere with German rail operations from Germany into France. Doubts about the ability of the US Army to undertake complex operations on its own led Foch initially to decide to use the US Army by itself to reduce the St Mihiel position but then be split to fight amongst parts of the French army. However, Pershing refused to allow this and Foch finally agreed, after considerable argument, to allow US 1 Army to operate in its entirety on the Meuse-Argonne front, supported on its left by French IV Armée. Once the Americans had taken St Mihiel, they would drive towards Mézières through the Meuse-Argonne area, with IV Armée on their left also pushing towards Mézières. The US operation at St Mihiel was designated as *opération A*, the subsequent US advance was to be *opération B* and IV Army's concurrent advance was *opération C* (the latter is discussed in the next chapter). *Opération A* was to be undertaken while the forces were

being concentrated for B and C. Four battalions of light tanks, two *groupes* of Schneiders and three *groupes* of St Chamonds had been attached to the US Army for *opération B*.

Opération A – The Battle of St-Mihiel, 12 September 1918

On 17 August, Colonel Wahl, commander 1 AS Brigade, was instructed by Estienne to undertake reconnaissance in the US army's area of operations. After a detailed examination of the ground that might be fought over by two of Wahl's battalion commanders, a report was sent to Estienne on 24 August suggesting that in some areas tank combat was feasible. On the following day, after considering these reports, Estienne appointed Wahl to command all the French tank units that would be attached to the US army and a liaison officer, AS Lieutenant Dubois, was sent to co-ordinate operations between Wahl and the head of the US tank force, Brigadier General Rockenbach. The German salient was sixteen miles deep and was in front of three important Allied objectives; the fortified city of Metz, the railway running from Metz and Sedan to Flanders and the coal fields at Briey. As long as the salient was in German possession, it threatened the Verdun area and the rail communications between Paris and Lorraine.

Preparations for the battle

On 5 September, 13, 14, and 15 BCLs from RAS 505 and AS14 and AS17 (along with SRR 102) from Groupement IV, now equipped with ten Renaults and eighteen Schneiders, were ordered to begin preparations to move to the American zone. Over the next four days, the tank units were moved by rail, with surprisingly few delays, and it was decided to add to the US support by moving Groupement XI with thirty St Chamonds into the area. By 11 September all the tank units were in position.

The US operation was envisaged as follows. The St Mihiel salient was to be eliminated by two simultaneous attacks; one from the south by US 1 Corps and US 4 Corps, with US 5 Corps attacking from the west. French 2 Colonial Corps would advance through the salient one hour after the US advance to mop up German forces left in the area. There were seven German divisions in the salient, organised in three groups under the command of Lieutenant General Fuchs. The Germans were well aware that they could not resist a determined Allied attack and plans had been long established to evacuate the position in an orderly fashion. Although the US army made every effort to disguise preparations for the operation, the German defenders of the salient were warned by OHL on 1 September that an attack was imminent and during the following day heavy equipment began to be transferred out of the arca and the narrow-gauge railway lines began to be dismantled. However, for unclear reasons, the HQ of Army Group Gallwitz (with overall command of the salient) delayed putting into action the full evacuation plan, despite growing daily evidence that the salient would be attacked in the very near future.

1 US Corps was given 13, 14, 15 BCLs and Groupement XI (AS34 and AS35), under the command of *Chef de bataillon* Mare (commander of RAS 505). The corps was attacking with three divisions in the first line; 3, 5 and 90 US Divisions, with each division initially having two battalions in the first line. The advance was expected to cover 100 metres every four minutes and the final objectives were to be taken within six hours. AS34 and 14 BCL were attached to US 5 Division and AS35 went to US 2 Division along with 13 BCL, with 15 BCL acting as the corps reserve. AS34 and AS35 were to clear the way for the US infantry through the wire up to the German trenches and then, subject to the US engineers successfully constructing passages for the tanks across the German trenches, help the US infantry advance. The US divisions were initially advancing in column of brigades, with a tank *groupe* attached to each leading brigade. 13 and 14 BCL would only come into action when the first line of German trenches had been passed. 15 BCL was with the reserve US division, with its commander stationed at the Corps HQ.

To ameliorate language problems, each tank section attached two English-speakers to each US battalion commander that they were supporting and a TSF tank was placed with each leading infantry battalion, with another stationed at the leading brigade's HQ. There would be artillery support for the tanks in the form of smoke shells in the barrage, smoke attacks on known German observation posts and dedicated batteries to fire on anti-tank guns.

US 4 Corps had three divisions attacking in line; US 1, 42 and 89 Divisions, which had the same rate of advance and time on final objective as the divisions of US 1 Corps. Lieutenant Colonel George S. Patton Jr. was in charge of the tank units in this corps, which consisted of Groupement IV (commanded by *Chef de bataillon* Chanoine) and US 2nd Tank Battalion. US 42 Division was attacking with two brigades in line and Groupement IV was attached to the brigade on the left; US 83 Brigade. This brigade was advancing with two regiments in line; on the left US 166 Infantry with AS17 and on the right US 165 Infantry with

AS14. One tank battery was placed with each forward infantry battalion, with one battery held back as the regimental reserve.

12 September

The attack commenced at 05.00 on 12 September, after a four-hour artillery preparation. The tank attack on the front of US 4 Corps benefitted on the day from a very effective US smoke and gas barrage and the tanks helped the US infantry all the way to the banks of the Rupt de Mad river. The tanks took shelter in a nearby ravine while passages were made over the German trenches and then advanced again in support of the US infantry. AS17 assisted in the capture of forty prisoners by the US infantry.

On US I Corps' front, with US 5 Division, AS34 only managed to send two tanks forward of the infantry to clear the barbed wire, as all the other tanks had either ditched in the broken terrain or broken down. By 17.00, six tanks were available at an assembly position but they were to see no action. 14 BCL sent two companies into action, AS340 and 341, with AS342 in reserve. These two companies advanced with the US infantry but they encountered no resistance and the infantry moved so rapidly that the tanks were unable to keep up with them. Unusually, AS340 lost a tank when it hit a mine, but it had twelve tanks in working order at the end of the day. AS341 had a similar experience to AS340, with the infantry disappearing into the distance and the tanks having no way of catching up with them. By the evening, AS341 had eleven tanks operational.

With US 2 Division, AS35 was unable to get into its departure position until 07.00, when it was discovered that the passages for the tanks had not been adequately built by the Americans. This resulted in only two tanks, out of the nine that had left the departure position, getting to the final objective, the others being victims of the very difficult terrain, which included particularly loose and muddy soil.

The light tanks of 13 BCL had as many difficulties as the medium Schneider tanks had crossing the slippery and crater filled ground and, as the tanks were unable to catch up with the US infantry, at 15.30 the US divisional commander ordered the tanks to retire. AS338 managed to get all of its tanks back to the assembly position but AS337 left most of its tanks on the battlefield, requiring later salvage. AS339 had been placed in reserve and was not called into action and nor was 15 BCL, the corps reserve.

13 September

There was less action on 13 September, with no action at all on US 5 Division's front (AS34 and 14 BCL) and only AS34 seeing a small-scale combat supporting US 2 Division. There were no tank actions on the following day on either division's front and the French tank units were regrouped to the rear. The operation was now over

The primary result of the Battle of St Mihiel was that the Paris to Avricourt railway was no longer in danger and the salient, which the Germans had held for four years, was now in Allied hands. The Allied forces had captured 13,251 prisoners, 466 guns and 752 machine guns, only suffering light losses in the process.

Lessons for the AS from St Mihiel

Although the St Mihiel operation had been a success for the AS, a number of issues had arisen. There were considerable difficulties with the railway wagons supplied to move the tank units as well as the trains themselves, a number of which had broken down. There had also been much congestion on the rail network, particularly from the ALGP supply trains, and the road network was equally disorganised in the view of the AS officers. The AS officers also felt that they had received their orders at a very late stage, due to the requirements of secrecy, and they had difficulties getting clear orders from the Americans. They also noted that as the German resistance diminished after 12 September, they were called on less because the US infantry 'wanted to preserve for themselves the glory of success', according to Wahl.

German anti-tank defences had been of four types; traps, mines, field guns and anti-tank rifles, some of which were more dangerous than others. For example, the camouflaged traps only managed to catch one tank, from AS337, and it was able to escape under its own power. The German anti-tank guns seemed little more effective than the traps had been. However, Wahl's report noted that the German anti-tank mines seemed to be more powerful than had been encountered before, one blowing the turret off a Renault from 14 BCL. A similar mine had blown the tracks off a St Chamond and Wahl pointed out that these mines were difficult to avoid while in combat and recommended that areas where mines were suspected to be should be cleared by artillery fire prior to tank attacks.

Technical issues included the known problem with the fan belts of the light tanks, on average thirty per company failing during the 12 September attack. There were difficulties with towing immobilised

Renaults; they simply could not be moved by another light tank, as this usually just resulted in putting both tanks out of action, and the Baby-Holt tractors were very conspicuous on the battlefield and thus could not be used while a battle was raging. Wahl suggested that each light battalion should have two unarmed Schneiders for tank recovery purposes. He also suggested that the light tank battalions needed either some unarmed Schneiders or St Chamonds attached to be used for battlefield supply, as this was impossible for the AS wheeled vehicles to do, as well as trailers carrying petrol reserves, such as had been used by Groupement II at Malmaison. Wahl also noted that the AS regiments had insufficient telephone wire, suggesting that twenty kilometres of wire per regiment should be issued and that an AS regiment should be as well equiped with telephones as an artillery regiment.

Over the period of 12 to 16 September, the AS units attached to the US infantry had lost six men killed and twenty-eight wounded, including five officers. Out of the 250 tanks available on the night of 11 September, only two light tanks were destroyed in the fighting that followed, one by shell and one by a mine, with one St Chamond being damaged by a mine. However, by the evening of 14 September, forty-six tanks were out of action due to mechanical issues, largely caused by the state of the terrain. For example, the Americans reported that the mud on the battlefield had been a major problem, as it was particularly sticky and many of the US light tanks had sunk into muddy shell holes, requiring difficult salvage operations to free them.

Opération B – The Battle of Meuse-Argonne, 26 September–8 October 1918

Now that the St Mihiel salient was in Allied hands, the next phase of the operation could commence; the American part designated *opération B* by the French. On 17 September, the number of French tanks with 1 US Army was as follows; 13 BCL (sixty Renaults), 14 BCL (fifty-eight Renaults), 15 BCL (sixty-five Renaults), Groupement XI (seventeen St Chamonds) with SRR105 and Groupement IV (sixteen Schneiders and eight Renaults) with SRR102. All of these tank units, with the exception of Groupement IV, were organised together as 505 RAS, under the command of Wahl. 505 RAS was subsequently joined by 17 BCL, and the tank regiment was attached on 23 September to US 5 Corps. Groupement IV was attached to US 1 Corps and would be fighting with US 35 Division and US 1 Tank Brigade. The heavy fighting that US 1 Tank Brigade was involved in, which Groupement IV played a fairly minor part of, is well covered in US accounts (see Further Reading) and I will therefore concentrate on the actions of 505 RAS with US 5 Corps.

The planning for the battle

The engagement plan for US 5 Corps attached the tanks to the infantry in the following manner; 13 BCL was with US 37 Division, 14 BCL, 15 BCL and Groupement XI were with US 79 Division, with 17 BCL as the corps reserve. 15 BCL was then called to support US 4 Division in US 3 Corps. The AS units moved to a holding position in the northern edges of the Forêt de Fays et de Sivry on the night of 23 September and on D-1 they moved to their departure position just north of the Bois de Esnes. From the point of view of the AS, the execution of the operation unfolded in three major stages; the operations from 26 to 29 September, a period of reinforcement and reconstitution until the reprise of operations from 4 to 8 October.

First stage of the battle, 26–29 September 1918

On 26 September, the tanks of 13 BCL set off at 05.30, supporting US 79 Division, and by 13.00 AS337 and AS339 were 400 metres south-east of the Bois de Cuisy, with AS338 echeloned 300 metres to the rear. Their advance to this position had been beset with difficulties; such was the terrain, the battalion only had twenty tanks in action, leaving thirty-seven tanks left broken-down in either the French or German lines. After some work, twenty tanks were sufficiently repaired to return to their units but not all of these tanks were in a combat-ready state.

The infantry from US 79 Division were at this moment halted by heavy enfilading fire from the Bois de Cuisy. The tanks were 300 metres behind them and waiting for orders. Lieutenant Colonel Pullen arrived (commander of US 5 CA's tanks) and told the French tank company commanders to support US 79 Division in the fight for the woods. A row now broke out between the French and the Americans about the former's orders, largely the result of the tank officers being keen to operate according to their tank regulations and being initially unwilling to improvise an attack in what looked like unpromising circumstances. The French officers pointed out that they were attached to US 37 Division, not US 79 Division, but Pullen 'insisted' that the tanks go to the aid of 79 DI. The report from Pullen to Rockenbach said that the French tank officers refused to attack the Bois de Cuisy, as their orders required the US infantry to have seized the woods before the tanks advanced, which the US troops were too disorganised to do. The

French tank officers according to Pullen insisted on written orders from the Brigade commander before advancing but the Brigade commander could not be found. Finally, an exasperated Pullen turned to Captain Gaëtan Liaras, commander of AS337, and asked him if he was prepared to act with or without written orders to which the AS officer replied; 'I do not need written orders, I am ready to fight; it is not important when, it is not important who.' Liaras then ordered the tank companies into action. AS337 and AS339 both sent a section into combat against the Germans in the woods, the former's section to the right and the latter's section to the left. When the tanks halted after clearing the edges of the Cuisy woods, Liaras took command of the section from AS337 and the tanks advanced into the woods, which prompted the US infantry to jump from their trenches and follow them. By 17.00, the woods were entirely cleared and occupied by the US infantry. Pullen told Liaras that 'it was not the [American] infantry that took the woods, it was the [French] tanks'. An hour later, the commander of US 313 Infantry asked AS338 to supply a tank section to assist him, the section being under the command of Lieutenant Franchomme with five tanks. The US infantry then attacked the German position in the copses lining the Malancourt-Montfaucon road but by the time the tanks arrived the Germans had retreated and the positions were easily occupied by US infantry.

At 19.00, AS339 was asked to supply a section to support an advance towards Montfaucon. Section Corbier destroyed several machine guns on the plain and enabled the US infantry to advance up to the fortified position south of Montfaucon. As night fell, the tanks returned to the reassembly position on the north edge of the Bois de Cuisy. The results were that the following day the Germans abandoned the woods and the heights of Montfaucon.

14 BCL set off behind 13 BCL in a line of companies, with AS342 at the head followed by AS340 and AS341, reaching the Bois de Cuisy by the end of the day without being engaged. Preparations were made overnight to support the American attack on Montfaucon scheduled for the following day and the commander of AS342, Lieutenant Jacquot, met with the commander of US 313 Infantry, Colonel Sweezy. They agreed that the tanks would intervene at 07.00 and would attempt to manoeuvre around Montfaucon before attacking it, Montfaucon being unassailable from the front. Two tank sections would attack from the west, with the third section advancing from the east, the tanks' main objective being to clear the slopes around Montfaucon for the US

infantry. The plan initially went well, with the tanks' advance in the west forcing the Germans to evacuate Montfaucon, but the tanks and US infantry were then hit by increasingly accurate German artillery fire. This fire pinned the infantry down and then the tanks began to be specifically targeted, resulting in three tanks being quickly knocked out. Lieutenant Revel, commander of 1 section, realised that remaining in position was impossible but that retreat would be dangerous and 'without profit'. He used his flag to order all tanks forward, at which point the German barrage lifted enough for the US infantry to advance into Montfaucon and the tanks moved to a position just north of the position. The section to the east, from AS340, had a rather easier day and had seized all of its objectives with the US infantry by midday.

Around 14.30 on 27 September, the commander of US 73 Brigade asked for a tank section to support an attack in the direction of Cierges by US 154 Infantry. However, when the tanks arrived the US battalion commander told them his troops were too tired to undertake the operation. By this stage of the operation, friction between the Americans and the French tank officers was such that the AS company commander insisted on receiving written orders from the US battalion commander that the tanks could return to the resupply position. The tanks arrived back there at 20.00, the day's efforts adding quite unnecessary wear and tear to the tanks and being a complete waste of time for the crews.

14 BCL sent two companies to raise morale in the US infantry but saw no action unlike 15 BCL, which participated in a successful action near Nantillois, supporting US 79 Division. AS343 and AS344 were attached to the leading US infantry regiments, while AS345 was placed in reserve. The action did not get off to an auspicious start as the US divisional staff changed their plan of attack during the morning, forcing the AS company commanders to recast their plans and re-establish liaison with the infantry commanders. Due to these holdups, the attack did not start until 16.30, by which time the Americans were still somewhat unprepared. Although the two tank companies were able to advance without much difficulty, destroying a number of machine guns as they went as well as a German heavy-artillery emplacement, the US infantry did not follow them. The tanks took Nantillois, one AS lieutenant actually walking through the village without seeing any Germans, and advanced beyond it but the US infantry remained over a kilometre behind the area that the tanks had conquered. However, 15 BCL had still helped the infantry push two kilometres into the German positions across a front of three kilometres. The battalion took no

casualties that day, although two men were hospitalised with gas injuries, and one tank was lost to an artillery shell.

On 28 September two companies from 14 BCL successfully attacked the Bois de Beuges et Nantillois. Three tank sections from 13 BCL were requested for US 74 Brigade by the divisional commander to support an attack on the village of Cierges. One section duly set off at 10.00 and arrived at the departure position at 15.00. When the French company commander met with the US colonel commanding the infantry attack, he was told by the latter that the US troops were not ready for the operation and it would thus take place on the following morning at 07.00. Although the French tank officers were not pleased to have to wait again because of US disorganisation, they were able to make use of the delay to resupply the tanks with petrol, many tanks being on the verge of running out of fuel. The tanks remained at the departure position overnight while planning for the morning attack.

The Bois de Ogons and Ferme de la Madeleine were attacked by one company (AS344) of 15 BCL and one *groupe* of St Chamonds from Groupement XI. The three sections from AS344 had a similar experience to that of the previous day; the tanks neutralised numerous German machine-gun positions in their advance but the US infantry failed to follow them and occupy the positions the tanks had taken, although to be fair to the Americans there was a particularly heavy weight of German fire on the battlefield. Those positions that the US infantry had occupied were abandoned during the night. This operation had cost AS344 two tanks hit by shells, with one man killed, three wounded and three missing.

The St Chamonds of Groupement XI were in four batteries with three tanks each and one battery of four tanks, these tanks being concentrated north of the Bois de Montfaucon. At 11.00, the *groupement* received orders to support US 79 Division whose troops were halted along the Nantillois-Cunel road in front of the Bois des Ogons. US 79 Division decided to mount its attack at 14.30, with support from Groupement XI and a company of light tanks from 15 BCL. Two St Chamond batteries went to the east of the Nantillois-Cunel road and two went to the west of the road. At 13.00, the tanks moved into their sectors.

The four tanks of 1 Battery (Lieutenant Guignabaudet) advanced quickly but were not followed by the US infantry. The battery stopped and Guignabaudet went back to talk to the commander of US 2 Battalion/315 Infantry who claimed that he could not advance because of the machine-gun and artillery fire his battalion had suffered. After a 'difficult conversation', the US commander was persuaded to continue the attack with the tanks' support. The US infantry formed up behind the French tanks and advanced to a crest, where they were fired upon from the edges of the Bois des Ogons. The tanks swept the edges of the woods with machine-gun fire and the US infantry resumed their advance, only stopping as they reached the woods. Here they needed persuading by Guignabaudet to enter the woods, which was complicated by the fact that the US battalion commander had been killed and his replacement, a captain, was reluctant to advance at all, saying his troops had not eaten in three days. However, the Americans did eventually penetrate the woods, only for small groups of the US infantry to retire from the position until it was left abandoned.

The other batteries had similar experiences with the Americans, in 3 Battery's case its tanks advanced without any infantry support and 4 Battery did not get into action because of US disorganisation. During the night of 28 September, the *groupement* was stood down and it remained on the southern edge of the Bois de la Tuilerie until 3 October.

Such was the growing tension between the AS and the Americans, 1 AS Brigade commander, Colonel Wahl, issued a *note de service* on 29 September that instructed the AS officers not to disparage their American colleagues and to set a good example. Wahl's note acknowledged that fighting with the Americans had produced 'numerous difficulties' due to their inexperience and fatigue, the lack of orders and the language problems. However, these difficulties would have to be overcome with 'good will', he said. It is worth noting that criticism of the more senior US infantry officers did not only come from the French tank officers; Pullen wrote to Rockenbach to say that there should be an official enquiry into the behaviour of the commanders of US 313 Infantry, as Pullen believed that Montfaucon would have been taken if they had acted more competently.

That same day, the commander of US 148 Infantry requested the support of 13 BCL as the infantry regiment advanced towards Cierges, the attack setting off at 07.00. The order was sent verbally at 05.50, which gave the French tank officers of 13 BCL a very limited amount of time to organise themselves and liaise with the infantry officers. The tanks set off with two sections in front and one following 300 metres behind them. When the French arrived at the US front line at 07.30 they found that the US infantry were only just setting off. Two tank sections advanced in column, one section behind the other, while the third used neutralisation fire on the area of advance. The second tank section (commander, Lieutenant Maurel of AS339) then advanced towards Gesnes in order to bring neutralisation fire on the village of Cierges, disappearing from view and not being seen again. The bulk of the US infantry now stopped behind the rear third tank section and could not be induced to resume their advance. The situation was exacerbated when the various US infantry elements that had kept up with the forward tank sections, decided to retreat back to their comrades behind the rear tank section. The two forward tank sections were now left without infantry support and in a dangerously exposed position. Despite all the efforts of the AS officers, including a plea from the company commander, the US infantry remained 'deaf' to all pleas to follow the tanks forward. The AS section commanders decided to leave the tanks in position until Maurel's section returned but by 10.30 there was still no sign of him. The tanks were then subjected to an artillery barrage, whereupon it was decided to retire the two tank sections to a safer position. A three-tank patrol was sent out to try and establish contact with the US infantry but 'this was in vain' and the tanks were forced to retire by enemy artillery fire. By 12.00, the US infantry had retired 300 metres back to a position south-east of the woods and the day's action was over.

One company of 15 BCL (AS345) attacked the Ferme Madeleine in conjunction with US 315 Infantry (from US 158 Brigade). This was to prove a hard fight as the Allied artillery had not managed to seriously damage the German defences in the farm and the Americans were rather disorganised; as the commander of AS345, Lieutenant Ragaine, said in his report; 'I spent the whole night [28 September] asking for orders [from the Americans]'. The AS officers were further dismayed to find the American front line had moved during the night one kilometre further back, a situation they had not been informed about. Although the tank company only received its orders for the attack two hours before its commencement, the tanks were highly successful, overcoming all resistance, including eliminating a German field artillery battery, but once again they were not followed by the US infantry, leaving the farm largely destroyed but still in German hands.

Second stage of the battle, 30 September to 4 October
On 30 September, 13 BCL had twenty tanks operational, 14 BCL had thirty-two, 15 BCL had fifty-four and 17 BCL, which had not been engaged, had fifty, giving a total of 156 light tanks available, with eleven St Chamonds. This stage of the battle saw little fighting as the by now very tired US divisions were being replaced by fresh ones. However, the

tank units were constantly put on alert and frequently moved into departure positions and then moved out of them, something that was, as an AS report noted; 'extremely tiring for both personnel and material'. (For example, on 3 October, AS343 was put on alert for an attack that was cancelled an hour later and then moved twice before receiving its final orders to stand down.) During this period, 13 BCL and 14 BCL were moved into the reserve and retired to a position near the Forêt de Hesse.

Third stage of the battle, 4–8 October
The third stage of the battle began on 4 October, as US 5 Corps resumed its operations. It had the following changes to its order of battle; US 32 Division replaced US 37 Division and US 3 Division replaced US 79 Division. Groupement XI was attached to US 80 Division in US 3 Corps, 17 BCL was attached to US 32 Division, with 15 BCL attached to US 3 Division.

At 05.25, AS343 and AS344, from 15 BCL, began their advance in the direction of Romagne, supporting US 4 Infantry. The infantry-tank co-operation was very good thanks to the US regimental staff and the attack was successful, the objectives being obtained by 09.20. The light tanks continued in action, however, and supported US 7 Infantry's attacks into the early evening. There had been many breakdowns, including numerous cases of broken fan-belts, and in one section four of its tanks broke-down almost immediately after leaving the departure position.

17 BCL was supporting an attack by US 32 Division on German positions north of Gesnes and the Bois de la Marine. The attack commenced at 07.30 in a heavy morning mist, AS349 being with US 63 Brigade and AS350 with US 64 Brigade. The tanks advanced to the south-west edges of Gesnes but were not followed by the infantry, causing the former to retire. The attack recommenced at 16.00 but once again the US infantry failed to follow the tanks. This fruitless activity had cost 17 BCL three tanks destroyed by a single German artillery piece and a number of others seriously damaged by anti-tank rifle fire, personnel losses being six presumed dead and five wounded. However, on 5 October the attack was resumed and this time the US infantry followed the French tanks, resulting in Gesnes being captured and the Bois de la Marine being cleared of enemy troops.

On 2 October, Groupement XI was attached to US 3 Corps and then to US 4 Division, with the infantry and tank officers liaising the following day. On 3 October, Herlaut was visiting the US Corps HQ when he discovered to his astonishment that US 4 Division was now being replaced by US 80 Division in that sector and that the tanks would now be supporting the latter. There were further issues with the US plans from the point of view of the AS. The jump-off time (05.25) was too early according to Herlaut, as there would be insufficient light for the tanks to move safely. He was unable to persuade the Americans to change their plans but, at his insistence, the corps orders to the US division included an annexe detailing how the tanks would operate, which was largely a brief resume of the French tank regulations, emphasising that the US infantry should never be more than 100 metres behind the tanks.

On 4 October, the *groupement* could only muster a *groupe de marche* under the orders of Captain Balland. At 04.15 the tanks moved from the Bois de Tuilerie to the departure position, which they left at 05.30. The *groupe* had one battery of four tanks and two batteries of three tanks, two batteries were supporting the right-hand infantry battalion and one battery was supporting the left-hand infantry battalion. On arriving at the departure position, one tank got stuck in a shell hole.

The first battery attacked the south-east edges of the Bois des Ogons but quickly found itself without infantry support. The battery eventually found a US infantry battalion pinned down in a ravine where it had been receiving heavy fire from German artillery and machine guns. The US battalion commander agreed to let two infantry companies support the tanks in an advance but the company commanders insisted on delaying the operation. After waiting for an hour, the tanks were spotted by German observation planes and when at 11.00 the US infantry were still not ready to advance, the tanks were forced to retire to the resupply position south of Nantillois. This was just as well because just after the tanks moved, a violent artillery barrage came down on their former position.

The second battery destroyed a number of machine guns on the edge of the Bois des Ogons but the US infantry did not follow. The tanks went back for the US infantry but 'they never appeared' and the tanks resumed the advance on their own. Because of the mist and smoke on the battlefield, two of the tanks got lost and moved into US 4 Division's sector, the terrain of which was badly broken up, resulting in one tank losing its tracks and another getting bogged down. The remaining tank continued in combat until 12.30 when it ran out of petrol just outside of the Bois de Tuilerie.

When the third battery's commander, Lieutenant Thepenier, entered some woods in his search for the US infantry he was arrested by an American patrol, who failed to understand that he was French, and he only escaped when the patrol took cover during a bombardment. Eventually finding a group of US infantry, Thepenier's efforts to get them to advance were in vain and he retired the battery when it was subjected to an artillery bombardment which included gas shells.

On the afternoon of 5 October, Groupement XI went into reserve, followed the next day by 15 BCL, the battle now being over for most of the AS. 17 BCL, however, was engaged one last time on 9 October, for an attack on Romagne and the heights to its west. There were two days to prepare this operation, undertaken to support US 32 Division, which resulted in a relatively smooth operation; the attack was a success, with Romagne being captured, and at 16.00 the tanks were released by the infantry commander and retired.

Conclusion

In relation to the operations along the Meuse, the French reported that the Americans were inexperienced in offensive operations and their dense formations made ideal targets for the German artillery. Reports from German prisoners were damning; they told the French that the Americans were not 'a dangerous adversary'.

The experience of fighting with the Americans that had started so well at Cantigny had become for the AS in the Argonne a very disagreeable task. For example, Adrien Balland was disgusted with the Americans' disorganisation, as was made clear in one of his reports. In one case, the US infantry had refused to advance because they said they had not eaten in three days, which Balland dismissed as a 'pretext'. He finished his report by stating bluntly; 'I request not to have to continue in these conditions.' Herlaut attached a note on the morning of 29 September to this report, addressed to *Commandant* Mare (commander 505 RAS), stating that he was entirely in accord with Balland. The 'fatigue of the American infantry who need to be raised from their inertia' made further action by the tanks futile, he said. An attack 'this morning' by a battalion of light tanks had the same results. 'The tanks are serving nothing; we are wearing out our material and killing our crews for nothing . . . it is pointless to continue like this.' Captain Maitre, commander of AS340 had such difficulties with the Americans that he reported; 'I do not know what more I can say or do'. Only US 4 Infantry avoided this opprobrium; US Lieutenant Harris was told by AS officers (from 15 BCL) that this regiment was the equal to a French infantry regiment.

In fact, all of the reports from the AS units involved in the Argonne operations were critical of the Americans. The commander of 14 BCL, *Chef de bataillon* Guillo, reported that the American infantry did not always follow the French tanks and when they did, they always abandoned captured positions the moment they came under bombardment. 'In fact, the personnel are completely appalled by working with the Americans', said Guillo.

17 BCL had similar problems; the American organisation, or rather lack of it, had caused serious difficulties for the tank battalion's officers. For example, before the battalion's engagement on 4 October against the Bois de la Mornie and the Bois du Chene Sec, it proved impossible to establish any liaison with the US artillery, which therefore gave the tanks no supporting fire. One of the US regiments was relieved overnight just prior to the attack by another regiment that, to the surprise of the AS officers, failed to get into position on time. The attack started at 05.21 and the French tanks were lucky that a thick mist had descended across the battlefield as there was no US artillery support, specifically smoke and gas, to cover the tanks' advance. However, the US infantry never caught up with the tanks and they were forced to return to the Allied lines. Another attack at 16.00 unfolded in much the same manner; the tanks advanced but the US infantry did not follow them and the tanks were forced to retire. The attack was mounted yet again the following day but with greater success as the US infantry actually followed the tanks and occupied all of their objectives. However, the lack of both infantry and artillery support left the French tanks very exposed on many occasions; three Renaults were destroyed by one German field gun and all the tanks engaged had been subjected to heavy German anti-tank rifle fire, which seems to have been more effective in this area than it was in French IV Armée's zone (as discussed in the following chapter).

There had been a variety of difficulties encountered by Groupement XI. Herlaut reported that the US divisional command-posts had been moved forward with 'extraordinary rapidity', which usually left their telephone communications entirely out of action. This resulted in there being no communications between the division and its constituent parts, in particular seriously affecting infantry-artillery liaison. For this reason, Groupement XI had to use runners and pigeons (which worked 'perfectly') to keep in touch with the infantry commanders. Herlaut believed that the serious traffic jams that his unit had encountered in the operation, some of which had lasted forty-eight hours, were the result of poor US organisation and these had made any motorised liaison impossible.

Despite the general French exasperation with the Americans, the latter were very impressed by the AS units that they had fought with. The commander of the US Tank Corps, Brigadier General Rockenbach, wrote to Chanoine on 2 October 1918:

> Having fought your groupement to its mechanical exhaustion it becomes necessary to relieve it from duty with 1st American Army and return it to its depot for repairs . . . I desire to record with great satisfaction the efficient and brilliant service that has been rendered us by you and your command in the St Mihiel salient and the Aire. It will always be a matter of great satisfaction to myself and the others of the American Tank Corps to have you and your command with us in our first encounter with the common enemy. You and your command have set us an example that will always be inspiring and which your country and army may well be proud of.

Major General C. S. Farnsworth (commander of US 37 Division) wrote to Estienne on 30 Sept to commend the commander of 13 BCL, *Commandant* Duclos, and his company commanders. His division, Farnsworth said, regretted the loss of Lieutenant Maurel's section and referred to the 'splendid conduct' of Lieutenant Franchomme who had been wounded in combat. The US commander of US 5 Corps, Major General George Cameron, wrote to Mare to express his satisfaction with the French tank units, saying that he wanted to express his appreciation of the 'excellent service' from the AS and asked Mare to pass this message on to his officers and men.

There had been technical problems as well, with the St Chamonds being particularly hard worked. Groupement XI had left Martigny camp in early September with thirty tanks and six *chars-caissons*. By the time the tanks were engaged at Thiaucourt and Montfaucon, they had travelled more than twenty kilometres on their tracks in very bad weather. This had caused numerous breakdowns and SRR105 made repairs on twenty-eight tanks but the availability of spare parts was a problem. The most common problems were throwing tracks on the difficult terrain, some structural problems with the front of the tank, along with various other engine and electrical issues.

The AS was to fight one more minor action with the American army on 16 October, with AS350 (17 BCL) participating in an attack on the Bois de Haumont, south of Damvillers. Fifteen Renaults got into action with US 104 Infantry, two tanks being lost, with six killed and thirty-eight wounded. From this point on, the US Tank Corps would supply the American armies with their tank support, the AS moving its attention back to the final operations of the French army on the Western Front.

Chapter 9

Fourth Champagne –
The Battle of Somme-Py,
28 September–3 October 1918

The Battle of Soissons had proved to the French army that tanks could be used as a substitute for an artillery preparation in semi-mobile warfare but it remained to be seen if this approach would work in an attack on strongly fortified positions. The Battle of Somme-Py, part of the Allied battle for Champagne in the autumn of 1918, thus provides an interesting case-study to examine the effectiveness of the AS in rather more challenging conditions than had been encountered previously that year, in particular as the area's fortified positions had been consistently upgraded since 1916. As we saw in the previous chapter, Foch had set in motion a widespread offensive across the Western Front that involved US 1 Army working in conjunction with French IV Armée, based in the Champagne area. US 1 Army was advancing across the Meuse-Argonne front, supported on its left by IV Armée. We have seen how *opération A* and *B* unfolded and now we will look at IV Armée's *opération C*.

Planning for Fourth Champagne
Although IV Armée was only attacking across part of its front, it was nonetheless heavily reinforced, particularly in relation to artillery; in addition to its already formidable organic artillery, thirty *groupes* of field artillery, forty-five *groupes* of heavy artillery and ninety-one ALGP guns were moved into its area from 8 September. It was determined by GQG that IV Armée was to have five corps, plus another eight divisions, available for the operation, as well as a large number of light and medium tanks; seven battalions of Renaults and six mixed *groupes*, comprising of Renaults and Schneiders. Maistre at GAC did not believe that IV Armée had enough artillery and pestered Pétain for more but the

latter initially refused to further increase the artillery allocation, although he agreed to slightly augment it just prior to the operation. Inevitably, the number of tanks initially attached to IV Armée were reduced because of delays in reconstituting the AS units. In the end, IV Armée received five Renault battalions and three Schneider *groupes* for *opération C*, totalling thirty Schneiders and 326 Renaults. Transportation was also increased within IV Armée's transportation assets were also enhanced; *Service Automobile* Groupements XI and XII, both with around 360 lorries, were in the army's rear area by 23 September, as well as a further 100 lorries from the cavalry.

General Henri Gouraud (commander, IV Armée) issued his orders for the operation on 19 September. IV Armée was operating in conjunction with US 1 Army between Sainte-Marie, Py and Fontaine-en-Dormois and the operation would begin with a strong attack in a general northern direction. The operation was to be in two phases; a *manoeuvre de rupture*, followed by a *manoeuvre d'exploitation*, each of these phases having a number of sub-phases of its own, illustrating how complex planning had become by this stage of the war. The *manoeuvre de rupture* was the fight through the first German positions, setting off in the early morning after an overnight artillery preparation. The aim was initially to push the infantry through to the limit of the French field artillery's range, then use the tanks to continue the advance while the artillery was limbered up and moved forwards, along with supplies. The *manoeuvre d'exploitation* would take place the following day and would consist of a series of attacks up to the ridges behind Somme-Py. This phase would be made in conjunction with US 1 Army on the right and French V Armée on the left. Four French corps (11, 21, 2 and 9) would break into the first German position; all the corps had four divisions, except 9 CA which had three. The attack would be supported on the flanks by 14 and 38 CA. Exploitation would be then undertaken by 38 and 9 CA on the right of IV Armée, supported by two fresh divisions from the army reserve.

IV Armée's artillery was told that it was to be used in a 'new mode', which would 'rupture' the heavily-fortified front. This consisted of moving to the battle-zone a large quantity of artillery in secret, using a reduced preparation, 'rigorous' protection of this artillery by numerous heavy and super-heavy artillery batteries for counter-battery fire and an immediate advance by horse-drawn batteries to exploit the infantry's success.

The terrain in Champagne and the German defences

The zone that 167 DI (the division on the left of 21 CA) was fighting in was typical of this operation and will be used here to illustrate the strength of the German defences and the difficulties of the terrain. In the main combat zone, the defences comprised of two lines of double trenches, the second of which was placed on the reverse-slope of a crest. This trench line, the Wiesbaden trench line, was at the very limit of the French field artillery's range and was furnished with good communication trenches and strong shelters. The trenches were all covered by an extensive network of barbed wire, with deep shelters in the trenches and concrete emplacements for the machine guns and observation posts. The French would be attacking towards Somme-Py across an area covered in small woods, with successive undulations and crossed by the Somme-Py to Manre railway line. The German second position was on a dominating crest north of Somme-Py (Blanc Mont) and similar in strength to the first position, comprising of several successive trench lines, again wire and concrete fortifications. The ground became very difficult after the second German position; it was heavily wooded with a series of deep ravines, the two principal ridges being held in strength by the Germans. Further north, the Orfeuil-Médéah ridge was fortified by two trench lines that were awkward to attack, due to the numerous woods and the lie of the ground. The Germans had also brought numerous reinforcements into the area as well as additional equipment, including machine guns, mines, artillery and a great number of anti-tank rifles.

Preparations for the tank attack

Gouraud issued an instruction to his senior commanders on the employment of tanks in the coming battle. The use of tanks in an action to rupture a long-established fortified front was, he said, a 'delicate operation', requiring 'deep study and minute preparation' at all levels of command. The state of the ground from the French lines to the former German front lines, the latter now behind the German first position, was such that the tanks could only enter the battle after these had been taken by the Allied infantry. These positions marked the limit of the French field artillery's range and the tanks would advance in support of the infantry, while the mobile artillery units moved forward. If the tanks were able to help the infantry advance far enough, then the artillery could be moved in one 'very large' bound. However, the tanks were not guaranteed to cross the 'overturned' zone in good time and possibly not at all, therefore it would not be possible to fix exactly which units would receive tank support and when. At divisional level and above, commanders were told to plan so that they could use the tanks at the most opportune moments as these revealed themselves. The tanks could not be used until after the German first position was taken, unless specifically authorised by Gouraud. He pointed out that it was 'in everyone's interest' for the tanks to make an easy crossing of the battle zone. This needed a series of actions to be taken; the camouflaged departure positions were to be as far in advance as possible, so that the tanks could follow the infantry closely. The ground needed to be prepared for the tanks behind the French lines during the night preceding the attack and a route through the German lines was to be planned in detail for each section or battery, ensuring that the minimum number of trenches were to be crossed. The tanks were to advance by bounds from cover to cover, each bound only to be made when the ground had been prepared. Work would commence on enemy trenches the moment they were captured by the first elements of the infantry and the commanders were to make sure there was sufficient equipment and men for this task. Work crews were to be taken from the second-line divisions, who would go into action with the tanks. Men from 262 RI would accompany the individual tanks during combat and were only to be used for that purpose; they would be reinforced with some work crews from the first-line divisions. The tanks were to have priority on all tracks, even those not made for them, such as the artillery re-supply routes. The infantry battalion commanders were instructed to make a 'systematic' assault plan for each centre of resistance in their zone, which would then be given to the AS section or battery commanders when and if they were attached to the battalion. In 'combat of this genre' the tanks had to precede the infantry, although the latter were instructed that they should plan as though there would be no tank support. In line with the *Instruction* of 14 July 1918 and the GAN *Note* of 9 September, the dangers from enemy artillery were emphasised and it recommended that areas where anti-tank guns might be situated, such as the edges of woods and villages, should be shelled continuously as the tanks approached them. In relation to all other matters to do with the tanks, such as liaisons, Gouraud referred infantry commanders to the 9 September *Note*. His note makes clear that Gouraud understood how the tank regulations were supposed to be implemented, although this understanding did not extend to all his subordinate commanders, as was to become apparent.

General planning for the Champagne operation

The AS was still reconstituting its units after the heavy fighting in July and August and elements from 501, 503, 504 and 506 RAS were brought in to support IV Armée, under the command of Colonel Chédeville (commander, 2 AS Brigade). The distribution of the tanks was weighted according to the tasks of the individual corps and the practicality of the ground in the corps' zone. 21 CA had the principal role in the operation, including an assault on the important defences in front of Somme-Py, and it was thus given two Schneider *groupes* from Groupement I and two battalions of light tanks (2 and 3 BCL), 180 tanks in all. This corps was flanked by 11 and 2 CA, which, as they were advancing over more difficult terrain, were given fewer tanks than 21 CA. From 30 September, 18 BCL would become available and act as the army tank reserve.

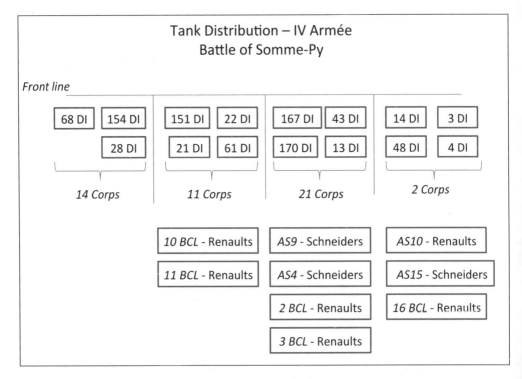

As the important fighting occurred mainly in the zone of 21 CA, we will look at this in more detail than the actions on other parts of the front. 21 CA, with 2 CA on the right and 11 CA on the left, was attacking towards Orfeuil in two phases; the first was an advance up to the German artillery line, the second an advance through the rear German lines. The infantry advance of the second phase would be supported by 'all the artillery that can be moved forward' and, 'when needed', the AS. The corps would be attacking in a 'square' formation; that is two divisions in the first line and two behind them. The first line of 21 CA had 167 DI on the left and 43 DI on the right, with 170 DI and 13 DI in the second line. The first-line divisions were moved into position two nights prior to the operation, while the second-line divisions were only moved on the night prior to the attack. The first-line infantry was advancing behind a creeping barrage and would capture the main resistance points, the minor ones being left to second-line units. The infantry were instructed that it was imperative not to lose contact with the enemy and that they were not to wait for artillery or tank support if they encountered centres of serious German resistance. Mixed groups of infantry and machine guns, half a company of the former and two sections of the latter, were formed to maintain contact between the front and rear divisions.

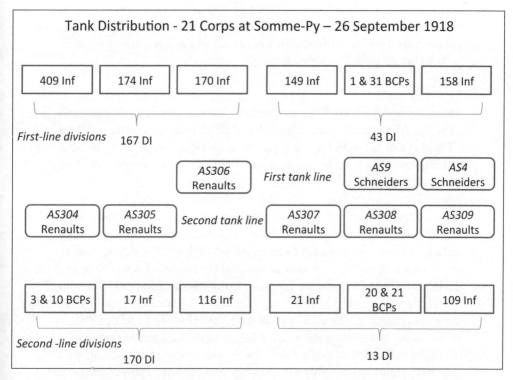

There was to be a nine-hour artillery preparation, with the priority targets being enemy observation posts and known artillery batteries. As it was doubtful that such a comparatively short artillery preparation would destroy all the German defensive positions, 21 CA was to concentrate its artillery fire on making a number of corridors through the enemy lines. These corridors would be masked by smoke barrages on their flanks, which would also help the tanks. Artillery sections were to follow closely the infantry of the first line, in order to give them direct fire support.

Once the first objectives had been taken, the second phase would commence. Only the general outline of this phase was planned by IV Armée's staff, it being left to the divisional commanders to devise their own plans after the capture of the first objectives. In principle, the second-line units were not to be engaged until the commanders of the first-line divisions decided that their units were no longer able to continue. Once the second phase began, all the units within a division's zone would come under the direct orders of the divisional commander, who would be in command of how the operation would then unfold. It was thus not possible to set an hour at which the first-line divisions would be passed by those following them and the support units (tanks, aviation etc.) had to be prepared to transfer to the new front-line units without waiting for further orders.

21 CA's front

The commander of 501 RAS, Lieutenant Colonel Velpry, took command of all the AS units attached to 21 CA and he arrived at IV Armée HQ on 17 September to begin planning for the forthcoming operation, his staff arriving two days later. In conjunction with the corps commander, Velpry devised the following plan. As per the instructions from IV Armée, the state of the ground meant that the tanks were in principle not to be engaged until the second phase, although the tanks were permitted to help the infantry pass through the forward defences along the Somme-Py railway, as this was expected to be a difficult fight. The AS units were to begin their employment as soon as the infantry reached the line Clairière du Talon to Bois de Corbeau, the tanks being instructed to catch up with the infantry as quickly as possible. AS9 and 4 (Schneiders) and 3 BCL were operating with the divisions on the right, 43 DI and 13 DI, 3 BCL's commander being stationed with 43 DI's commander and taking charge of all the tank units in this sector. The Schneiders were advancing with the first infantry line, with 3 BCL only coming into action when the medium tanks were spent. 2 BCL was on the left with 167 DI and 170 DI, with one company forward in support of 167 DI, the other two companies not to be engaged until the second phase of the operation. The tanks were thus to be in two lines. The first line had the Schneider *groupes* on the right with 43 DI and AS306 on the left with 167 DI. The second line had 3 BCL on the right in front of 13 DI, two companies of 2 BCL on the left with 170 DI. The first line of tanks was advancing behind the infantry but had to be close enough to intervene in combat immediately. The approach march was to be made in bounds from cover to cover, the bounds reducing as the tanks approached the first line of French infantry. The tanks' movement would be conducted with 300 metres between sections or batteries and twenty-five metres between tanks in these units. The battalion and *groupe* commanders were reminded to 'avoid in all circumstances' allowing their tanks to be stationary, unless they were under cover and hidden from ground and air observation, these plans being in accordance with the tank regulations.

Within the divisional zones, the infantry division commanders decided on the distribution of the tanks but they were instructed not to distribute the tanks uniformly across their zone, being told that the tanks must be reserved for assaults on those important points of German resistance that the operation required to be taken. As the tanks were coming into action in the second phase of the operation, it was thus not possible to determine exactly in advance which infantry regiments or battalions would receive tanks and the tank commanders were ordered to liaise and attack with whatever infantry they found themselves with at this moment. Theoretically, this was a sensible arrangement but it was to prove very difficult to implement effectively in practice.

Velpry took great care in the planning of the passages that the tanks would require to move through the battlefield. Six carefully-chosen paths (three for each first-line division) were planned for the tanks and those within the French lines were examined in secrecy by the AS company and *groupe* commanders. The proposed tank routes in the German lines were intently studied on maps and with photographs. An AS officer from each *groupe* or company was tasked with organising the work on the paths during combat and was to have a company of workers available to make trench crossings for the tanks. The forward AS officer had six liaison agents and an infantry detail to help monitor the work crews. This AS officer and his troops were to follow the first-line of infantry as closely as possible, preparing the way for the tanks. Once this work was complete, he would signal and then guide the tanks forward.

As per the tank regulations, considerable effort was made to ensure adequate communications between the tank units; there were couriers and cyclists to liaise between the *groupement* and the *groupes*, couriers for *groupe* to battery communications, with motorcycles, cars and telephone lines for communications between the *groupements* and the rear area. The *groupement* commander was to be stationed with the ID commander, with the *groupe* commanders being stationed with their respective infantry regimental commanders.

There was also specific advice given to individual AS units. For example, the crews of Groupement I were reminded that all fire should only commence under the orders of the tank commanders and that they should never fire near the French infantry. They were reminded of the usefulness of 'neutralisation fire' during combat, a new technique that was to prove to be decisive in protecting the tanks during their advance. AS battery and section commanders were instructed to remind the infantry machine-gun batteries that they should concentrate their fire on any anti-tank guns or machine guns firing on the tanks and that the French infantry should fire on any Germans who tried to close-assault the tanks.

2 CA's front

On the right of 21 CA, AS10 (Renaults) and AS15 (Schneiders), along with 16 BCL, were attached to 2 CA, under the orders of one of the most experienced AS commanders, *Chef d'escadron* Lefebvre, Groupement III's commander. Lefebvre also had SRR103 and two companies from 262 RI. 2 CA was attacking in a square formation with two divisions in the front line, 14 DI on the left and 3 DI on the right, with 48 DI and 4 DI behind them. After considering the situation, Lefebvre recommended to the commander of 2 CA that AS10 and AS15 should be with the left division, AS346 and 348 with the right one, leaving AS347 as the corps reserve.

The arrangements were rather different in 3 DI's zone as there were no tanks with the leading infantry regiments, 87 and 272 RI, which were advancing 'by infiltration and encirclements', through the heavily overturned terrain. The third infantry regiment, 51 RI, was held as both the ID and divisional reserve, along with AS346 and AS348. As in 21 CA, extensive reconnaissance was undertaken and contacts made with the infantry commanders, down to the battalion level. After examining the available maps, air photos and intelligence on the mines and other defensive positions, Lefebvre decided that the AS needed more infantry support, which came from the second-line divisions. The corps artillery was supplying counter-battery fire to protect the tanks, particularly directed against those known enemy batteries with a field of fire over the tanks' routes. There was also to be a smoke barrage on the enemy observation posts by a reserved howitzer *groupe* within each division, the fire to be directed by aircraft. The artillery plan was well organised; when the tanks' artillery protection came to limber up and move, other batteries would cover for it until it was in its new position. In addition to the normal communications equipment of the divisions, the AS had sixty messenger pigeons (PV), two birds per battery or section.

Planning on 11 CA's front

On the left of 21 CA was 11 CA, with 10 and 11 BCL (504 RAS) under the orders of the commander of 504 RAS, *Commandant* de Forsanz. Like the other corps, 11 CA was attacking in a square formation, leading with 151 DI on the left and 22 DI on the right, 21 DI and 61 DI behind them. The orders given to the tank companies conformed to the employment plan of IV Armée; at H-hour the tanks were to proceed in section columns behind the infantry, until the moment when the tanks reached the line formed by the Rhenans-Heidelberg trenches, where they would deploy into combat formation. They would then attack their first objective, the Manheim and Dusseldorf trenches. In order to maintain sufficient reserves for subsequent operations, only one tank section in each company was to be engaged with each infantry regiment. To assist the tanks crossing the enemy positions, 4 Coy/262 RI and a detachment from 137 RI were distributed between the tank sections, as well as an engineer detachment tasked with discovering any anti-tank mines on the tanks' routes.

Preparatory Moves

The aim of all the tank plans was to bring the tank units in as close as possible to the front, so that the tanks would not need to move much under their own steam prior to combat. 21 CA's tanks assembled on its front without any problems; 2 and 3 BCL left their camp on 20 September, with Groupement I moving out the next day. By 23 September, when SRR106 joined them, the corps' AS units were at their assembly positions. However, both 10 BCL and Groupement III had difficulties moving onto IV Armée's front. The Renaults were moved by lorries without the regulation tank-disembarking ramps, resulting in very slow unloading, it taking nearly two hours to unload each company. The movement of 2 CA's tanks was even more difficult. Groupement III arrived to detrain at Suippes station too late in the evening to disembark and when the station was hit by an artillery bombardment, the trains carrying the tanks being forced to divert to Auve. However, this station was without a suitable platform and unloading was 'laborious'. It was evening before the tanks were all unloaded and they then had to move straight off by road to Croix-en-Champagne. One half of 16 BCL detrained successfully after leaving Mailly-Poivres on 21 September but the other half's train was first seriously delayed and then broke down. There were no ramps to unload the tanks with and one had to be acquired from 2 AS Brigade, the Renaults then having to disembark in daylight. This was extremely dangerous as the train was easily within range of German heavy artillery and the tanks were lucky not to be spotted. The tanks then moved under their own steam to join AS10 and 15 in a ravine near the Grossetti-Laval road. By the night of 25 September, the AS units, with the exception of 16 BCL which was being held in position until just after H-hour, had left their waiting positions and were in the departure positions north of the Romaine road.

The Battle
26 September
The artillery preparation for the offensive started at 23.25 on 25 September, the infantry advance starting at 05.25 the following day. In some places the infantry advanced easily through the initial German positions but in others the advance was more difficult. For example, 22 DI's infantry found itself in a thick mist as it set off and 'several errors of navigation' had to be corrected to avoid mixing up its units. Although the Germans had manned their advance posts, these offered little resistance because, according to prisoners, the French infantry followed the barrage so closely. The division did not meet with serious resistance until around 06.30 and from then on it was engaged in heavy fighting across well-defended ground. However, by the end of the day the division had fought its way to the Darmstadt trenches, capturing over 200 prisoners and destroying 'numerous' machine-gun nests.

On 21 CA's front, the AS units initially advanced behind the infantry as planned but by midday the tanks were all halted waiting for their paths to be completed and the infantry had continued to move forward, having met only weak resistance. The work crews making these paths were unable to continue in their task as they were receiving very accurate German artillery fire being directed by several balloons. The tanks were only able to move forward at 16.00, after French aircraft had destroyed the balloons, with several Schneiders breaking down while they waited. On 167 DI's front, the right-hand regiment (170 RI) had reached all its objectives by 07.30. However, the central regiment (174 RI) moved through the German forward positions easily but then got stuck fighting over the former French GMP trenches in the German zone, not reaching its objective until 10.20. The regiment on the left, 409 RI, had even harder fighting and only reached its initial objectives at around midday. It was then ordered to advance on its second objective but there was sufficient residual German resistance to make this difficult; the leading elements of the division only occupying the Butte de Souain at 16.00.

On 11 CA's front, the Renaults of 10 BCL were obliged to intervene almost immediately to help the French infantry take the first German lines, as the latter were subject to heavy machine-gun fire from these positions. The tanks successfully eliminated the machine guns and the infantry continued their advance to the line formed by the Cattaro and Schleswig trenches. 11 BCL saw barely any combat, although three of its accompanying infantrymen were the only AS casualties for the day.

On the right of 2 CA's front, AS346 and AS348, with 3 DI, found the going slow due to the state of the ground and the infantry's slow advance. By the evening, the infantry were close to the Dormoise line, with the tanks just behind them. On the left of the corps, AS15 crossed the battlefield reasonably easily, arriving at the Anglais trench around 16.00. There was no suitable passage for the tanks over the Dormoise river, so the rest of the day was taken up trying to find a passage to the west of the river. AS10 advanced without much difficulty, arriving around midday at the woods just north of the Moskova trench. Although an infantry and tank attack was planned on the Kronprinz trench, by the time the attack was organised night had fallen and it was sensibly called off.

27 September

It started to rain on 27 September, making operations even more difficult by turning the ground into a quagmire. It rained continuously for the next two days, ruining the half-prepared tank passages and making resupply additionally difficult.

21 CA's AS units had crossed the damaged zone during the night and made contact with the infantry regiments they were attached to. AS4 was attached to 158 RI and AS309 was held ready to support it immediately and, if necessary, continue the advance. In 1 and 31 BCPs' zone, AS9 was to go into action concurrently with AS308 as the

chasseurs' front was wider enough to require this. The French infantry advanced at daybreak but were quickly halted by the strength of the German resistance, particularly from the Wurtzbourg trench lines. The AS units only caught up with the infantry at 07.00, due to difficulties crossing the battlefield, and the attack resumed an hour later. The tanks broke the German resistance and the French infantry were able take possession of the heights of La Pince. Three companies of 3 BCL then had a tough struggle fighting off successive German counter-attacks and covering their infantry while they got in position.

On the corps' left flank, the infantry was halted at 09.00 in front of the Wiesbaden trenches. An hour later, a section from AS305 was ordered to support 174 RI, the tanks' movements initially being covered by fog. This extemporised mission quickly ran into difficulties when the fog lifted; the tanks were fired on by German artillery and two were knocked out and two ditched while trying avoid the fire. 21 CA staff saw that these piecemeal attacks were not going to succeed and gave instructions that the tanks were not to be used the next day, unless at company strength and with available artillery support. Velpry instructed his subordinates that they were not to be engaged in isolated sections on the following day and that they should not hesitate to remind the infantry commanders of this. The AS commanders were also told to insist on dedicated assistance from the French machine-gun units, clearly implying that this had been lacking.

On 2 CA's front, two tank companies were attached to 3 DI and these had to cross the Dormoise River over bridges prepared during the night. One company crossed without incident but when the other company tried to cross over the bridge, it collapsed. A delay ensued but the rest of the tanks managed to cross the Dormoise and, by midday, the companies were in position, each with nineteen working tanks. An hour later, the colonel of 51 RI asked the tanks to support an attack on the Bois de Tourterelle and two tank sections were attached to the infantry. The tanks came under artillery fire almost immediately they set off and all but one broke down or ditched as they tried to race through this hostile fire, manoeuvring made difficult by the quantity of smoke on the battlefield. In the afternoon, AS348 was ordered by one of 51 RI's battalion commanders to support an advance on Manre. The commander of AS348 made it clear that the tanks could not get into position on time, causing the attack to be postponed for thirty minutes. However, forty-five minutes later, the foremost AS section was only just arriving at the departure position. Fortuitously, this did not matter as Manre had just been flanked by another French division, resulting in the attack being cancelled and AS348 retiring for the night. The medium tanks only got two sections of eight tanks from AS10 into combat but half of these quickly broke down. The four working tanks were a success in forcing the Germans to retreat but the French infantry did not follow and no ground was gained. During the afternoon, AS10 got three sections into combat, although two sections had only four tanks between them, but once again the tanks' gains were lost when the French infantry failed to follow up.

On 11 CA's front, 22 DI and 151 DI continued their advance, trying to reach the Sainte-Marie-à-Py to Somme-Py road, with support from 21 DI and 61 DI. The infantry officers were reminded that the tank regulations required that the tanks were not used in 'small fractions' or on heavily-damaged ground. The infantry advance resumed at 05.15 but the fighting quickly bogged down and the infantry were unable to make much progress, despite help from the Renaults. For example, AS331 and AS333 were used to support infantry attacks with only two sections, despite which the tanks were successful, capturing a number of prisoners, although both companies lost seven tanks.

28 September
The following day, the struggle continued. The experience of 21 CA's tanks can illustrate the varied fortunes of the AS units that day. On the left flank of the corps, infantry from 167 DI set off at 05.15 from the Wiesbaden trench to attack the Prussiens and Essen trenches, along with three companies from 2 BCL. As the tanks were able to advance behind a thick smoke barrage, which successfully blinded the German observation posts and masked the flanks of the tank units, the infantry were able to quickly take their objectives, capturing over 100 prisoners. By 10.00, the leading regiment of the division (409 RI) had reached the Prussiens and Mecklenbourg trenches, with the help of the tanks. Velpry reported that the operation was a complete success, noting that this was because all of 2 BCL had been used in one attack that was prepared in accordance with the tank regulations.

In contrast, on the right flank of 21 CA, only two companies from 3 BCL were used, supporting 149 RI and 1 BCP in an attack starting at 07.00. German resistance was strong, with the woods used as cover for a large number of anti-tank rifles and field gun batteries. Most of the French infantry was very tired after two days of combat, so progress was slow, which meant that the combat was very onerous on the AS; the tank companies were engaged for long periods and losses were heavy despite, said Velpry, 'the tenacity and valour of their crews'. During the afternoon, the Schneider *groupes* managed to cobble together two batteries, which helped the infantry advance north of the Nassau trench and the edges of the Bois de l'Araignée.

On 2 CA and 11 CA's fronts, there were no AS battalion-scale attacks and the tanks were engaged section by section throughout the day. For example, only one tank section was available from AS346 on 2 CA's front and it was used to support an infantry battalion attack. The tanks successfully crossed the infantry line and went into battle formation, destroying several machine-gun positions, forcing the Germans to retreat. All the tanks but one were immobilised during the fighting and only a small element of infantry had followed them. By the time the last tank was hit and immobilised, it was 1,200 metres forward of the infantry. On 11 CA's front, 10 BCL had a similarly mixed day. AS330 was only given orders to attack half an hour before the start and the tanks arrived after the French barrage had moved past the first German observation posts. The tank attack was thus too dangerous and it was called off, the company taking no further part in the day's action. AS329 was tasked with supporting an infantry attack across the Py river but the tanks got stuck crossing the river and within twenty minutes the majority of the tanks were out of action. A similar attack by AS328 got several tanks successfully across the Py but the heavy machine-gun fire prevented the infantry from joining them, forcing the tanks to retire.

29 September

September 29th saw the rear infantry divisions relieve the now tired forward divisions of IV Armée. In 2 CA, only AS347 was combat-ready and sections from this company were used individually throughout the day in piecemeal attacks, giving unsurprisingly mixed results. 2 CA's AS units were ordered to move into army reserve during the night of 29 September. In four days of combat, the AS in 2 CA had lost sixty-four officers and men, although only eight were killed. Four Renaults and two Schneiders had been destroyed, with a further twenty-three Renaults and three Schneiders damaged.

On 21 CA's front, the Renault companies supported a series of battalion-sized attacks, which were of only limited success largely due to increased German resistance. The tank units with 21 CA were retired that evening to IV Armée's reserve. Casualties had been heavy during this operation; 3 BCL lost eight of its nine section commanders, along with two junior officers, fourteen tank commanders and twenty drivers, requiring replacements to be rushed in from Groupement I.

On the front of 11 CA, 10 BCL supported an attack by 21 DI, which had replaced 151 DI. This attack was as unsuccessful for the tanks as it was for the infantry; two entire tank sections were annihilated by anti-tank guns and the weight of German machine-gun fire was such that the infantry could not take the village of Sainte-Marie. From 26 to 29 September, 10 BCL had lost fifteen Renaults, all totally destroyed, with four others damaged and fifty men killed, wounded or missing. 16 BCL was in no state to field any tanks at all on 29 September and the whole day was taken up with repairs and essential maintenance. Sixteen of its tanks were out of action due to combat, of which four were completely destroyed and five seriously damaged, although only one man had been killed in the battalion and twenty men wounded.

A brief pause in the battle, 1–2 October
October 1st and 2nd were, by necessity, occupied in reconstituting the very battered tank units. Both AS personnel and material had been sorely tested, although this was largely due to their intensive employment; the tanks had been in action for four days without repairs or maintenance. Personnel and material were quickly shifted around the tank units to bring some of them up to combat strength, priority being given to the Renault units. On 1 October, 16 and 18 BCL were moved to 21 CA's AS command.

The battle resumes, 3 October 1918
On 3 October, 11 and 21 CA, which had spent the previous day reorganising, resumed their attacks. 21 CA now had three relatively fresh divisions; the objective being the crest formed from Blanc Mont to Ferme Médéah to Orfeuil. As the primary effort was to be on 21 CA front, it received the majority of the tanks; 2, 3, 16 and 18 BCLs. 11 CA was covering the left flank of 21 CA, supported by a *bataillon de marche* from 10 and 11 BCL, attached to the division on the right of the corps.

On 21 CA's front, *Commandant* Fischbach, commander of 3 BCL, was only told at 16.00 on 2 October that his unit would be supporting US 2 Division the following day and his battalion officers were thus forced to make a general reconnaissance of the probable operation areas. The battalion had twenty-six tanks available, with five coming in from AS10. The mission was somewhat disorganised, like so many in the days after the initial attack. It proved impossible for the AS officers to liaise with the US officers during the night because there were no interpreters available. In addition, communication within the US division was very disorganised. On the plus side, the smoke element of the US barrage was very effective, smoke shells comprising 20 per cent of those fired. The tanks largely followed the US infantry during the operation, seeing little combat, except for two sections from AS309 that helped the Americans attack Ferme Médéah, capturing 'a good number' of prisoners. However, the tank companies had taken heavy losses from the German artillery; by nightfall, twenty-five tanks were out of action (although only five were beyond repair) and two men had been killed, with eighteen wounded. It is an indication of how little fighting the tanks did that the entire battalion only fired 100 shells.

2 BCL was attached on 2 October to US 4 Marine Brigade in order to execute an operation the following day. It was intended to have two Renault companies (with three sections each) in action but one section was so delayed that it arrived too late to join the leading tank company, forcing it to join the support company. This left two tank sections with the leading infantry battalion, whereas the support battalion had four. Unlike 3 BCL, 2 BCL's officers were able to meet with the American officers from the brigade commander to the battalion commanders, so at least a minimum level of liaison was achieved before combat. The infantry and the leading tank company started the advance at 05.45, arriving without any difficulties at the objective. The infantry commander then released one tank section but kept the other. This was fortunate as a strong German counter-attack took place at 14.00 that was seen off by the infantry with help from the tanks. The supporting tank company got its four sections over the Py without difficulty, covered by the heavy smoke barrage. All four tank sections went into action, destroying numerous machine guns and three anti-tank guns, one of the latter being a new 57mm model. 2 BCL had only five tanks damaged, all easily repaired, and the personnel losses were equally light; with only two fatalities. An indication of the intensity of the fighting is that the two tank companies fired over 900 shells during the day.

On 11 CA's front, 10 BCL, with four sections, joined 21 DI in an attack on German positions north of the Py, after a five-minute artillery preparation. One company failed to get over the Py, as its crossing had not been completed, but the other crossed the river and helped the infantry take their objectives. By 13.00, the French infantry were installed in their new positions and the tanks retired. Losses had been relatively light; one man killed and eighteen wounded, with only two tanks, hit by shells, left on the battlefield. 11 BCL attached a three-section *compagnie de marche* to 137 RI. As with 10 BCL, the tanks found that their planned bridge over the Py was not completed and it took them some time to find a way across. There was little resistance as they attacked the Elbe trench but the French infantry failed to follow them and the tanks were forced to retire due to intensified German artillery fire. The weak German resistance can be gauged by the fact that 11 BCL only had two men wounded, with no tanks lost on 3 October.

Final Tank Operations in Champagne

One more tank operation would take place in the Champagne region in October 1918. 3 BCL, with thirty tanks, was attached to US 71 Brigade and moved into a waiting position near the Bois de Vipère on 6 October. 3 BCL had only one of its original company commanders and two section chiefs left, the replacement officers were only transferred into the battalion over the previous three days, with barely enough time to contact their troops and check their tanks. Reconnaissance of the front was made the following day but the AS officers could not make effective liaison within US 71 Brigade, largely because the US divisional commander and the brigade commanders were not in contact with a number of their battalion commanders, the whereabouts of whom were unknown. This was the first time in combat for this US brigade and it had received no training at all in relation to tanks. Almost as soon as the tanks began their advance, they were subjected to heavy artillery fire, the Germans being alerted by the noise of the tanks when they moved into position. This fire was so intense that both the tanks and the US infantry became completely disoriented, with one tank section coming under fire from some confused US troops, killing the AS liaison officer. The artillery fire resulted in four out of the six section commanders being rendered *hors de combat*, along with numerous drivers and tank commanders, which meant that it was necessary to reform the companies before any further action could be taken. AS Captain Clermont reorganised the tank sections into a *compagnie de marche* but the US infantry commander, Colonel Jackson, had decided not to continue his advance. However, Jackson was so concerned about his casualties that he kept the tanks on station with him for the rest of the day, to guard against counter-attacks. In his report, Fischbach was highly critical of Jackson for leaving the tanks in an 'exposed position' for nearly nine hours. They were fortunate that day to avoid heavy casualties; only four tanks were completely destroyed and another twelve were damaged.

Nineteen men had been wounded, including five officers, notably all of them had been hit while outside their tanks. It is indicative of the engagement that no shells or bullets were fired by the tanks that day.

On 11 CA's front, 10 BCL and 11 BCL each formed a *compagnie de marche* to support 7 DI. The operation began inauspiciously as one infantry regiment failed to get to its jump-off position in time, forcing its tank section to set off with no infantry support. The fighting seesawed across the ground as several German counter-attacks pushed the French infantry back but by the evening the French had made some progress. Fighting had been relatively light; the two tank battalions had one killed and six wounded, with six tanks breaking down while crossing the Arnes River. Only two tanks were left on the battlefield, being unrecoverable, and *Commandant* Darnay (commander of 10 BCL) considered that the operation had been a 'very great success', marred only by the lack of progress of the adjoining infantry divisions. The AS units remaining with IV Armée on the evening of 8 October were retired to the general reserve over the following days and took no further part in the Champagne operations.

By 4 October, Foch had become very impatient with Gouraud and IV Armée's advance; he wrote to Pétain to complain that the previous day's fighting had seen a 'battle that was not commanded, a battle that was not pushed . . . and, it follows, a battle where there was no exploitation of the results obtained'. Gouraud told Clemenceau that he had been forced to slow down his advance after the initial success because the US Army was unable to keep pace with IV Armée and he did not want to leave himself with an uncovered right flank. This was not an unreasonable position for Gouraud to take, as the Americans were still having considerable difficulties with their logistical arrangements. For example, when Clemenceau and his military advisor General Mordacq visited Montfaucon, on 29 September, they were forced to abandon their vehicle because of the chaos in the US rear area. Mordacq later wrote that he had never seen such a 'spectacle' in the entire war. However, Gouraud admitted to US General John Lejeune, commander of US 2 Division, that the French troops were 'worn out' by 1 October, when he asked Lejeune for the use of his division for an attack on Blanc Mont. Certainly, the experience of the AS units shows that after four days of fighting, effective operations required fresh, or at least rested, infantry. Gouraud had planned the offensive very carefully and his failure to repeat the gains made on the first day of the offensive is indicative of the wider difficulties of maintaining momentum in offensive operations on the Western Front, rather than any fault in his planning.

The Results of the Battle

Despite Foch's desire for a higher tempo to the operations and considering the strength of the German defences on the Champagne front, IV Armée's operations had been successful, particularly in relation to wearing down the increasingly exhausted German divisions. For example, by 4 October, the three German divisions that had been engaged on the front of 167 DI were completely worn out and had to retire, with another three German regiments taking serious losses. 176 DI captured thirty-two German officers and 1,684 men, along with forty-seven guns, fifteen minenwerfer, more than 300 machine guns, seven anti-tank rifles, and various munitions and other supply dumps. The division's casualties for the period were fifty-two officers and 1,362 men, of whom 250 had been killed. On 11 CA front, 22 DI had advanced nearly seven kilometres, capturing over 500 prisoners from four German divisions, along with ten field guns and 'numerous' machine guns. Over three days of hard fighting, 22 DI lost fifty-five officers (including three battalion commanders) and 1,548 men. *Commandant* Darnay praised the German defenders for their slow and methodical retreat that had been made with machine guns and anti-tank pieces crewed by troops of the 'first order'. There were few prisoners taken and not many bodies left on the battlefield; Darnay could not but admire the tenacity of the defenders in these 'formidable positions'. The area where the Champagne operations took place was also particularly difficult to assault, as it was so heavily fortified. As Gouraud had pointed out to Pétain in September; 'this region is perhaps the most solidly organised of all the fronts'.

Results for the AS

In relation to the AS, the Champagne operations had been relatively successful, particularly as they had taken place against a well-entrenched enemy. The Germans had received plenty of warning about a possible tank attack and had plenty of time to prepare for it. For example, the area around Tahure was typically well provided with anti-tank defences; isolated field guns, minefields, traps and anti-tank rifles. It seems that it was only the rapid advance of the French infantry that prevented most of these isolated anti-tank guns from coming into action. Not all the defences were a problem; while it had not been possible to identify many of the tank traps and mines in advance, they were 'easily identified' on the ground and avoided, unlike in the US army's sector where mines were more than a nuisance for the tanks. Lefebvre believed that the German anti-tank rifles 'were always a threat' and had caused several losses. In some cases, the Renaults' armour had been penetrated by anti-tank rifle fire, causing death or serious injury. As so many of these had been found on the battlefield, he believed the AS should take this weapon 'very seriously'. However, Forsanz (commander of 504 RAS) disagreed with Lefebvre, believing that the anti-tank rifles were relatively ineffective, there only being two Renaults under his command penetrated by anti-tank bullets. Although in one case this had killed the tank commander, Forsanz believed that this was an 'unusual accident'. French experiments with captured anti-tank rifles demonstrated their 13mm cartridges could easily penetrate the Renault's armour at 200 metres or less and could often penetrate at up to 250 metres, unless they hit the sloped front armour around the driver and ricocheted. However, the general unwieldiness of this huge weapon, which weighed nearly 18 kilograms, meant that its theoretical effectiveness against the light tanks was never fully realised by the Germans. Field guns, both batteries and single guns in forward positions, continued to be the main danger to the tanks. Forty-one Schneiders and 631 Renaults were engaged in the Champagne operations, of which five Schneiders (12.1 per cent) and fifty-two Renaults (8.2 per cent) were seriously damaged. Fifty-eight officers and men had been killed, with 320 wounded, the majority from the Renault units.

Velpry's initial report for RAS 501 emphasised a lesson already noticed from the July battles; that the personnel casualties of the light tank units were much higher than their material losses. After only two or three engagements, the Renault units would not have enough remaining section commanders, tank commanders and drivers to crew the surviving tanks, whereas in the medium tank units the reverse was the case. In anticipation of this problem, cadres were taken from Groupement I and placed with the regiment's light tank battalions, for a three week training period over August and September. This paid off as is illustrated by the experiences of 2 and 3 BCL on 26 September. On 26 September, the two battalions had lost thirteen out of eighteen section commanders and 40 per cent of their drivers. During the same day, all the regiment's Schneiders were rendered *hors de combat*, although the personnel casualties were minimal. Only by moving crews from the Schneiders to the Renaults were the light tank battalions able to go into action on 3 October. That was a hard day for 3 BCL; by evening, the battalion did not have a single original captain, section commander or rear echelon commander uninjured. Only further transfers of crews from Groupement I permitted the two light tank battalions to be reconstituted by 6 October with three companies, of two sections each. From 26 September to 8 October 1918, Groupement I had only lost three killed and fifteen wounded but, by contrast, 2 BCL had lost two killed and forty-two wounded, including seventeen officers. The situation was even worse in 3 BCL, which had twenty-one killed, including five officers, and seventy-five wounded, including twenty-nine of whom were officers. In the light of this, Velpry recommended for the future that each light tank should have two crews, serving alternately in combat.

The AS in Champagne had been operating under the tank *Instruction* of 14 July, Pétain's *Note* on light-tank use, the light-tank regulations and the 9 September *Note*. A number of issues connected with these regulations had been revealed by the fighting in Champagne. A new fire tactic for the tanks had been tried; neutralisation fire, that is firing on areas where machine guns or anti-tank guns might be hidden, such as the edges of villages and woods, without the necessity for a visible target. This was not in line with the tank regulations, which emphasised that a tank should always use aimed fire, although neutralisation fire against visible targets was permitted. (Constantin-Weyer mentions that his Renault section from 19 BCL practised area-fire in training during August 1918, conceding that this was not according to the regulations. However, as he says, most of his section were combat veterans, albeit not in tanks, not 'theoreticians', and thus they trained as they intended to fight.) Velpry considered that this new practice had been a great success; those companies which had practised neutralisation fire during August and September (AS306 and AS309) had significantly lower losses than those that had not. No tanks from these units were hit by anti-tank rifle-fire, despite the considerable number of these weapons found abandoned on the battlefield. The sections had practised making a field of fire; the section commander would open up with his 37mm gun on a point at around 300 metres range and this would then be fired on by the rest of the section. This method was claimed to have eliminated a number of anti-tank minenwerfer. Both Vigneron (commander, 2 BCL) and Fischbach felt that the machine-gun tanks had been more successful at neutralisation fire and that the light tank section should have in future three machine-gun tanks and only two gun tanks, a recommendation supported by 16 BCL's commander. This largely settled a discussion that had been going on within the AS since the summer about the ideal proportion of machine-gun to gun tanks.

There had been considerable argument between the AS officers and many of the infantry commanders at regimental and occasionally battalion level. Some colonels had welcomed their AS advisors but many did not; one colonel claimed to have no room in his command post and put his AS liaison officer with the telephonists, a situation that required the intervention of 10 BCL's commander to rectify. In another example on 28 September, the commander of AS304 made prior contact with the commander of the leading battalion from 409 RI but the latter then proceeded to 'ignore' the AS officer throughout the battle. *Commandant* Laurent (commander of Groupement I) believed that it was always necessary to remind infantry commanders that it was in everyone's interest to allocate to the AS commanders an adequate means of communication, telephone personnel alone being insufficient.

In contradiction to the tank regulations, many infantry officers decided to intervene in the tanks' tactical dispositions, often overruling the relevant AS commander's plans. Laurent argued that it was urgent to remind the infantry commanders that they should be indicating the aim to be achieved but that the AS unit commanders had to decide how this would be undertaken, in line with the tank regulations. Vigneron thought it was necessary to 'insist' to the infantry commanders that the tanks must be used *en masse*. Although all of the tank regulations emphasised the necessity to use the tanks *en masse*, Vigneron's experience was that his subordinate AS commanders, at 'every level', had been forced to resist orders from the infantry commanders who wished to employ the tanks by the section, 'if not individual tanks'. 16 BCL's commander agreed; 'the infantry need to know that a tank section cannot be treated like an infantry section'. These discussions about tactics between the infantry and AS officers had clearly been heated; Vigneron refers to remarks made by the infantry officers that could only be excused by the stress of the situation. Laurent complained that many orders had arrived too late for the AS units to undertake adequate reconnaissance or make even contact with the infantry, once again contrary to the regulations.

Although the regulations insisted that the tanks should be used *en masse* on a wide front, it was generally agreed by the AS officers involved in the Champagne operations that this would not always be possible. Velpry, rather accurately, stated that tank attacks made after the first day of any operation would inevitably be weaker than desirable but this was an 'inevitable obligation' for the AS, as it would be impossible for the tank units to regroup after every two or three hours of combat without seriously damaging the infantry's morale and halting the advance. Angeli (commander, 11 BCL) agreed, although he recommended that the AS units should be held further back, to avoid the infantry calling them forward too soon. Lefebvre, too, criticised the way the tanks had been used by the infantry commanders, the tank attacks being scattered 'not just in space but time too'. In particular, after 27 September the AS attacks had been too hastily mounted, without sufficient reconnaissance or liaisons and without the necessary artillery support, which had caused 'useless losses' and 'mediocre results'. His other recommendation was 'that until the moment where the AS units go to be engaged in combat, they should remain under the direct orders of the divisional commander'. By keeping the AS units to the rear of the infantry, the divisional commander could ensure that the tanks were only engaged at an opportune moment.

The artillery support for the tanks was also subject to criticism and a common complaint was that the smoke element of the barrage was initially good but the artillery crews tended to abandon their smoke shells when the artillery batteries moved forward because the crews did not want to move them instead of HE shells. Once again, the tank regulations were clear but had been largely ignored.

There was a strong call for direct artillery support for the tanks. Velpry argued that in order to be successful in these small-scale attacks, the tank units must be given their own means to fight off German anti-tank batteries, his solution being field artillery accompanying the tanks. Velpry stated that experience showed that this would be effective; on 28 September, a company from 2 BCL had been engaged by two 77mm and two 105mm guns. The artillery liaison officer stationed with the infantry colonel saw this situation and used an abandoned German 77mm gun, with his liaison team as crew, to fire on the Germans and quickly silence the four guns. He said that there was a need to organise permanently a section of accompanying artillery for each tank company, something Darnay certainly agreed with; the defence against anti-tank pieces in his sector had been 'non-existent'. He gives the example of a German anti-tank gun that was identified coming into action at 11.00; it took an hour before the first shells from a French battery arrived, by which time five tanks had been destroyed.

However, an experiment using tanks to haul 75mm field artillery pieces for close support had not been a success. Lieutenant Mousset

(Groupement I) had been given six Schneiders and some field guns, plus a replacement tank and one Renault. The tanks were fitted with an improvised hook to pull the guns, these only being made and installed several hours before the operation. The column was delayed due to numerous breakdowns, caused by the state of the ground and the fact it that it was a very dark night. It took over five hours for the column to make the eight-kilometre journey to the rendezvous point. Mousset made contact with the artillery unit's officers and the six tanks were split into three sections, with two tanks, each tank pulling one 75mm gun, as well as carrying sixty shells. These three sections had considerable difficulty crossing the broken terrain and the gun-hooks all broke and were replaced by cables. Eventually one section was able to bring its guns into action, firing around twenty shells at a German machine-gun position. It became clear to Mousset by the afternoon that the operation was over and the eight tanks returned to Savette the following day, all 'more or less' in working condition. The experiment had not been a success because, according to Velpry, the organisation was 'embryonic' and the equipment had been inadequate, which was clearly true. Velpry did concede, however, that the proposed 75mm Gun Renault might mean that accompanying artillery might prove to be unnecessary.

The AS officers also highlighted a number of other areas where the co-operation with the infantry was less than ideal. They were unanimous in believing that only fresh infantry should be used with the tanks. For example, Vigneron compared his unit's experience fighting with French 167 DI and US 4 Brigade. The former had never trained with tanks whereas the Americans had received some previous training. In addition, the French infantry had been fighting for several days before the tank engagement and were thus tired, whereas the US troops were fresh. Although his battalion was considerably weakened by the time it fought with the Americans, the tanks were able to give effective assistance to the US infantry. Moving under a 'very dense smoke barrage', the US brigade had advanced four kilometres, in comparison with the adjoining French division that made no headway and no worthwhile advance. Angeli made an interesting observation about the effect of the tanks on the morale of the French infantry; as the arrival of tanks usually indicated an operation, fresh infantry would view the tanks as an encouraging addition, whereas tired troops would see them as an unwelcome indication that there was to be further fighting.

Fischbach noted that the French infantry divisions were now generally attacking with three regiments in line, in battalion columns.

There was thus one infantry battalion of each regiment in the first line and, according to AS regulations, one tank section should support this battalion but this, Fischbach said, was 'too little'. He recommended that there should be two sections with each leading battalion, with the third section following behind with the second infantry battalion.

In relation to communications, everyone agreed that this had not been satisfactory but opinions varied as to why this was. At the battalion level, Vigneron said that the AS 'did not have a proper telephone network'. This made it difficult for him to communicate by phone with his immediate superior and he was reliant on couriers, although these gave 'satisfactory results'. By contrast, 16 BCL had found that couriers sometimes took over eight hours to deliver messages. Velpry claimed that the problems with the telephone network were less to do with what was available and more to do with 'insufficient employment' of the equipment by the AS battalion and company commanders. There was a general agreement that the pigeons had worked well, messages often taking less than half-an-hour to arrive. It was remarked in several reports that TSF tanks would have been very useful if they had been available.

In relation to the tanks themselves, the Schneiders exhibited no new problems. In relation to the Renaults, the fan belts continued to break in worrying numbers, although Vigneron thought that it was 'incontestable' that careful driving (and thus better training) could ameliorate this problem. All of 3 BCL's tanks had their fan-belts checked on 27 September but by 8 October forty-four tanks had broken fan belts, all of which had to be replaced. The situation with the tank's tracks unsurprisingly varied according to the circumstances; by the end of the Champagne operations, all of 3 BCL's tanks needed their tracks repaired due to serious wear and tear, some of the tanks having been run with little maintenance for 195 hours. By contrast, 2 BCL had no problems with their tracks. There were various miscellaneous problems, which included engine failures caused by leaking oil and a variety of gearbox seizures. Darnay also complained that the Berliet light tanks were not well built; the majority of his had broken down before getting into combat.

There were a variety of other issues that the operations in Champagne had thrown up. All of the AS commanders complained about the disembarking arrangements used when moving to the front, particularly the ramps used on the trains. Only 10 BCL had an easy journey because its tanks had been moved by tractor. Velpry complained about the automatic pistols that had been issued to the AS personnel because these had caused numerous accidents, of which several were fatal. 'I am not aware that they have killed any Germans but I know that in my regiment they have killed Frenchmen', he said. He recommended that the AS crews be given carbines for dismounted use, a measure which he thought would also improve morale. Vigneron was unhappy with the amount of motor transport available to each tank company, there not being enough wheeled vehicles to move the unit's equipment in one go. Darnay thought the system of signal panels had worked well except that it indicated to enemy aircraft the AS positions, which then attracted heavy artillery fire.

The difficulties of continuing the initial success of the first day of battle, already seen in previous operations, remained. Although giving the divisional commanders considerable discretion as to how to fight this engagement after the first day was in theory a good idea, in practice it often meant that from the second day onwards there was a complete lack of co-ordination across VI Armée's front between the various attacking infantry units. For example, on 28 September, the two forward divisions of 21 CA started their attacks nearly two hours apart, one of them initially using only part of its allotted tanks and then feeding the others into the battle piecemeal. Darnay also noted that there had been a lack of co-ordination between some of the infantry divisions which had resulted in some captured trenches being only partially cleared. The lack of co-ordination was also apparent within the French infantry divisions; for example, on 28 September on 3 BCL's front, there was little co-ordination within the division and its three infantry regiments attacked at different times. In particular, many of the divisional commanders had passed responsibility for the tanks to their subordinate regimental commanders who, the operation had made clear, were less familiar with the tank regulations than they should have been.

The operations in Champagne reinforced the AS officers' belief in the soundness of the tank regulations, this time proved in the context of a difficult attack on a heavily-fortified and well-defended area. If the tanks were used according to the regulations, as on the first day of the Champagne battle, they could offer significant assistance to the infantry but this became inevitably diluted as operations became smaller and more extemporised. The Champagne operations' primary lesson for the AS was the same as that of Soissons; it was essential that the tank regulations were thoroughly understood and adhered to by the infantry commanders and that there was no need to revise the current tank doctrine. There were no further tank regulations issued before the end of the war.

Chapter 10

The Final Battles of 1918 and the Armistice

October 1918 would see the culminating battles of the war fought, as the Germans were relentlessly pushed back out of France and Belgium, fighting in which the *Artillerie Spéciale* would participate. This fighting would not see any new tactics developed by the AS or any change in the German response to the tanks and we will therefore only take a snapshot look at these final battles. Before turning to the battle along the Serre river in France, a brief look at the AS actions in Flanders will be undertaken. As might be imagined, the terrain in Flanders was unpromising for tanks and by this point in the war the Allies were chasing a demoralised German army which required a tempo of operations that the tanks were hard-pressed to keep up with. In Flanders, the AS participated in the Battle of Roulers and the Battle of the Lys & Escaut (20 October to 11 November) but only the former will be discussed as it is typical of the fighting in Belgium.

The AS in Flanders
On 6 October 1918, Lieutenant Colonel Velpry arrived in Belgium to take command of the AS of the *Groupe d'Armées des Flandres* (GAF). This consisted of 7 and 34 CAs and 2 CC and was nominally under the command of the Belgium army, although by September 1918 French General Jean-Marie Degoutte and the staff of French VI Armée were calling the shots at the Belgian King's HQ and co-ordinating the Allied armies in Flanders.

GAF had begun an offensive in September that had already made significant progress by the first week of October but, despite German strength diminishing every day, the French had ground to a halt in the region of Cartemark, Hooglede and Roulers. By 4 October, there were fifteen German divisions in front of GAF; seven between Armentières and Ledeghem, five between Ledeghem and Wercken and three on the passive front between Nieuport and Ostende. There were a further three in the rear which the French thought capable of intervening given a few days of rest. It was therefore necessary to reinforce GAF and this was duly done, GAF receiving 30 CA and 11 DI, as well as 12 BCL from RAS 504. Although Foch pressed for the attack to begin on 10 October, the Belgians could not get sufficiently organised in time, particularly in relation to the their reserves, and asked that the offensive be postponed until 13 October.

On 6 October, the Belgian high command gave its orders to GAF. The French corps were ordered to break through the German lines in front of them and then advance without stopping in the direction of Thielt and Gand. 7 CA with 5 and 41 DIs in line had its principal effort north of Roulers and would then encircle the crête de Hooglede by the south, supporting the main effort by 34 CA (70 and 77 DIs in line with a further division in reserve) which was attacking this position from the north. On 8 October, it was clear that the Belgians would not be ready by 13 October and the operation was postponed to the next day. The infantry attack would start at 05.30, with the artillery preparation starting two minutes later, laying down a dense smoke barrage. The first objectives would be marked by the line Haagebrok, Hooglede, Roulers and the second objectives marked by Gits, Gitsberg and Beveren, the latter followed by exploitation of the success.

The AS units available for this operation were a full-strength 12 BCL, two reduced companies from 1 BCL and Groupement XII (three *groupes* of St Chamonds). It was not clear during the planning for the operation if Groupement XII would arrive in time to participate, as it was in transit, so it had to be assumed that the St Chamonds would not be there. As the main infantry effort was being made by 77 DI against the heights of Gits and Hooglede, it received AS336 and AS334 from 12 BCL along with potentially two *groupes* from Groupement XII (one of which would be in reserve), 12 BCL's other company (AS335) going to 70 DI to the north with one St Chamond *groupe*, with 5 DI (7 CA) to the south receiving 1 BCL's two companies (AS301 and AS302).

The St Chamonds in Flanders

As expected, Groupement XII (commanded by *Chef de Bataillon* Azais) arrived too late for the necessary reconnaissance (after a very difficult road and rail journey), which resulted in several disagreeable surprises on 14 October. AS38, reinforcing 159 RI, found itself in trouble from the moment its St Chamonds left the departure position and ran into an area of deep shell holes, many of which were filled with water. The tanks ditched one after the other and only one St Chamond advanced more than one kilometre before itself getting stuck, without ever catching up with the infantry. AS37, supporting 360 RI (70 DI), had a similar experience; its tanks set off from their departure position seven minutes before the infantry attack started and quickly passed the French lines. However, their part of the advance required driving down a narrow road, which proved very difficult as there was so much smoke and fog on the battlefield. (Azais pointed out in his report that this was one occasion when a smoke barrage was not needed for the tanks, as the weather provided enough cover, and the smoke actually became a serious hindrance.) Only one tank managed to navigate the road successfully but this broke down within the hour and the reserve tank battery had to be brought up to support the infantry.

The following days saw more breakdowns than combat casualties as the St Chamonds were asked to traverse terrain that could not have been more unsuitable for them and this pattern continued until the evening of 18 October when the *groupement* was retired. At this point, it had only managed to get eight tanks into combat (out of thirty) over five days.

The light tanks in Flanders

The light tanks, by contrast, were able to deal with the Flanders countryside rather better than their heavier cousins, although once again the tempo of operations would prove challenging. On 14 October, AS335 (12 BCL) helped the infantry of 70 DI take Geite St Joseph at great speed and with very light casualties, while AS336 was similarly successful, helping the French take Hooglede and advance up to Gitsberg. 1 BCL, by contrast, received heavy fire during its advance due to the failure of AS38 and 159 RI to clear its left flank and the battalion's two already reduced companies were badly hit, taking nine casualties and losing four tanks to anti-tank gun fire. Despite these losses (and three other tanks to breakdowns), the light tanks and the infantry were able to continue their advance and take their objectives but it took 1 BCL an entire day to recover from this combat. It could only get two sections into action on 16 October but these tanks were of considerable assistance to the infantry of 74 RI in their attack and capture of the village of Beveren. Although by 17 October the Germans were in full retreat, combat was still risky and on that day a section from AS302 lost three of its tanks to a single anti-tank gun near Thielt. By 19 October, 1 BCL was no longer fit for combat, due to both losses and breakdowns, and it was retired

ˈ back to France. 12 BCL, although having started with more tanks, could by 17 October only field three sections from AS336 and AS334 and it was placed in the army reserve the following day.

The results

What became known as the Battle of Roulers had important results; on the first day parts of the Allied army had advanced over eight kilometres and had captured over 10,000 prisoners as well as a considerable quantity of enemy equipment. On 17 October, the Germans were in full retreat and between 16 and 26 October the ports of Zeebrugge and Ostend were captured as well as Courtrai, Thielt and Bruges. Despite the difficult terrain, which had rendered the St Chamonds fairly impotent, the light tank units had performed well but the pace of the operation took its inevitable toll on them, reducing their effectiveness day by day.

From 17 to 19 October in Flanders, the Germans were rapidly retreating in some disorganisation but by this time the AS units had been whittled away to such an extent that their ability to support the Allied infantry was very limited. However, the state of the light tank units was primarily the result of moving the tanks significant distances on their tracks, rather than by lorries as per the regulations, across difficult terrain. Once again, operational necessity required that the tank regulations were not followed and the inevitable wear and tear tested the Renault design to the limit. The St Chamond tank would not be used in action again but the Renaults would continue in combat until the very end of the war. While the tanks had been fighting in Belgium, heavy fighting was still underway in France.

The Battle of the Serre, October 1918

On 18 October, 1 AS Brigade made 4 and 6 BCL from 502 RAS available to V Armée, which had been pursuing the retreating German army in a north-easterly direction since 11 October. By 13 October, German resistance had solidified and the French advance was stopped near the Hunding line. The German position in front of V Armée was a seven-kilometre salient, bounded by the Aisne and the marshes at Sissonne, with good observation for their artillery across the battle zone. The defenders were well equiped with machine guns and artillery. The AS part of the operation against this salient was entirely undertaken by light tanks and it is thus an interesting example of late-war tank combat.

It was decided after a reconnaissance that the tanks could operate effectively in the zone between Nizy-le-Comte and La Croix (east of Bethancourt). The tank battalions were moved by rail to Reims and then by lorry to their assembly position. This move poignantly took them through the village of Berry-au-Bac, where their predecessors had advanced through the previous year in somewhat more hazardous circumstances. On the morning of 22 October, 6 BCL set off with sixty-three tanks, the first of these arriving at the assembly position at 15.00. By dawn on 23 October there were fifty-five tanks at the assembly position, the remaining eight tanks being either delayed by traffic or having broke down, all joining the other tanks during the course of the morning. 4 BCL set off on 23 October with fifty-nine tanks in three convoys, all of which arrived without incident, the remaining tanks arriving the following day. 4 BCL and 6 BCL were both attached to 21 CA.

General situation

21 CA had 5 CA on its left flank and 13 CA on its right, its zone delineated by Saint-Quentin-le-Petit to the west and Seraincourt to the east. 6 BCL was attached to the left division (170 DI) and 4 BCL to the right-hand division (43 DI), with one division (167 DI) in reserve. The infantry's mission was to assault the Hunding position and within three hours to be pushing through it to the second and third objectives beyond. The tanks were to pass the infantry after their departure and support their attack on the first objective, after which they would retire and wait under camouflage until advancing again to support the infantry attack on the other objectives six hours after the jump-off time. Reconnaissance and liaison were undertaken right up until the evening of 24 October and numerous passages were made by the divisional *genie* under the supervision of AS officers. The jump-off time was set for 06.30 on 25 October, the tanks getting into position during the evening of 24/25 October.

170 DI had three regiments in line with a tank company per regiment, with each tank company having a section in reserve. 43 DI was attacking Banogne in two infantry columns from the north-west and south-east, a tank company with each column, with AS310 in reserve. The noise of the tanks moving on the evening of 24 October would be covered by low-flying aircraft from 19.00 to 24.00. The divisions' artillery would be required to use smoke to blind the observation posts with a field of view of the tanks' action zone. There would be artillery sections with

the leading infantry battalions tasked with immediate counter-battery fire whenever German anti-tank guns appeared. A divisional aircraft would keep the tanks constantly in view and report their position, as well as identifying any active anti-tank defences/positions. An artillery *groupe* was dedicated to destroy any identified anti-tank resistances.

6 BCL's battle

AS316 was attached to 116 RI on the left of 170 DI. Two tank sections passed the infantry as planned and destroyed a number of German machine-gun nests placed forward of the defensive network around Saint-Quentin-le-Petit, advancing to the west and east up to the station, taking the village. During this advance, two tanks had mechanical failures and three tanks got into difficulties in a minefield but only one AS officer was killed (a section commander) and another wounded. The remaining tanks fought on until 11.00, at which point they retired back to the departure position.

AS317 was with 17 RI, the centre regiment of 170 DI, and the tanks were able to push through the Hunding position, causing severe enemy casualties and destroying numerous machine guns. Four tanks were knocked out by field guns or minenwerfer and one tank suffered a mechanical failure. The remaining tanks continued their advance until they were met with such heavy machine-gun fire that they could not continue, retiring around 11.00. The reserve section was then brought forward for another attack on the same objectives but, this time, the tanks were met with ferocious anti-tank fire, five tanks being quickly knocked out. Two others had mechanical failures, leaving only one operational tank to return to the French lines.

AS318 was with the *Groupement de chasseurs* (3 and 10 BCP) on right of 170 DI. At 07.15, two tank sections were called forward to clear the way for the infantry that had been halted at the intermediate position; the tanks passed the infantry and forced the enemy to retire but they were then engaged by a single field gun that knocked out all the tanks except one. At 18.00, the tanks were assembled 600 metres north-east of Lor and the unit regrouped into four combat sections, two from AS318 and one each from AS316 and 317. Three sections were sent to the departure position on 26 October and had the same affectations as the day before but this time the tanks were more concentrated. However, there were only enough tanks to push into the second trench line, which they were unable to hold because the French infantry could not advance. 6 BCL was withdrawn to the corps reserve on the evening of 26 October.

4 BCL's battle

AS311 was with the right-hand column of 158 RI, being first engaged at 08.40 when it was asked to attack some machine guns that were holding up the French infantry's advance. The tanks destroyed the German positions, allowing the infantry advance to continue. The Renaults passed the infantry again shortly afterwards, clearing the way for them right up to the Neptune trench, which the tanks successfully attacked. Two tanks were damaged by enemy fire and immobilised, while another broke its fan belt. At 11.00, the tanks retired to shelter in a sunken road as the infantry could not progress further. One tank section failed to get into action because it did not receive any orders.

AS312 was attached to the left hand infantry column (1 BCP), the tank company getting into action before the jump-off time as they were needed to clear some German machine guns that were preventing the French infantry from getting into their departure positions. One section continued the advance, destroying important machine-gun positions but not able to clear enough to allow the French infantry to advance. Two entire crews were badly wounded. Another section (Laugier) helped clear machine guns but three tanks were quickly knocked out by cannon fire, with another tank suffering a mechanical failure. Section Le Gargan had an easy advance until it met a 'special cannon' which set the section commander's tank on fire. This gun was then destroyed by the combined fire of the other tanks, who then went on to continue clearing the terrain. Three tanks successively had mechanical breakdowns and the last tank had its machine gun completely destroyed. Those that could returned to the departure position at around 11.00. As the infantry division had not been able to obtain all of its objectives, particularly on the left, the attack was recommenced at 15.30, after a new artillery preparation. A TSF tank called down French heavy-artillery fire on the south-east edges of Recouvrance in order to destroy an anti-tank battery it had identified.

AS310 was in reserve but, in the afternoon, it was called forward to support elements of both AS311 and AS312 fighting with the *chasseurs*. Its four tank sections passed the infantry at 15.30 and cleared the ground in front of them and then neutralised the first German line, which was then occupied by the French infantry. The tanks continued forward but were unable to clear all the enemy machine guns, many of which were in escarpments inaccessible to the tanks. Despite the heavy resistance, only three tanks were rendered *hors de combat* by cannon fire and, after night fell, the tanks returned to the departure position.

The battle continues, 26 October

The attack resumed at 09.00 on 26 October with two sections of AS310 supporting the *chasseurs* who were attacking Banogne from the west. Their mission was to support the *chasseurs'* attack on the Neptune trench and then against the second line of the Hunding position. The tank sections passed the French infantry and made easy work of their advance, this being eased by the thick fog that covered the battlefield. However, the infantry could not advance due to heavy fire coming from Banogne which the tanks could not suppress. The two tank sections retired behind an escarpment 100 metres north of the road where they remained until night fell, waiting in vain for the opportunity to intervene again in the battle, at which point they returned to the departure position. In the evening of 26 October, 4 BCL was placed in the corps reserve and retired to a position south of Ferme Roberchamp.

The results

To sum up, 6 BCL's tanks had enabled the capture of St-Quentin-le-Petit village and the Neptune trench as well as capturing numerous machine guns, anti-tank guns and prisoners. 4 BCL had also been of considerable assistance to the French infantry; for example, on 26 October, the tanks had assisted the left of 43 DI to advance over one kilometre. The six tank sections had lost fourteen officers and men killed, with sixty-one wounded. Of these roughly 40 per cent were killed or injured inside their tanks while 60 per cent were hit outside their tanks. Fifty-one Renaults had been left on the battlefield (although a number of these would be recovered), with a further sixty-five out of action for one reason or another, leaving the two light tank battalions with just thirty-three tanks immediately available. (Seventeen tanks had been hit by shells, six by minenwerfer.) 4 BCL had fired 2,354 shells and used 202 machine-gun belts, with 6 BCL firing 4,970 shells and using 590 belts.

5 BCL enters the fray

As 4 and 6 BCL were now in urgent need of rest and reconstitution, 5 BCL was drafted in to continue the fight. The light-tank battalion was at Bourron when it received instructions on 24 October to join 502 RAS and by the 27th it was at Bois d'Avaux waiting for orders. It was attached to 13 CA, which was to resume its attack and push through the Hunding positions, as it had tried to do on 25 and 26 October unsuccessfully. The attack was to start at 11.00 on 29 October, the corps divisions advancing in line; 16 DI on the left, 151 DI in the centre and 45 DI on the right.

AS314 and AS315 were attached to 151 DI, as this was making the principal effort, with AS313 being held as the corps reserve. The tanks were instructed to join the infantry as the latter jumped off and provide them with support until the night. After spending 27 and 28 October planning and liaising with the infantry commanders, the companies moved to their assembly positions thirteen kilometres away at 18.00 on 28 October. 151 DI was advancing with 407 RI on the left in battalion columns with two sections of AS315 with the lead battalion, 410 RI on the right had two battalions in line, with a section from AS315 with each infantry battalion. Two tank sections were left with the ID commander as a reserve. Artillery fire would cover the noise of the tanks moving into their assembly positions and the approach march would be covered by a barrage of explosive and smoke shells, with 1,200 smoke shells supplied specifically to blind the German observers. A fighter squadron was to fly protection for the tanks during the entire morning and the division and corps were to supply one aircraft each to keep track of the tanks. As usual, AS officers were stationed with the relevant infantry commanders (for example, the tank battalion commander was with the corps commander) and a TSF tank was attached to the left-hand battalion of 410 RI, with a second one stationed at 151 ID PC.

5 BCL's Battle
The attack commenced at 11.00 after a thirty-minute artillery preparation. The tanks set off before the infantry and used neutralisation fire on known machine-gun nests and other German positions close to the French lines. The two tank sections with 407 RI cleared out the resistance in front of the French infantry, capturing both prisoners and machine guns. The tanks were planning to cross over the French lines but 407 RI had not prepared any passages and the tanks were obliged to retire. During this action, numerous tanks broke down due to fan-belt failure. The two tank sections with 410 RI had been forced to cross a thick gas barrage but this failed to halt them and the tanks destroyed a number of German resistance points, fighting for over three hours and helping to catch over 200 prisoners. The operation had been a qualified success, although the French division could not fully succeed because the adjacent divisions (without tanks) had failed to take their objectives.

The operation continues, 30 October
To resume operations, 13 CA was given 13 DI and 28 DI from the

adjacent 1 CAC, as well as AS313 which was attached to 13 DI. 13 DI was adopting a lozenge formation; 109 RI at the head with two battalions then in line, with one in reserve; 21 BCP to the right, 20 BCP on the left and 21 RI in reserve. A tank section went with each of the two leading battalions of 109 RI, with a section in reserve with the ID, the tank protection measures being those taken on previous days. Reconnaissance showed that the ground was good for the tanks but there were steep slopes in the battle area that would slow their movement. One tank section was given the wrong orders by the infantry commander and advanced at 15.00 without the infantry, requiring a return to the departure position and then setting off again, this time with the infantry, at 15.40. Two tanks broke down for mechanical reasons and the remaining tanks continued the advance, clearing machine-gun positions for the infantry. The tanks were then able to destroy a significant centre of resistance emplaced in a wood that had stopped the French infantry in their tracks. The situation stabilised around 16.30 and the tanks retired having enabled the infantry to advance 600 metres. The other tank section ran into heavy machine-gun fire immediately upon setting off, setting the scene for a day of hard fighting. By the end of the day, this section had captured twenty prisoners, losing two tanks and having three men killed. Out of the battalion's seventy-five tanks, it had left two tanks on the battlefield and a further two needed repair, 2,300 shells had been fired and eighty machine-gun belts used.

AS observations on the operation

There were many complaints about the new tanks that the battalions had received, both 6 BCL and 4 BCL receiving a mix of new and repaired Renaults when they mobilised. In the case of both the repaired and the newly-built tanks, extensive work was required on them before they were usable. In particular, the renovated tanks were supplied with their armament in a terrible condition; for example, one tank's machine gun exploded when it was first fired. An additional problem was that many of the tank motors would not function at full power.

Chef de bataillon Chaubès, commander of 502 RAS, reported that the French tanks and infantry had faced a disorganised and demoralised enemy but, except for the encirclement of St-Quentin-le-Petit, there were simply not enough tanks to suppress the great number of enemy machine guns. He pointed out that the Germans were now preparing their anti-tank defences meticulously and thus it was imperative for special counter-battery measures to be taken against them. Increasing German proficiency in anti-tank work meant there was a constant danger to the tanks from minenwerfer hidden in undergrowth and field guns that were camouflaged, often in the heads of ravines. Although most of the mines laid by the Germans had been identified by aerial reconnaissance and avoided, two tanks still ran into mines hidden in barbed wire and were seriously damaged. The radio officer of 43 DI reported that the TSF tanks had worked well, giving the front-line AS units quick and easy communication with the artillery protecting them to the rear.

507 RAS with I Armée
As V Armée's offensive on the Serre progressed, I Armée was fighting on its flank, aided in the final stages by 507 RAS, which only formed on 5 October 1918 and comprised 19, 20 and 21 BCLs, the AS regiment joining 1 Armée at the end of October. This fighting was to introduce no more surprises to the AS than had the combat with V Armée, so I will consider just one action that typifies the engagements of 507 RAS in October 1918.

On 25 October, AS362 (21 BCL) supported an operation to capture the village of Villers le Sec in conjunction with infantry from 153 DI, a battalion from 79 RI in the lead, with support from its flanking infantry regiments. The infantry battalion was to capture Villers in two bounds; the first taking the west half of the village and the second taking the east half and the Parc du Chateau. One company of tanks from 21 BCL was attached to 79 RI, with each tank section having a different mission. One section was attacking the village from west to east, neutralising the western and southern edges as it advanced while another section was advancing into the village by the north-east, taking the station and then exiting the village by the north. The third section was operating with 161 RI to the north of Villers attacking a German strongpoint that could enfilade the left flank of the tank attack on the village. Once this position was captured, the tanks would enter the village from the north and take up a covering position on the Villers-Pleine-Selve road. The tanks got into their departure positions on the night of 24 October, the two sections attacking the village being stationed just under two kilometres from it and the third a similar distance east of Ribemont. The company commander received his instructions from 21 BCL's commander (*Chef d'escadron* Wattel) at 20.00 on 24 October and the AS officers of the company met with their infantry counterparts over the course of that night. The tanks set off fifteen minutes earlier than the infantry (05.45) so that they caught up with the infantry as they jumped off.

The light tanks neutralised the edges of the village fairly easily, although a 77mm anti-tank was engaged while doing so, but the French infantry had been delayed and the tanks had to turn around and go back for them. Once they returned to their advance, with the infantry, the tanks cleared out much of the village by 09.30 but fighting continued until the early evening against the remnants of the German defenders and the tanks had to fight off a strong counter-attack around 11.00. Section commander *Sous-Lieutenant* Bagneris was awarded the *Chevalier de la Légion d'Honneur* for his part in this battle.

The section supporting 161 RI ran into a minefield almost immediately it set off from the departure position, two tanks being blown up and one reversing into a trench and getting stuck. The remaining two tanks were subjected to fierce machine-gun fire at short distance, resulting in all the section's crews being wounded. The section commander, *Sous-Lieutenant* Sambart, himself wounded, returned to the departure position where the company commander decided that this section was no longer needed as the attack on the village was successful.

At the end of 25 October, 79 DI was fully in control of the village of Villers, having captured a considerable amount of material (forty machine guns and one 77mm gun) and 700 prisoners. AS362 had lost four men killed as well as nine wounded, with two tanks destroyed by mines and three destroyed by accidents and break downs. As with combat in the previous couple of months, this action only confirmed what was already known. For example, Wattel confirmed that neutralisation by machine guns was the most efficient method of helping the infantry advance and also the strongest method of dealing with anti-tank guns, as well as being a 'necessity' against ill-defined targets. Wattel made the by-now regular complaint about the light tanks' fan belts being fragile.

After the Armistice
The operations with GAF and I and V Armées during October were the last gasp of the AS and the end of the line for the medium tanks, as they would be quickly retired from service. (The Renault tanks, by contrast, would continue to be used for decades to come and would shortly be fighting in both Russia and Morocco.) Pétain wrote a memo to Foch on 8 September 1918 setting out his plans for 1919. He said that 'the battle of 1919 will be the battle of aviation and the tanks'. He was planning to use 360 heavy tanks (the new Char 2C) and 3,360 light tanks per thirty kilometres of front for the next year's offensives. However, most

of the AS units were still reconstituting when the war ended, Estienne having reported to Pétain on 9 October 1918 that only five Renault battalions would be ready for operations at the end of the month and no Schneider or St Chamond units at all. Pétain asked Estienne to make every effort to make available nine Renault battalions and two medium tank *groupements* by 15 November but the Armistice intervened making this request redundant. For the officers and men of the AS, the war was now over.

Almost immediately the war finished, the AS was integrated into the infantry branch of the French army. This was totally against Estienne's advice, as he thought it should remain a separate arm, just like the artillery and air services. Estienne realised that the limitations shown by the tanks in the war would soon be overcome by improvements in technology but mainstream French military thought now saw tanks entirely in terms of direct infantry support. Estienne was moved away from the tank service in 1919 to become commander of the fortified area around Nice. He returned to the tanks in 1921, as assistant to the *Inspecteur Général de l'infanterie et inspecteur des chars de combat*, but his influence was minimal and he was retired to the reserve in 1922 due to his age. Despite being a highly-respected figure in the French army, by the time he died in 1936 he had little influence on French military thought.

Estienne wrote in 1931 that 'in my opinion, the intervention of mechanised chariots on the field of battle gives the historian the appearance of an event as important as the invention of gunpowder and cannon'. While we may not agree entirely with Estienne on the importance of the tank's appearance in the Great War, I hope this book goes some way to show how important the AS was to the French army's success in the war. It took the French a comparatively short amount of time to arrive at a relatively successful system of tank, infantry, artillery and air co-ordination, with all the pressures of unprecedented industrial warfare to contend with at the same time. Considering the resources devoted to the tanks, they repaid the investment in full. In addition, Estienne created a military organisation that can justly be considered to be manned by soldiers of the highest quality, both in their bravery and their technical expertise, whose contribution to the Allied victory in 1918 was, if not crucial, certainly very important. Looking at the performance of the AS officers and men during the war, it is hard to argue with the German officer who told his captors that the troops of the *Artillerie Spéciale* were more than just men.

Appendix 1

Artillerie Spéciale Order of Battle, 26 October 1918

Staff or Unit	Company or Groupe	Location	Situation
General Cdt AS	AS100	Montigny	
1 AS Brigade Parc	AS251 AS202 AS298	Mailly Camp	
502 RAS	AS502	V Armée	Operations
4 BCL	AS310 AS311 AS312	V Armée	Operations
5 BCL	AS313 AS314 AS315	V Armée	Operations
6 BCL	AS316 AS317 AS318	V Armée	Operations
Groupement II	AS3 AS8 AS11 AS12	Mailly-Poivres Camp	Reconstitution
SRR	AS101	V Armée	Operations
504 RAS	AS504	Sompuis	Reconstitution
10 BCL	AS328 AS329 AS330	Recdoses	Reconstitution

Staff or Unit	Company or Groupe	Location	Situation
11 BCL	AS331 AS332 AS333	Sompuis	Reconstitution
12 BCL	AS334 AS335 AS336	VI Armée	Operations
Groupement IV	AS13 AS14 AS16 AS17	Mailly-Poivres Camp	Reconstitution
SRR	AS102	US Army	Battlefield salvage
506 RAS	AS506	Mailly-Poivres Camp	Reconstitution
16 BCL	AS346 AS347 AS348	Mailly-Poivres Camp	Reconstitution
17 BCL	AS349 AS350 AS351	Mailly-Poivres Camp	Reconstitution
18 BCL	AS352 AS353 AS354	Mailly-Poivres Camp	Reconstitution
2 AS Brigade Parc	AS252 AS204 AS300	Coye Barbery	
501 RAS	AS501	VI Armée	Operations
1 BCL	AS301 AS302 AS303	VI Armée Armée d'Orient VI Armée	Operations Salonika Operations
2 BCL	AS304 AS305 AS306	Chantilly	Reconstitution
3 BCL	AS307 AS308 AS309	Chantilly	Reconstitution

Staff or Unit	Company or Groupe	Location	Situation
Groupement I	AS2 AS4 AS5 AS9	Chantilly	Reconstitution
SRR	AS105	IV Armée	Battlefield salvage
503 RAS	AS503	Orry-la-Ville	
7 BCL	AS319 AS320 AS321	Survilliers	Available
8 BCL	AS322 AS323 AS324	Survilliers	Available
9 BCL	AS325 AS326 AS327	Survilliers	Available
Groupement III	AS1 AS6 AS10 AS15	Villiers sous Grez	Rearmament with Mark VI* Tanks
SRR	AS103	Survilliers	Reconstitution
505 RAS	AS505	Orrouy	
13 BCL	AS337 AS338 AS339	Champlieu Camp	Reconstitution
14 BCL	AS340 AS341 AS342	Champlieu Camp	Reconstitution
15 BCL	AS343 AS344 AS345	Champlieu Camp	Reconstitution
3 AS Brigade Parc	AS253 AS203 AS299	Martigny Camp	
507 RAS	AS507	I Armée	Operations

Staff or Unit	*Company or Groupe*	*Location*	*Situation*
19 BCL	AS355 AS356 AS357	I Armée	Operations
20 BCL	AS358 AS359 AS360	I Armée	Operations
21 BCL	AS361 AS362 AS363	I Armée	Operations
508 RAS	AS508	Lamarche	
22 BCL	AS364 AS365 AS366	Martigny Camp	Instruction
23 BCL	AS367 AS368 AS369	Martigny Camp	Instruction
24 BCL	AS370 AS371 AS372	Villiers sous Grez	Instruction
509 RAS	AS509	Cercottes	Being formed
25 BCL	AS373 AS374 AS375	Cercottes	Being formed
26 BCL	AS376 AS377 AS378	Cercottes	Being formed
27 BCL	AS379 AS380 AS381	Cercottes	Being formed
Groupement X	AS31 AS33 AS36	Martigny Camp	Reconstitution
SRR	AS104	X Armée	Battlefield salvage

Staff or Unit	Company or Groupe	Location	Situation
Groupement XI	AS32 AS34 AS35	Martigny	Reconstitution
SRR	AS105	Martigny	Reconstitution
Groupement XII	AS37 AS38 AS39	VI Armée	Operations
SRR	AS107	VI Armée	Operations
Groupement XIII	AS40 AS41 AS42	Martigny	Reconstitution
SRR	AS108	I Armée	Operations
518 RAS Instruction regiment	AS518	Grez sur Loing	
BIAS Instruction battalion	AS496 AS497 AS498 AS499	Grez sur Loing	Instruction
Inspection General GPAS TSF School	AS297	Bourron	
Ateliers	AS201	Bourron	

Estienne wanted to keep the AS brigade and regimental commanders current with the situation of the AS and to allow them to communicate 'laterally' with each other. He therefore proposed issuing an order of battle every ten days, a draft of which was attached, that would keep officers *au fait* with which units were where and who their commanders were. This annexe is based on that draft order of battle. Estienne asked for observations to be made to him by 2 November but nine days later the Armistice ended this project.

Source – Estienne, GQG Artillerie d'assault, *Note de Service*, 26 October 1918. SHD 16N2156.

Appendix 2

Table of *Artillerie Spéciale* Engagements, 1917–1918

Key to Table of Engagements
Btn de marche – extemporised unit, consisting of parts of several battalions.
Gt. – *Groupement.*
K – Killed, includes those missing in 1919.
W – Wounded.
Tank losses – Tanks very seriously damaged or destroyed.
Area of operations and the names of battles follow the French Official History.

Under 'AS Units', the highest AS unit is in bold. If it is followed by subordinate units (not in bold), these are the only ones to participate in that engagement. For example, **1 BCL**, AS301, AS302 shows that only the two named companies of 1 BCL entered combat. **1 BCL** indicates that the entire battalion or parts of the entire battalion were engaged.

I have amalgamated some engagements, for reasons of space, when they occurred on consecutive days.

The figures for wounded personnel and tank losses are the same as those in; GQG de AFE, Chars Blindées, no 24.387, *Tableau rectifié des pertes en Chars et personnel, par engagement, au cours de la campagne*, 9 September 1919. 16N2120, with the exception of the 28 June 1918 engagement where the *Tableau rectifié* has left out the five wounded from 2 BCL. Thus the wounded total in my table has five more wounded than the *Tableau rectifié*'s total. In relation to personnel killed or missing, the *Tableau rectifié*'s figures are surprisingly low, listing only 555 officers and men. This compares to the *Etat Nominatif des Officers, Sous-Officiers & Soldats Tués* that lists 903 officers and men killed and the table below which has a total of 767 killed or missing. Note that the *Etat Nominatif* includes AS personnel killed when not participating in a tank engagement.

The material losses listed in *Tableau rectifié* are those of 'tanks seriously damaged by the enemy'. Aside from the after action reports, in 16N2120 there are two other casualty documents; *Etat Nominatif des Officers, Sous-Officiers & Soldats Tués* and *Liste Nominative des Officiers des Chars d'Assaut Tués* (both undated). The figures in these do not entirely concur with the figures in the *Tableau rectifié*. In addition, there is a table of engagements and losses of the AS, undated, in 16N2120. This gives more detail than the *Tableau rectifié*. Its provenance is unclear, although it appears to be part of the material collected for the internal history of the AS. There is also Perré and Gouest, 'Chars et statistique; Les constructions et les pertes', *La Revue d'infanterie*, July 1935, pp. 75–113. *Tableau no. III, Pertes en matérial at en personnel du fait de l'ennemi*, pp. 92–103. Perré's table appears to be taken from the list of engagements in 16N2120, mentioned above. However, he adds a column for percentage losses and combines several entries from the original document in the Soissons section. This leads to a mistake on the total wounded column, which should read 2,350 rather than 1,459. However, the total casualties listed are correct. For these reasons, the figures from the *Tableau rectifié* have generally been used in this volume.

Date	Infantry Units and Army	AS Units	No of Tanks in Action	Tank Losses	AS Personnel Losses	Operations Area	Comments
16 April 1917	69 DI 42 DI 10 DI V Armée	**Gt. Bossut & Gt. Chaubès**	82 S 50 S	57	71 K 109 W	Juvincourt, 4km north of Berry-au-Bac	The Nivelle Offensive. *Chef d'escadron* Bossut killed in action. See Chapter 1.
5–6 May 1917	1 CAC 37 CAC VI Armée	**Gt. Lefebvre**	19 S 12 SC	1	11 K 44 W	Laffaux, 8km north-west of Vailly	One tank destroyed by artillery. See Chapter 2.
23–25 October 1917	11 CA 14 CA 21 CA VI Armée	**Gt. II Gt. X**	38 S 20 SC	2	20 K 62 W	Laffaux, 8km north-west of Vailly	Battle of Malmaison. See Chapter 3.
5–18 April 1918	179 RI 132 RI 355 RI 18 DI I Armée	**AS4 AS2 AS3**	23 S	9	21 K 47 W	Mailly-Raineval, 3km south-west of Moreuil	2nd Battle of Picardie. There were three engagements during this period.
28 May 1918	28 RI US 1 DI US	**AS5**	12 S	1	1 K 1 W	Cantigny, 6km north-west of Montdidier	See Chapter 9.
31 May 1918	DM X Armée	**2 BCL** 2 Sections AS304 1 Section AS306 AS305	31 R	5	5 K 6 W	Chaudun, 7km south-west of Soissons	

Date	Formation	Unit	Tanks	Losses	Casualties	Location	Notes
3 June 1918	8 RI VI Armée	**1 BCL** **2 BCL** 1 Section AS304 2 Sections AS301	15 R	1	2 W	Chavigny, 6km north-west of Soissons	3rd Battle of the Aisne.
3–6 June 1918	167 DI 128 DI 136 DI 131 DI 91 RI X Armée	**1 BCL** **3 BCL** AS309 1 Section AS307	50 R	2	5 K 17 W	Actions around the vicinity of the Forêt de Retz	3rd Battle of the Aisne A series of section and company-sized engagements.
11–12 June 1918	48 DI 165 DI 152 DI 129 DI III Armée	**Gt. XI** **Gt. XII** **Gt. IV** **Gt. X**	103 SC 56 S	73	158 K 233 W	Méry Courcelles, 15km south-east of Montdidier	Battle of the Matz. All AS units were attached to *Groupement Mangin* (35 CA). See Chapter 4.
12 June 1918	33 RI X Armée	**3 BCL** AS309	15 R	0	7 W	Corcy, 9km east of Villers-Cotterêts	
13 June 1918	152 DI III Armée	**Gt. III** 1 battery AS10	4 S	0	2 K 3 W	Bois du Merlier, 5km south-east of Maignelay	One tank was hit by a shell during the engagement and was immobilised. It was successfully recovered that night.
15 June 1918	9 Zouaves 418 RI X Armée	**1 BCL** AS303	15 R	1	2 K 2 W	Coeuvres, 10km north-east of Villers-Cotterêts	Two tanks hit by shells.
18 June 1918	1 RMZT 72 RI X Armée	**1 BCL** 1 Section AS301 1 Section AS302	10 R	0	5 W	Montgobert, 7km north-east of Villers-Cotterêts	

Date	Army/Division	Unit	Tanks	No.	Casualties	Location	Remarks
28 June 1918	153 DI X Armée	**2 BCL** AS305 **3 BCL**	60 R	3	6 K 28 W	Cutry, 3km north of St. Pierre-Aigle	Surprise attack without an artillery preparation.
9 July 1918	36 RI 404 RI III Armée	**Gt. IV** 2 batteries AS16 2 batteries AS17	16 S	2	0	Antheuil, 5km south of Ressons-sur-Matz	Battle of Fermes Portes et Loges. Surprise attack without an artillery preparation.
15–17 July 1918	73 DI VI Armée	**5 BCL**	85 R	6	9 K 10 W	Courtemont, 6km west of Dormans	4th Battle of Champagne.
18–23 July 1918	X Armée	**Gt. I** **Gt. III** **Gt. IV** **Gt. X** **Gt. XI** **Gt. XII** **1 BCL** **2 BCL**	67 R 86 S 85 SC	173	108 K 463 W	West and south-west of Soissons	Battle of Soissons (2nd Battle of the Marne). See Chapter 6.
18–23 July 1918	VI Armée	**503 RAS** 7 BCL 8 BCL 9 BCL	100 R	11	11 K 61 W	South of the Ourcq river	2nd Battle of the Marne. A further forty-six Renaults were very seriously damaged. Groupement XIII (SC) was attached to 503 RAS but did not get into action.
18–24 July 1918	V & IX Armées	**502 RAS**	100 R 4 S	25	25 K 67 W	Chateau Thierry and south-west of Reims	2nd Battle of the Marne. All the tanks lost were Renaults. A further eleven Renaults were left on the battlefield and recovered later.
26–27 July 1918	V Armée	**4 BCL** AS310 **6 BCL** AS317 AS318	20 R	2	5 K 5 W	Forterelle Espilly	On 27 July, elements of 4 BCL fought with British 22 Corps.

Date	Army	Units		Location	Battle
1 August 1918	X Armée	**10 BCL**	45 R 10 10 K / 14 W	Grand-Rozoy South of Soissons	
8–9 August 1918	I Armée	**9 BCL** AS325 AS326 **11 BCL**	60 R 9 4 K / 14 W	Hangest-en-Santerre 9km south-east of Moreuil	3rd Battle of Picardie.
10 August 1918	III Armée	**10 BCL**	30 R 1 2 W	Ressons-sur-Matz, 15km north-west of Compiègne	Battle of Montdidier (3rd Battle of Picardie).
16–18 August 1918	I Armée	**Gt. III** AS8 **Gt. II** AS3 AS12 **11 BCL**	32 S 70 R 5 14 K / 68 W	Tillolloy 8km south-west of Roye	3rd Battle of Picardie.
20–21 August 1918	X Armée	**5 BCL** AS313 AS315 **AS2** **Gt. XIII**	30 R 12 S 28 SC 6 5 K / 36 W	The Aisne	2nd Battle of Noyon (3rd Battle of Picardie).
28–30 August 1918	X Armée	**9 BCL** AS326 AS327 **5 BCL** **4 BCL** AS310 **7 BCL** AS319	85 R 33 15 K / 70 W	The Aisne	Advance towards the Hindenburg Position.

Date	Army	Units				Location	Notes
31 August 1918	X Armée	**RAS 502** 4 BCL 6 BCL 12 BCL **RAS 503** 7 BCL 8 BCL	90 R	27	12 K 42 W	The Aisne	Advance towards the Hindenburg Position.
1–3 September 1918	X Armée	**7 BCL** **4 BCL** **5 BCL** **12 BCL** **8 BCL** **9 BCL**	100 R	23	35 K 69 W	The Aisne	Advance towards the Hindenburg Position.
12–13 September 1918	1 US Army	**Gt. XI** AS34 AS35 **Gt. IV** AS14 AS17 **13 BCL** **14 BCL**	28 SC 33 S 90 R	3	6 K 28 W	Saint-Mihiel	By coincidence, tank losses were one of each make. See Chapter 7.
14–17 September 1918	X Armée	**7 BCL** **8 BCL** **9 BCL**	69 R	26	6 K 38 W	Celles & Vailly	Battle of Vauxaillon.
26 September–10 October 1918	1 US Army	**Gt. IV** **Gt. XI** **13 BCL** **14 BCL** **15 BCL** **17 BCL**	68 R 16 S 12 SC	46	44 K 116 W	Meuse-Argonne	By this stage of the war, the Schneider *groupes* were so short of tanks, they had to be supplemented with Renaults. For example, AS14 (Gt. IV) was composed of eight Schneiders and five Renaults. See Chapter 7.

Date	Army	Units			Casualties	Location	Notes
26–30 September 1918	IV Armée	**2 BCL** **3 BCL** **10 BCL** **11 BCL** **16 BCL** **Gt. III** **Gt. I**	18 S 138 R	41	28 K 249 W	Montfaucon, 20km north-west of Verdun	Battle of Champagne and the Argonne. See Chapter 8.
30 September 1918	V Armée	**Gt. II** AS11 AS12	24 S 10 R	7	7 K 40 W	The Vesle river	Battle of Champagne and the Argonne. Battle of Saint-Thierry.
3 October 1918	V Armée	**2 BCL** **3 BCL** **10 BCL** **11 BCL**	86 R	0	12 K 35 W	The Suippe and the Aisne rivers	Battle of the Suippe.
3 October 1918	IV Armée	**16 BCL** **18 BCL**	60 R	10	5 K 13 W	Montfaucon, 20km north-west of Verdun	Battle of Champagne and the Argonne.
3–4 October 1918	VI Armée GAF	**1 BCL** AS301 AS302	25 R	16	9 K 20 W	Hooglede, 4km north-west of Roulers Belgium	
8 October 1918	IV Armée	**3 BCL** **16 BCL** **18 BCL** AS352 AS355 **10 & 11 BCL** Btn de marche	137 R	9	10 K 58 W	Montfaucon, 20km north-west of Verdun	Battle of Champagne and the Argonne.
14–18 October 1918	GAF	**1 BCL** **12 BCL** **Gt. XII**	16 SC 68 R	13	14 K 66 W	Roulers Belgium	Groupement XII had only eight tanks available by 15 October. By 18 October, it had only two tanks in service, although none of its tanks was out of action due to enemy action.

16 October 1918	104 USRI 1 US Army	**17 BCL** AS350	15 R	2	5 K 4 W	Bois d'Haumont, 8km south of Damvillers	
25–31 October 1918	V Armée I Armée	**4 BCL** **5 BCL** **6 BCL** **19 BCL** **20 BCL** **21 BCL**	202 R	72	61 K 185 W	Herpy, 2km south-west of Château-Porcien	Battle of the Serre. Destroyed; thirty-one Renaults with V Armée, forty-one with I Armée. A further twenty-three Renaults were severely damaged in I Armée. See Chapter 9.
31 October–2 November 1918	GAF	**7 BCL** **8 BCL** **12 BCL**	50 R	10	5 K 16 W	Lys Belgium	Battle of the Lys and the Escaut.
Totals				743	**767 K** **2,355 W**		

Appendix 3

Brief Technical Specifications

Schneider Medium Tank
FO: Weight – 13.5 tonnes
Length – 6.3m
Width – 2.00m
Height – 2.40m
Armour – 11mm (front), 5mm (sides)
Engine – Four-cylinder Schneider engine, giving 60hp @ 1,000rpm
Maximum speed – 8km/h
Main Armament – 75mm Schneider with ninety shells
Secondary Armament – Two Hotchkiss machine-guns, 1917 model
Crew – Six men including commander/driver

St Chamond Medium Tank
Weight – 23 tonnes
Length – 7.9m
Width – 2.67m
Height – 2.36m
Armour – 11mm (front), 8.5mm (sides), 8mm (rear)
Engine – Four-cylinder Panhard engine, giving 90hp @ 1,450rpm
Maximum speed – 8km/h.
Main Armament – 75mm Model 1897, with 106 shells
Secondary Armament – Four Hotchkiss machine-guns, 1917 model
Crew – Eight men including commander/driver

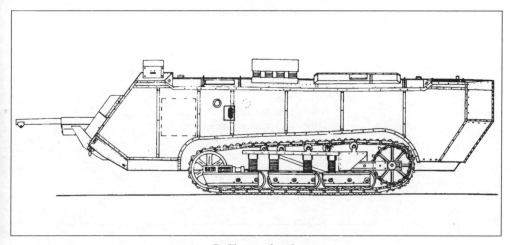

St Chamond tank.

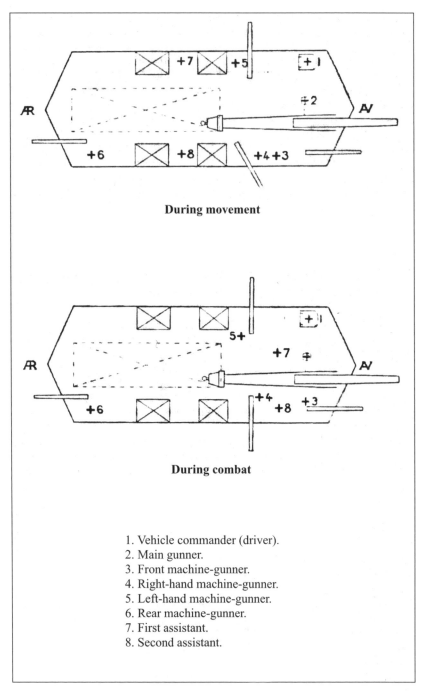

During movement

During combat

1. Vehicle commander (driver).
2. Main gunner.
3. Front machine-gunner.
4. Right-hand machine-gunner.
5. Left-hand machine-gunner.
6. Rear machine-gunner.
7. First assistant.
8. Second assistant.

Crew positions in a St Chamond tank.

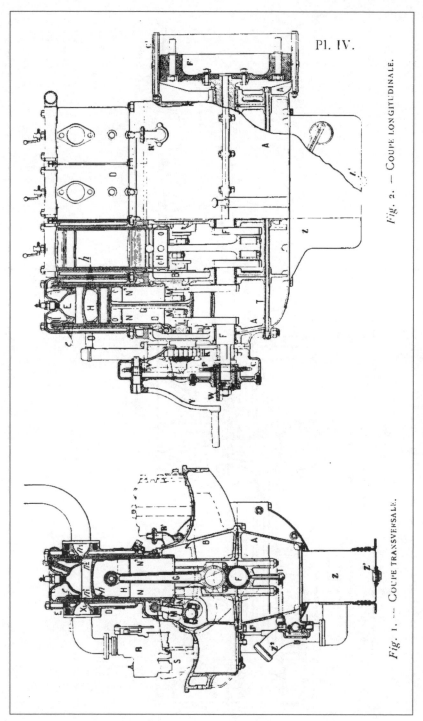

Pl. IV.

Fig. 2. — Coupe longitudinale.

Fig. 1. — Coupe transversale.

Engine of a St Chamond tank.

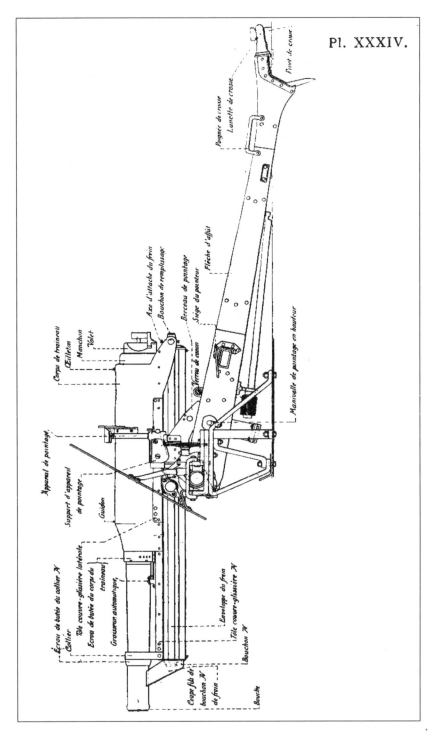

Pl. XXXIV.

75mm gun from a St Chamond tank. This was the most powerful gun to be mounted in a tank until the middle of the Second World War.

Renault Light Tank
Weight – 6,500kg (machine-gun tank), 6,700kg (gun tank)
Length – 4.1m (without tail)
Width – 1.74m
Height – 2.14m
Armour – 16mm (front), 6–8mm (sides and rear)
Engine – Four-cylinder Renault engine, giving 39hp @1,500rpm
Maximum speed – 7.78km/hour.
Main Armament – One Hotchkiss machine-gun, 1917 model, or one 37mm
Puteaux gun, with 237 shells
Crew – Two including commander/gunner

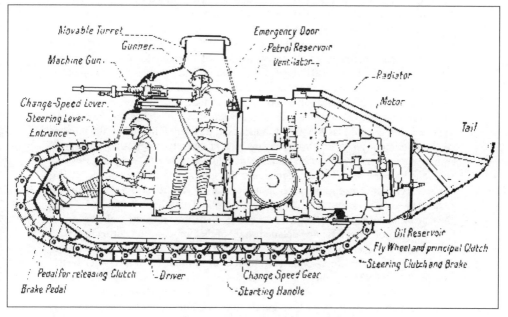

Cutaway of a Renault machine-gun tank.

Sources and Further Reading

In relation to the French army in the Great War, three volumes are required reading; Robert Allan Doughty's *Pyrrhic Victory: French Strategy and Operations in the Great War* (London: Harvard University Press, 2005), Elizabeth Greenhalgh's *The French Army and the First World War* (Cambridge: Cambridge University Press, 2014) and Michel Goya's *La Chair et l'Acier: L'invention de la guerre moderne (1914-1918)* (Paris: Tallandier, 2004). William Philpott's *War of Attrition – Fighting the First World War* (New York: Overlook Press, 2014) is the best modern overall introduction to the war and thus well worth consulting.

The French official history is an invaluable source. Issued by the *Ministère de la Guerre, Les Armées françaises dans la grande guerre* (AFGG) was published in Paris from 1923 in what became 105 volumes. Each year of the war is covered in (usually) two volumes of text (called a Tome), with a variable number of annexe volumes, each containing very large numbers of reproduced documents (there are twenty-four text volumes, fifty-five annexe volumes and twenty-six map volumes). For example, the Tome covering the Western Front from 18 July to 26 September 1918 is Tome 7, which is split into two volumes of text, with three annexe volumes. (Thus the first text volume is usually abbreviated as AFGG 7/1. A document in an annexe volume would be AFGG 7/1, annexes 1, 2, 3 etc, followed by the number of the document.) The text volumes are almost entirely a narrative account of military operations, with the barest analysis. However, nearly every page of text will refer to many reproduced documents in the appropriate annexe volume, giving the researcher much original material to ponder on. As the AFGG is now online (except the map volumes) at *Gallica*, where possible I have quoted documents from the official history as these are more accessible to readers than the archives.

The first port of call for any detailed study of the French Army during the Great War is the *Service Historique de Défense* (SHD) archives at the Chateau of Vincennes. There are forty-eight cartons relating to the AS in the GQG series, 16N2118 to 16N2166, plus the AS units' surviving *Journals des Marches et Opérations* (JMOs) (series 16N1244). There are a number of important units' JMOs missing, such as Groupement I, although other documentation for these units has survived. SHD has placed all the existing JMOs from the Great War online, which both allows easy access and prevents further deterioration of these often delicate documents. As with the various unofficial unit histories published after the war, the JMOs vary considerably in their usefulness; some are very comprehensive whereas others are somewhat sketchy.

In relation to the other documentation, cartons 16N2120 and 2121 contain comprehensive documentation on the history of the AS, although combat operations are not covered, with the exception of the Battles of the Aisne (April/May 1917) and Malmaison (October 1917) in 2121. These two cartons collect together a useful range of documents about a wide variety of AS topics, from orders relating to uniforms and security to correspondence between GQG and the *Ministère de l'Armement*. Tactical and doctrinal issues are dealt with in 16N2142. The cartons on AS units and their operations (16N2151-2166), usually one carton for two *groupements*, contain copious documentation, often down to individual tank commander's reports.

There are also a number of useful secondary sources written before the Second World War, which include a number of memoirs of AS service. Of these, the most useful is Léon Dutil's *Les Chars d'Assaut – Leur Création et leur Rôle pendant la Guerre (1915-1918)* (Paris: Charles Lauvazelle, 1919). Dutil was a member of Estienne's staff from 1917, acting as chief of 2 Bureau. His work received Estienne's approval, who described the book as 'magisterial'. Dutil concedes in his introduction that he does not cite his sources but he points out that he was writing about what he personally saw and heard. Where Dutil proves to be a very valuable source is that *Les Chars* is in effect an unofficial internal history of the AS. Combat operations are not covered in great detail, unlike in the work of Jean Perré discussed below, but the bureaucratic struggle with parts of the French government is comprehensively discussed, without any attempt to disguise the anger that this produced in parts of the AS. The only weakness in Dutil is that the behaviour of the *Ministère de l'Armement* is seen entirely from the point of view of the AS, with no attempt to consider other pressures on the ministry, particularly in relation to resources. In relation to accuracy, I have found no substantive errors in Dutil, although in some places his chronology is rather vague. There is a document in 16N2120 that suggests that *Service Historique* officers used Dutil's book to help identify the important documents and compile them for this carton and the other one containing general historical documents about the AS; 16N2121.

Post-war French professional military publications, such as *La Revue d'infanterie* and *Revue Militaire Française*, discussed various issues pertaining to the use of tanks during the Great War. The former in particular has numerous articles containing detailed analysis of both the overall tank effort and on specific engagements. One prolific author in *La Revue d'infanterie* was Lieutenant Colonel, later General, Jean Perré. He published numerous articles on the AS, largely in *La Revue d'infanterie*, many of which were collected together in two books; *Batailles et Combats des Chars français – L'Année d'Apprentissage 1917* (about the Nivelle Offensive and the Battle of Malmaison) and *Batailles et Combats des Chars français – La Bataille défensive, Avril-Juillet 1918*. Both books cover AS combat in great detail, often down to the level of individual tanks, with numerous good-quality maps, and his combat narrative for the battles covered is as detailed as most readers would need. His analysis is sound and his work is clearly compiled from material in the SHD archives. As with Dutil, I have found no substantive errors on factual issues. In relation to the analysis of the battles considered, Perré is both comprehensive and interesting. Outside of combat narrative and analysis, of particular use are the two articles he wrote for *La Review d'infanterie* under the title 'Chars et statistique'; 'Les constructions et les pertes' and 'Les comsommations en munitions.' The first is a detailed analysis of construction and losses, while the second is on ammunition and fuel expenditure.

Another interesting author is *Commandant* Adrien Balland. He fought with the AS during the war as a captain, in Groupements X and XI. He kept many of the orders and documents he received during this period, subsequently returning them to the *Service Historique* in 1930. One dossier contains orders received from October 1917 to October 1918, the other on the 18 July 1918 offensive, both of these are in 16N2164.

We have memoirs from commanders of Schneiders, St Chamonds and Renaults (all to be found in the bibliography) but none from the higher-level officers, although the archives contain reflections by *Chef de bataillon* Chaubès on his wartime experience with the AS. In general, these AS memoirs are not particularly useful, other than for impressionistic accounts of the battles fought and the social life of the writers. There are, however, snippets of tactical information in all of these accounts, which makes them worth consulting. Constantin-Weyer's memoirs are of particular interest as they cover the final six months at the end of the war, unlike most of the others which finish in mid-1918. A Renault tank section commander, Captain Aubert, left a detailed account of his part in the first combat action of the light tanks, with an analysis of the wider engagement. There are few articles and writings by Estienne from after the war, although copious documentation from him during the war remains in the archives.

Of the general histories of the French tank project (other than Dutil), F. J. Deygas' *Les Chars d'assaut: Leur passé, leur avenir* (Paris: Charles-Lavauzelle, 1937) is probably the best and certainly the clearest, although combat is not treated in detail. The 1923 textbook for the Centre d'Études des Chars de Combat, *Cours d'Emploi des Chars de Combat*, is a useful military analysis of key tank battles in the war; the Nivelle Offensive, Cambrai, 18 July 1918, Champagne September 1918.

There are a two very good illustrated books on the French tanks in the war. Francois Vauvillier's *The Encyclopaedia of French Tanks and Armoured Vehicles 1914-1940* (Paris: Histoire & Collections, 2014) is beautifully illustrated and carefully compiled and Steven J Zaloga's *French Tanks of World War 1* (Oxford: Osprey, 2010) is a good, largely accurate, brief introduction to the subject, again beautifully illustrated.

Chapter 2

On early French tank tactics, see; GQG, *Emploi tactique des cuirassés terrestres* [derived from a conversation with Estienne on 12 December 1915], 18 August 1916, AFGG 4/2, annexes 3, 2958, GQG, *Emploi tactique des chars d'assaut*, 20 August 1916. AFGG 4/2, annexes 3, 3002 and Estienne, *Bases générales de l'organisation et de la tactique de l'artillerie d'assaut (A.S.) (Projet soumis à l'approbation du général commandant en chef)* , 9 October 1916, AFGG 5/1, annexes 1, 49.

My account of the fighting on 16 April is largely derived from Estienne's report; GQG, Artillerie d'assaut, no 1266, *Rapport au sujet de la participation aux opérations de la V Armée des groupements Bossut et Chaubès de l'artillerie d'assaut*, 28 April 1917, SHD 16N2120. For more details, see SHD 16N2161, which contains all the surviving documentation for Groupements Bossut and Chaubès.

Jean Perré's *Batailles et Combats des Chars français. L'Année d'Apprentissage 1917* (Paris: Lavauzelle, 1937) has particularly fine large colour maps as well as a detailed narrative.

Chapter 3

The fighting on 5–6 May is covered in Estienne, *Rapport au sujet de la participation du groupement Lefebvre et du 17ᵉ BCP aux opérations de la VIᵉ armée, les 5 et 6 Mai 1917,* 18 May 1917. SHD 16N2120.

Jean Perré's *Batailles et Combats des Chars français. L'Année d'Apprentissage 1917* (Paris: Lavauzelle, 1937) is again recommended for its fine colour maps as well as a clear narrative.

On organisational matters, the SHD has extensive material, particularly in 16N2120 and 16N2121. See for example, *Le Général commandant l'AS à Monsieur le général commandant en chef du Nord et du Nord-est, Artillerie d'Assaut, secret,* 12 June 1917. 16N2120.

Chapter 4

Estienne's report on Malmaison; GAN Artillerie d'Assaut, *Rapport au Sujet de la Participation de l'Artillerie d'Assaut aux opérations de la VI Armée du 23 et 25 Octobre 1917,* 5 Novembre 1917. 16N2120.

For a detailed discussion on the logistical preparations for the Malmaison attack and the various depots set up for supply, see F. L. L. Pellegrin, *La Vie d'une Armée pendant la Grande Guerre* (Paris: Flammarion, 1921) pp. 161–74.

Pétain, *Note pour les groupes d'armées,* 22 August 1917, AFGG 5/2, annexes 2, 957.

The tank regulations; GQG, *Instruction Provisoire sur L'Emploi des Chars d'Assaut,* 29 December 1917 and the *Instruction sur l'emploi des chars d'assaut* of 14 July 1918. All in SHD 16N2142.

Perrè, 1917, has a good description of the tank battle.

Chapter 5

The French official history (AFGG V/2) has detailed coverage of this important battle.

Groupement X, XI and XII's carton (16N2164), Groupement III's (16N2163) and the personal papers of Groupement X's commander, Charles de Violet (1K128).

Artillerie d'Assaut, Groupement III, *Rapport,* undated. 16N2163.

Groupement X, no 392, *Le Commandant de Violet, commandant le Groupement X, à le Lieutenant Colonel l'AS de la 6° Armée,* 13 June 1918. 16N2164.

Groupement XI, *Rapport du chef de Bataillon Herlaut commandant le XIème groupement d'Artillerie d'Assaut sur les opérations du groupement les 9-10-11 et 12 juin 1918,* 20 June 1918. 16N2164.

Groupement XII, *Rapport du Commandant du Groupement XII au sujet de la participation du groupement a l'attaque de la 165 RI, 11 juin 1918,* 17 June 1918. 16N2164.

Capitaine Adrien Balland, Groupements X & XI, *Rapport sommaire sur les opérations du 35 groupe d'AS dans la journée du 11 juin,* 12 June 1918. 16N2124.

Groupement Mangin, 3/3 M, *Note pour les divisions,* 11 June 1918. AFGG VI/2, annexes 2, 1482.

For Lieutenant Orens' part of the battle, see AS15 report of the battle in 16N2163.

Chapter 6

GQG, Artillerie d'Assaut, no. 3508, *Réglement Provisoire de Manœuvre des Unités de Chars Légers,* 10 April 1918. 16N2142.

Pétain, *Note sur l'emploi des chars légers,* 9 June 1918. 16N2142.

GAN, Artillerie d'assaut, *Note pour les commandants d'AS de GA,* 20 April 1918. 16N2150.

GAN, 3 Bureau, *Note pour le Général commandant l'artillerie d'assaut,* 20 June 1918. 16N2142.

AS officer's accounts of Chaudun; Capitaine Aubert, 'Emploi d'une section de chars dans le premier engagement des chars "Renault" – Mai 1918', *La Revue d'infanterie,* 1 August 1935, pp. 309–20. Captain Delacommune and Captain Cornic, 'Le premier engagement des chars Renault en 1918', *La Revue d'infanterie,* August 1932, pp. 215–23. Maurice Velpry, 'Le premier engagement des chars Renault en Mai-Juin 1918', *La Revue d'infanterie,* December 1932, pp. 795–801. We have several documents that cover Charles Boudon's engagement; the report from AS309, the report from 1 Section/AS309 and the personal testimony of Boudon, in a letter written in 1938 to a member of the *Service Historique.* Michël Souquet has shown the latter to be not entirely accurate, as might be expected having been written twenty years after the event, but it is the only eyewitness account of this interesting small action of the Renaults.

3 BCL, AS309, 1 Section, *Compte rendu de l'engagement du 3 juin 1918,* 16N2165. Report by Boudon's second-in-command, *Maréchal de Logis* Bellavoine.

Perré, *1918,* p. 200.

501 RAS *JMO.*

Chapter 7

GAN, *Note pour les Armées; Enseignements Tirés des Combats Récents en ce qui concerne l'Artillerie d'Assaut,* 9 September 1918. 16N2142. The note's contents were addressed to all commanders, down to the level of infantry battalion and artillery *groupe.*

Michael Neiberg's *The Second Battle of the Marne* (Bloomington: Indiana University Press, 2008) is an excellent modern account of the battle.

AFGG Volumes VI and VII and their appendixes have extensive coverage of the battle and the planning for it.

Colonel Loizeau's *Le Combat d'une Division* (Paris: Charles-Lavauzelle, 1932) is a very detailed account of 58 DI in the battle, with good coverage of the tank actions with the division.

The *JMO*s of the various units involved are online.

Groupement Chanoine, *Compte rendu de l'attaque du 18 Juillet 1918,* 22 July 1918. 16N2163.

Groupement I, *Compte-Rendu relative a la participation du I groupement d'AS aux opérations des 18 et 19 juillet 1918,* 23 July 1918. 16N2162.

1 BCL, *Rapport sur les opérations exécutes par le 1 BCL pendent la période du 18 Juillet au 24 Juillet 1918.* 16N2165.

2 BCL, *Rapport d'ensemble des opérations exécutées depuis 14 Juillet 1918,* 25 July 1918. 16N2165.

501 RAS, *Compte-Rendu des Opérations du 18 au 23 Juillet 1918,* 2 August 1918. 16N2159.

30 CA AS, *Rapport sur l'action des chars du 3 BCL au cours de combats des 19, 20, 21 et 23 Juillet 1918,* 25 July 1918. 16N2159.

Groupement II, *Compte rendu du Capitaine Murat, commandant le 12 groupe sur le combat du 20 Juillet 1918,* 21 July 1918. 16N2162.

503 RAS, *Compte rendu Sommaire des opérations du 503 RAS au cours de la bataille du 18 au 26 Juillet,* 29 July 1918. 16N2160.

Chapter 8

Most of the material for this chapter came from SHD cartons 16N2156, 16N2160, 16N2164, 16N2166 and 1K128 (de Violet papers). The US Official History is useful as is the French Official History. In the latter, AFGG VII/1, Chapter 11 covers St Mihiel from the French perspective.

For US tank actions, see Dale E. Wilson's *Treat 'Em Rough! The Birth of American Armour, 1917-20* (Novato: Presidio Press, 1989).

For a detailed survey of the Franco-American relationship in the Great War, see Robert Bruce, *A Fraternity of Arms – America & France in the Great War* (Kansas: UKP, 2003).

For details on the AS during this period; all the tank battery accounts at Cantigny are from; Groupe AS5, *Compte-rendu, Capitain Noscereau, Commandant le 5 Groupe d'AS sur le combat du 28 mai 1918,* 29 May 1918. SHD 6N2162.

Artillerie d'assaut, Groupement XI, *Rapport du Chef de Bataillon Herlaut sur les opérations du XIème groupement pendant la période du 16 Septembre au 6 Octobre 1918*, 6 October 1918. 16N2164.

The reports of AS *1 Brigade* in 16N2156 are particularly useful.

Chapter 9

Gouraud's note on tank use; IV Armée, *Note au sujet de l'emploi des chars d'assaut,* 17 September 1918. AFGG 7/1, annexes 2, 1192.

501 RAS, groupement I, *Compte-Rendu du chef d'escadron Commandant le 1 groupement* [Laurent] *au sujet des opérations du 3 Octobre,* 4 October 1918. 16N2162.

501 RAS, groupement I, Lieutenant Mousset, *Compte-Rendu des opérations du 3 octobre 1918,* 5 October 1918. 16N2162.

For a detailed account of IV Armée artillery; Lieutenant Colonel Aublet, 'L'Artillerie du 21 Corps d'armée le 26 Septembre 1918', *Revue Militaire Française*, October 1929, pp. 322–45.

Centre d'Études des Chars de Combat, *Cours d'Emploi des Chars de Combat* (1923) has a chapter devoted to the AS part of the battle.

Chapter 10

507 RAS, 21 BCL, *Compte-rendu du combat de l'AS 362 le 25 octobre 1918,* 16N2166.

1 Brigade, 502 RAS, no. 2.127, *Compte-Rendu des Opérations du 502 RAS du 19 au 30 octobre 1918 sur le Territoire de la V Armée,* 10 November 1918. 16N2159 (502 RAS), report from *Chef de bataillon* Chaubès.

501 RAS, *Operations de l'armée Francaises des Flandres du 14 au 20 octobre 1918*, 16N2159 (501 RAS Flanders with GAF).

AFGG VII/2.

Paul Cornish, *Machine Guns and the Great War* (Barnsley: Pen & Sword, 2009).

Deygas, *Les Chars d'assaut.*

For more on the post-war life of the Renault, see Tim Gale, 'Mass Production – The surprisingly long life of the Renault light tank', in Alaric Searle (ed.), *Genesis, Employment, Aftermath: First World War Tanks and the New Warfare, 1900-1945* (Solihull: Helion & Co, 2015).

Bibliography

SHD Archive – Vincennes
AS series. (Only those cited in the text included here).
16 N 2120. General papers on the AS.
16 N 2121. More general papers.
16 N 2129. Consultative Committee, Inter-Allied Tank Committee.
16 N 2131. Schneider.
16 N 2132. St Chamond.
16 N 2133. Renault.
16 N 2142. Tank regulations.
16 N 2148. General orders, tank recovery, tank availability.
16 N 2149. AS HQ Operations, 1917–18.
16 N 2150. AS HQ Operations, 1918.
16 N 2156. 1 and 3 AS brigades.
16 N 2159. 501 and 502 RAS.
16 N 2160. 503 to 507 RAS.
16 N 2161. Groupements Bossut and Chaubès.
16 N 2162. Groupements I and II.
16 N 2163. Groupements III and IV.
16 N 2164. Groupements X to XIII.
16 N 2165. BCLs 1 to 6.
16 N 2166. BCLs 7 to 23.
IK 128. De Violet Papers.

AS JMOs.
26 N 1244/2 – Groupement II.
26 N 1244/3 – Groupement III.
26 N 1244/4 & 5 – Groupement XII.
26 N 1244/6 – Groupement XIII.
26 N 1244/7 – AS3.
26 N 1244/8 – AS5.
26 N 1244/9 – AS8.
26 N 1244/10 – AS10.
26 N 1244/11 & 12 – AS11.
26 N 1244/13 – AS12.
26 N 1244/14 – AS31.
26 N 1244/15 – AS33.
26 N 1244/16 – AS35.
26 N 1244/17 – AS36.
26 N 1244/18 – AS41.
26 N 1244/19 – 4e Section de réparations et de revitaillement.
26 N 1244/20 – 108e Section de réparations et de revitaillement.
26 N 1244/21 – RAS 501.
26 N 2144/23 – RAS 502.

Other JMOs
Armies
26 N 51/11 – X Army.
26 N 39/5 – VI Army.

Corps
26 N 99/4 – 1 CA.
26 N 134/6 – 11 CA.
26 N 145/4 – 14 CA.
26 N 193/6 – 20 CA.
26 N 195/4 – 21 CA
26 N 198/4 – 30 CA.

Divisions
26 N 292/5 – 13 DI.
26 N 314/3 – 27 DI.
26 N 315/4 – 28 DI.
26 N 333/4 – 38 DI.
26 N 344/7 – 43 DI.
26 N 463/17 & 18 – DM.

Regiments and Batallions
26 N 605/4 – 30 RI.
26 N 644/4 – 52 RI.
26 N 661/8 – 75 RI.
26 N 673/4 – 99 RI.
26 N 680/4 – 109 RI.
26 N 700/13 – 158 RI.
26 N 719/13 – 221 RI.
26 N 823/9 – 21 BCP.
26 N 832/29 – 64 BCP.
26 N 857/8 – 1 TM.
26 N 854/4 – 1 RMZT.
26 N 855/10 – 4 RMZT.
26 N 868/2 – RICM.

Printed Works in French
Anonymous, *Historique du 17ᵉ Bataillon de Chasseurs à Pied* (Paris: Berger-Levrault, undated, c. 1920).
Anonymous, *Historique du 501ᵉᵐᵉ RAS* (Tours: Mame et Fils, undated, c. 1920).
Anonymous, *Historique du 505ᵉ Regiment d'Artillerie d'Assaut* (Rennes: Francis Simon, 1920).
Aubert, Capitaine, 'Emploi d'une section de chars dans le premier engagement des chars "Renault" Mai 1918', *La Revue d'infanterie*, August 1935, pp. 309–20.
Aublet, Lieutenant Colonel, 'La préparation d'artillerie de 1914 à 1918', *La Revue d'infanterie*, May 1928, pp. 690–732.
Aublet, Lieutenant Colonel, 'L'Artillerie du 21 Corps d'armée le 26 Septembre 1918', *Revue Militaire Française*, October 1929, pp. 322–45.

Balland, *Commandant*, 'Le cuirassement et la protection des véhicules de combat', *La Revue d'infanterie*, March 1931, pp. 550–73.

_____, 'Un combat de chars le 18 juillet 1918 avec la Ire division américaine', *La Revue d'infanterie*, October 1935, pp. 693–718.

Barjou, Lieutenant Colonel, 'Les chars en liaison avec l'infanterie [Battle of the Matz -11 June 1918]', *La Revue d'infanterie*, June 1924, pp. 728–48.

Binet-Valmer, Jean, *Mémoires d'un engagé volontaire* (Paris: Flammarion, 1918).

Bloch, *Chef d'escadron*, 'La Protection des chars dans la bataille', *La Revue d'infanterie*, August 1922, pp. 309–23.

Bouchacourt, *Commandant*, *L'Infanterie dans la Bataille: Étude sur l'Attaque, Étude sur la Défense* (Paris: Charles-Lavauzelle & Co., 1931, 2nd Edition).

Boullaire, General, *Historique du 2e Corps de Cavalerie du 1er Octobre 1914 au 1er Janvier 1919* (Paris: Charles-Lavauzelle & Co., 1923).

Bourget, General P. A., *Le Général Estienne* (Paris: Berger-Levrault, 1956).

Breton, J. L., 'L'histoire des chars d'assaut', *L'Illustration*, 29 March 1919, no. 3969, pp. 340–4.

Carls, Stephen D., *Louis Loucheur: Ingénieur, Homme d'État, Modernisateur de la France 1872-1931* (Paris: Presses Universitaires du Septentrion, 2000, translation by Alice-Catherine Carls of English edition of 1993).

Centre d'Études des Chars de Combat, *Cours d'Emploi des Chars de Combat* (1923).

Chablat-Beylot, Agnès and Amable Sablon du Corail, *Guide des Sources Conservees par le Service Historique de la Defense Relatives à la Premier Guerre Mondiale* (Vincennes: SHD, 2008). Useful guide to the archives at Vincennes.

Chédeville, Charles, 'Étude sur l'emploi des chars de combat', *La Revue d'infanterie*, December 1921, January, February, March, April, May & June 1922, pp. 35–61, 172–88, 290–305, 395–405, 529–42, 650–75.

Chenu, Charles-Maurice, *Du Képi Rouge aux Chars d'Assaut* (Paris: Albin-Michel, 1932).

Civrieux, *Commandant*, *L'Offensive de 1917 et le Commandement de 1917* (Paris: 1919).

Clayeux, Lieutenant Colonel, 'Étude sur les opérations du 19e Bataillon de chars – Combattant en liaison avec le 15e corps d'armée du 17 au 20 octobre 1918, dans la région du Petit-Verly', *La Revue d'infanterie*, December 1922, pp. 710–30.

Cochet, François, *Survivre au front 1914-1918 – Les Poilus entre contrainte et consentement* (Paris: Éditions 14-18, 2005).

Colin, General H., *La Guerre de Mouvement 1918 : Souvenirs du commandant de l'ID 62, Le Matz, 2e Marne, L'Ourcq, La Vesle, L'Aisne, La Meuse* (Paris : Payot, 1935).

Constantin-Weyer, Maurice, *La Salamandre* (Paris: Les Etincelles, 1930).

Corlieu-Jouve, *Ceux des Chars d'assaut* (5th Edition, Paris: Éditions Jules Tallandier, 1933).

Corda, Lieutenant Colonel H., *La Bataille de 1918 sur le front Occidental* (Paris: Gauthier-Villars, 1921).

Daille, Maurice, *La Bataille de Montdidier* (Paris: Berger-Levrault, 1924).

_____, *Joffre et la guerre d'usure, 1915-1916* (Paris: Payot, 1936).

Dauzat, Albert, *L'Argot de la guerre* (Paris: Armand Colin, 1918).

Delacommune, Captain and Captain Cornic, 'Le premier engagement des chars Renault en 1918', *La Revue d'infanterie*, August 1932, pp. 215–23.

Delmas, *Commandant J.*, *L'Infanterie de la Victoire 1918* (Paris: Payot, 1932).

De Ripert d'Alauzier, Lieutenant Colonel, 'Essai synthétique sur les principes de

la guerre, application à cas concret – Le contre-attaque sur Méry (10 juin 1918)',
La Revue d'infanterie, January 1923, pp. 3–20.

Devos, Jean-Claude and Jean Nicot, Philippe Schillinger, Pierre Waksman, Josette
Ficat, *Inventaire Sommaire des Archives de la Guerre Série N 1872-1919:
Conseils 1-4 N to Généraux en Chef 14 N* (Troyes: la Renaissance, 1974).

Deygas, *Commandant* F. J., *Les Chars d'assaut: Leur passé, leur avenir* (Paris:
Charles-Lavauzelle, 1937).

Doumenc, *Commandant* Joseph, *Les Transport Automobiles sur le Front Français
1914-1918* (Paris: Librairie Plon, 1920).

Duffour, Gaston, *Joffre et la guerre de mouvement, 1914* (Paris: Payot, 1937).

Dutil, Capitaine Léon, *Les Chars d'Assaut. Leur Création et leur Rôle pendant la
Guerre (1915-1918)* (Paris: Berger-Levrault, 1919).

Estienne, General, 'Les Forces Matérielles a la Guerre', *La Revue de Paris*, 15
January 1922, pp. 225–38.

_____, 'Note au sujet du premier engagement des chars Renault en 1918', *La
Revue d'infanterie*, August 1932, pp. 213-4.

Fridenson, Patrick, *Histoire des Usines Renault, Volume 1, Naissance de la Grande
Entreprise 1898/1939* (Paris : Éditions du Seuil, 1972).

Gagneur, Captain Maurice and Lieutenant Marcel Fourier, *Avec les Chars d'Assaut*
(Paris: Hachette, 1919).

Galli, Henri, *L'Offensive Française de 1917 (Avril-Mai) de Soissons à Reims* (Paris:
Garnier Frères, 1919).

Gaudy, Georges, *Le Chemin des Dames en Feu (Décembre 1916-Décembre 1917)*
(Paris: Librairie Plon, 1923).

Gazin, Capitaine F., *La Cavalerie Française dans la Guerre Mondiale* (Paris: Payot,
1930). Good survey.

Grand Quartier Général, 3 Bureau, *Manuel du Chef de Section d'Infanterie* (Paris:
Imprimerie nationale, 1916).

Grasset, Colonel A., *La Guerre en Action: Le 8 août 1918 à la 42 Division –
Montdidier* (Paris: Levrault, 1933).

Goutard, Lieutenant, 'L'offensive de la Malmaison avec une section du 30 RI (23-
25 octobre 1918)', *La Revue d'infanterie*, December 1928, pp. 835–66.

Goya, Michel, *La Chair et l'Acier: L'invention de la guerre moderne (1914-1918)*
(Paris: Tallandier, 2004).

Guinard, Pierre, Jean-Claude Devos and Jean Nicot, *Inventaire Sommaire des
Archives de la Guerre Série N 1872-1919: Introduction: Organisation de l'Armée
Française, Guide des Sources, Bibliography* (Troyes: la Renaissance, 1975).

Hamp, Pierre, 'Louis Loucheur,' *Revue Hebdomadaire*, Volume 4, 1921, pp. 373–85.

Hatry, Gilbert, *Renault, Usine de Guerre 1914-1918* (Paris: Editions Lafourcade,
1978).

Herbillon, E., *De la Meuse à Reims – Le Général Alfred Micheler* (Paris: Librairie
Plon, 1934).

Herniou, Yvick, Eric Labayle and Michel Bonnaud, *Répertoire des corps de troupe
de l'armée française pendant la Grande Guerre, Tome 2: Chasseurs à pied, alpins
et cyclistes* (Château-Thierry: Éditions Claude Bonnaud, 2007).

Heuzé, Paul, *Les Camions de la Victoire* (Paris: La Renaissance du Livre, 1920).

Hellot, Frédéric, *Histoire de la guerre mondiale: Le commandement des généraux
Nivelle et Pétain 1917* (Paris: Payot, 1936).

Janet, *Commandant*, 'La défense de Chevincourt (10-11 juin 1918)', *La Revue d'infanterie*, July 1924, pp. 90–144.

_____, 'Attaques de la 48 Division – les 18 et 19 Juillet 1918', *La Revue d'infanterie*, February & March 1925, pp. 270–301, 389–422.

_____, 'Attaque du 6 régiment d'infanterie le 4 novembre 1918' [Second Battle of Guise], *La Revue d'infanterie*, January 1928, pp. 70–119.

Labayle, Eric, and Michel Bonnard, *Répertoire des corps de troupe de l'armée française pendant la Grande Guerre, Tome 1: L'infanterie métropolitaine Unités d'active, Régiments no. 1 à 176, Notices historiques* (Château-Thierry: Éditions Claude Bonnaud, 2004).

Lafitte, Lieutenant Colonel R., *L'Artillerie d'Assaut de 1916 à 1918* (Paris: Lavauzelle, 1921).

Lanquetot, Chef de bataillon, 'Emploi des mitrailleuses dans l'attaque – La conquête du casque par le 1er bataillon du 20e régiment d'infanterie (17-21 avril 1917)', *La Revue d'infanterie*, February 1923, pp. 197–228.

Laure, Emile, *Au 3ème Bureau du troisième G.Q.G (1917-1919)* (Paris: Librairie Plon, 1921, 8th Edition).

Laure, Lieutenant Colonel and *Commandant* Jacottet, Les Étapes de Guerre d'une Division d'Infanterie (Paris : Berger-Levrault, 1928).

Lestringuez, Pierre, *Sous l'armure – les chars d'assaut Français pendant la guerre* (Paris: La Renaissance du Livre, 1919).

Loucheur, Louis, *Carnets Secrets 1908-1932* (Ed. Jacques de Launay, Paris: Breplois, 1962).

Lucas, Lieutenant Colonel, *L'Evolution des Idées tactiques en France et en Allemagne pendant la Guerre de 1914-1918* (Paris: Berger-Levrault, 1925, 3rd edition).

Meilhan, Lieutenant Colonel, 'Les faits de guerre appliqué aux exercices sur la carte – La 152e régiment d'infanterie jeté dans la bataille 30 mai-4 juin 1918', *La Revue d'infanterie*, June 1923, pp. 821–54.

Ministère de la Guerre, *Instruction Provisoire du 30 mai 1916 sur le Canon de 37mm Modèle 1916 TR* (Paris: 31 Mars 1917).

_____, *Notice Sommaire sur la Télégraphie sans fil et les Appareils de Communication Électrique sans fil en service dans l'aviation et l'infanterie* (2 Edition, Paris: Imprimerie Nationale, 1918).

_____, *Les Armées française dans la grande guerre*. 105 volumes published in Paris from 1923.

Mordacq, General, *Le Ministère Clemenceau: Journal d'Un Témoin, Volume 1 Novembre 1917 – Avril 1918* (Paris: Librairie Plon, 1930).

_____, *Le Ministère Clemenceau: Journal d'Un Témoin, Volume 2 Mai 1918 – 11 Novembre 1918* (Paris: Librairie Plon, 1930).

Murray Wilson, G., *Les Chars D'Assaut au Combat 1916-1919* (French edition, A. Thomazi, ed., Paris: Payot, 1931, preface by General Estienne, dated 9 April 1931, pp. 7–18).

Ortholan, Henri, *La Guerre des Chars, 1916-1918* (Paris: Bernard Giovanangeli, 2007).

Pedroncini, Guy, *Pétain, Général en Chef, 1917-1918* (Paris: Publications de la Sorbonne, 1974).

Péraldi-Fiorella, *Commandant*, 'Exemple d'emploi des chars de combat dans la guerre de 1914-1918 – La contre-offensive de la Xe armée', *La Revue d'infanterie*, April 1923, pp. 691–726.

_____, Lieutenant Colonel, 'Le 3ᵉ bataillon de chars légers au combat de Cutry-Saint-Pierre-Aigle', *La Revue d'infanterie*, September 1924, pp. 394–417.

Pellegrin, Colonel F. L. L., *La Vie d'une Armée pendant la Grande Guerre* (Paris: Flammarion, 1921).

Perré, Lieutenant Colonel Jean, 'Naissance et évolution de la conception du char de combat en France durant la guerre 1914-1918', *La Revue d'infanterie*, January 1935, no. 508, pp. 13–30.

_____, and Captain Le Gouest, 'Chars et statistique: Les constructions et les pertes', *La Revue d'infanterie*, July 1935, pp. 75–113.

Perré, Lieutenant Colonel Jean, 'Chars et statistique: Les comsommations en munitions', *La Revue d'infanterie*, September 1935, pp. 477–509.

_____, 'Apropos du combat du 18 Juillet 1918 – Les chars à l'attaque d'un dispositif d'artillerie', *La Revue d'infanterie*, October 1935, pp. 719–27.

Perré, Général Jean, *Batailles et Combats des Chars français. L'Année d'Apprentissage 1917* (Paris: Lavauzelle, 1937).

_____, *Commandant* Aussenac and Captain Suire, *Batailles et Combats des Chars français. La Bataille défensive, Avril-Juillet 1918* (Paris: Lavauzelle, 1940).

Pissard, Chef de bataillon, 'Exemple d'emploi des chars de combat dans la guerre de 1914-1918 – Offensive de la IVᵉ armée en Champagne, 26 septembre 1918', *La Revue d'infanterie*, June 1923, pp. 877–903.

Poincaré, Raymond, *Au service de la France, Neuf années de souvenirs* (Paris: Plon, 1933).

Porte, Rémy, *La Direction des Services Automobiles des Armées et la Motorisation des Armées Françaises (1914-1918) – Vues au travers de l'action du Commandant Doumenc* (Paris: Lavauzelle, 2004).

Ramspacher, Colonel E., *Le General Estienne: Père des Chars* (Paris: Editions Lavauzelle, 1983).

Rimailho, Lieutenant Colonel, *Artillerie de Campagne* (Paris: Gauthier-Villars, 1924).

Rime-Bruneau, General Marcel, *Au Service de la France* (Colmar: Do Bentzinger, 2005).

Salanié, *Commandant*, 'Le tir des chars de combat', *La Revue d'infanterie*, August 1935, pp. 247–56.

Tournès, René, *Foch et la victoire des allies, 1918* (Paris: Payot, 1936).

Velpry, Lieutenant Colonel, 'L'Emploi des chars de combat dans la bataille, tiré de l'expérience acquise au cours de la dernière campagne', *La Revue d'infanterie*, July & August 1922, pp. 41–55, 183–212.

Velpry, General Maurice, 'Le premier engagement des chars Renault en Mai-Juin 1918', *La Revue d'infanterie,* December 1932, pp. 795–801.

English-language Sources

Bruce, Robert, *A Fraternity of Arms: America & France in the Great War* (Kansas: UKP, Lawrence: UPK, 2002).

Clayton, Anthony, *Paths of Glory: The French Army 1914-18* (London: Cassell, 2003).

Doughty, Robert Allan, *Pyrrhic Victory: French Strategy and Operations in the Great War* (London: Harvard University Press, 2005).

Foch, Ferdinand, *The Principles of War* (trans. Hilaire Belloc, originally published 1903, London: Chapman, 1920).

_____, *The Memoirs of Marshal Foch* (trans. T. Bentley Mott, London: Heinemann, 1931).

Fogarty, Richard S., *Race and War in France: Colonial Subjects in the French Army, 1914-1918* (Baltimore: John Hopkins University Press, 2008).

Gale, Tim, *The French Army's Tank Force and Armoured Warfare in the Great War* (Farnham: Ashgate, 2013).

Greenhalgh, Elizabeth, 'Technology Development in Coalition: The Case of the First World War Tank', *The International History Review*, Vol. XXII/4, December 2000, pp. 806–1008.

_____, *Victory through Coalition – Britain and France during the First World War* (Cambridge: CUP, 2005).

_____, *The French Army and the First World War* (Cambridge: Cambridge University Press, 2014).

Guderian, Heinz, *Achtung-Panzer!* (reprint, translated by Christopher Duffy, London: Cassell, 1992).

Johnson II, Douglas V. and Rolfe L. Hillman Jr., *Soissons 1918* (College Station: TUP, 1999).

Johnson, Hubert C., *Break-through! Tactics, Technology, and the Search for Victory on the Western front in World War 1* (Novato: Presidio, 1994).

Keiger, J. F. V., *Raymond Poincare* (Cambridge: CUP, 1997).

Kennedy, Paul, 'Military Effectiveness in the First World War', in Allan R Millett and Williamson Murray, (eds), *Military Effectiveness: The First World War* (Boston: Unwin Hyman, 1988). Outdated.

Krause, Jonathan, *Early Trench Tactics in the French Army – The Second Battle of Artois May-June 1915* (Farnham: Ashgate, 2013).

Lawrynowicz, Witold J., *Schneider CA, St Chamond* (Gdansk: AJ Press, 2008).

Neiberg, Michael S., *The Second Battle of the Marne* (Bloomington: Indiana University Press, 2008).

Philpott, William, *War of Attrition – Fighting the First World War* (New York: Overlook Press, 2014).

Porch, Douglas, *The March to the Marne: The French Army 1871-1914* (Cambridge: CUP, 1981).

_____, 'The French Army in the First World War' in Allan R. Millett and Williamson Murray (eds), *Military Effectiveness Volume 1: The First World War* (London: Unwin Hyman, 1988), pp. 190–228.

_____, 'The Marne and After: A Reappraisal of French Strategy in the First World War', *Journal of Military History*, Vol. 53, October 1989, pp. 363–85.

Renouvin, Pierre, *The Forms of War Government in France* (New Haven: Yale University Press, 1927).

Ryan, Stephen, *Pétain the Soldier* (New York: AS Barnes and Co, 1969).

Stevenson, David, 'French Strategy on the Western Front', in Roger Chickering and Stig Forster (eds), *Great War, Total War: Combat and Mobilisation on the Western Front, 1914-1918* (Cambridge: CUP, 2000), pp. 297–326.

Sumner, Ian, *The French Army 1914-1918* (London: Osprey, 1995).

Smith, Leonard, *Between Mutiny and Obedience: The Case of the French 5th Infantry Division during World War 1* (Princeton: PUP, 1994).

Vauvillier, François, *The Encyclopaedia of French Tanks and Armoured Vehicles 1914-1940* (Paris: Histoire & Collections, 2014).

Zaloga, Steven J., *French Tanks of World War 1* (London: Osprey, 2010).

Index